NEW POLITICAL ECONOMY

Edited by
Richard McIntyre
University of Rhode Island

A ROUTLEDGE SERIES

New Political Economy

Richard McIntyre, *General Editor*

RETHINKING MUNICIPAL PRIVATIZATION

Oliver D. Cooke

Routledge
Taylor & Francis Group

NEW YORK AND LONDON

First published 2008
by Routledge
711 Third Avenue, New York, NY 10017

Simultaneously published in the UK
by Routledge
2 Park Square, Milton Park, Abingdon, Oxon OX14 4RN

Routledge is an imprint of the Taylor & Francis Group, an informa business
First issued in paperback 2012
© 2008 Taylor & Francis

Typeset in Sabon by IBT Global

Library of Congress Cataloging in Publication Data
Cooke, Oliver D.
Rethinking municipal privatization / by Oliver D. Cooke.
p. cm.— (New political economy)
Includes bibliographical references and index.
ISBN 978-0-415-96209-4
1. Privatization—New York (State)—New York. 2. Municipal services—New York (State)—New York. 3. Central Park (New York, N.Y.) I. Title.

HD3890.N7C664 2008
338.9747'105--dc22   2007033927

ISBN13: 978-0-415-96209-4 (hbk)
ISBN13: 978-0-415-54311-8 (pbk)
ISBN13: 978-0-203-93106-6 (ebk)

Contents

List of Figures

Acknowledgments

I would like to thank Rick Wolff and Steve Resnick for their many years of thoughtful, patient guidance, and for encouraging me to pursue this book. Deep gratitude is due to Ric McIntyre whose careful reading of the original manuscript and insightful comments were critically important to the book's final form.

Thanks is also due to my mother, whose get-it-done approach to life I have always greatly respected and taken to heart, and to my father, whose willingness to read sections, provide comments, and visit for long hours were critical to my own thought process and mental health throughout the journey. My brother's seemingly endless work effort and dedication to excellence were also major sources of inspiration along the way.

Finally, I thank Jessica, whose patience, encouragement, support and steadfast belief in me never waned.

Chapter One
Municipal Privatization
An Introduction

The private production of municipal goods and services has a long history in the United States. Contracting-out, the most common form by which public goods and services are privately produced, existed long before the Constitution.[1] Corruption has often plagued the private production of public goods and services, and thus the public sector has often been forced to resume production following failed attempts at private production. Indeed, as far back as 1895 the Mayor of Detroit stated, "Most of our troubles can be traced to the temptations which are offered to city officials when franchises are sought by wealthy corporations, or contracts are to be let for public works."[2] Hence, responsibility for the production of municipal goods and services in the United States has long resembled a pendulum, swinging (sometimes slowly, at other times more quickly) back and forth between the public and private sectors. Many cities have swung between these two poles numerous times, experiencing first hand the benefits and disadvantages of each.[3]

Though debate over the extent of the growth in the privatization of municipal goods and services continues, much of the evidence suggests that, at least during the last two decades of the last century, the pendulum swung strongly in the direction of the private sector. As Jeffrey Henig notes, "The rapid dissemination throughout the world of the language and programs of privatization has been likened to a revolution or a boom."[4] Ronald Moe's comment that, "When administrative historians some years hence study the 1980s, they are likely to conclude that "privatization" was the single most influential concept of the decade," strikes a similar note.[5] Figure 1.1 shows increases in the use of contracting by city and county governments in the United States between 1988 and 1997 across several goods and services. As shown, the types of public goods and services that have been privatized vary widely and include: the operation and management of gas and electricity production units, hospitals, and daycare facilities, rodent control, and solid waste disposal.

The movement toward increased privatization of municipal goods and services in the United States during the past two decades reflects, in part, political trends dating to the Reagan era that ushered in a new federalism—one that significantly altered the relationship between the various levels of government. Subsequently, the movement was reinforced by the Democratic Party's efforts to "reinvent" government during the 1990s.[7] Others locate the movement's roots in the urban fiscal crisis that swept the country during the 1970s. Under serious fiscal duress, or in some cases nearly bankrupt, many cities were forced to adopt severe austerity and restructuring programs. Such programs often included the partial or full privatization of many publicly-produced goods and services.

Today, the movement towards the privatization of municipal goods and services continues. This movement's import (or, at least public consciousness of it) becomes especially apparent in times of economic distress,

Good/Service	% governments using contracting*	
	1988	1997
Gas operation/management	12	60
Operation/management of hospitals	24	71
Operation of daycare facilities	34	79
Electricity operation/management	11	43
Operation of homeless shelters	43	66
Drug and alcohol treatment programs	34	56
Solid waste disposal	25	41
Programs for the elderly	19	34
Ambulance services	24	37
Utility meter reading	7	18
Child welfare programs	17	27
Insect/rodent control	15	21

* The number of local governments varied with each survey and the number of local governments reporting varies within each service. Variations also existed in surveys' formats.

Figure 1.1 Increases in the Use of Contracting by Local and County Governments, 1988 to 1997[6]

when local governments confront fiscal pressures. Attempts to balance budgets amid declining employment, income, and tax receipts, in a political environment increasingly hostile to tax increases, often expands the list of publicly-provided goods and services thought eligible for privatization. The privatization movement remains critically important even outside locales experiencing fiscal stress, however. In fact, privatized water has fast-become the latest municipal-level privatization buzz issue, as hundreds of American cities have hired private companies to manage and upgrade their aging waterworks systems over the recent past.[8] The first-term proposal from the Bush administration to privatize nearly half of the federal workforce was yet another indication of the movement's continued salience on the national policy agenda.

It is this backdrop—the rapid expansion of the privatization of municipal goods and services in the United States over the past two decades; the continued mounting fiscal and budgetary pressures confronting many municipalities across the country; and, the apparent increasing likelihood that local governments will turn to the private sector to help provide vital public goods and services—that frames this book and underscores its current and future import.

1.1 INSTITUTIONAL FORMS AND CONCEPTIONS OF PRIVATIZATION

Among the most pressing problems in the discourse on privatization is the need to define precisely what the word means. Similar to many ideas or terms (e.g., globalization), the proliferation of meanings assigned to the word privatization, as well as the endless contexts in which it is thought to apply, has rendered the discourse's terrain exceeding difficult to navigate, while making communication difficult. The following remarks offer a primer on the most common (institutional) forms privatizations take. This primer is followed by brief comments on broader conceptions of privatization.

Privatizations take many forms at the municipal level. Indeed, subtle differences often lead to confusion about precisely what type of privatization is implemented in a certain locale. Nevertheless, the forms detailed below are common and are used across a broad range of service categories in a host of municipalities across the country.[9]

Asset sales and Long-Term Leases. The government divests an enterprise or property. Privatization qua asset sales is often the centerpiece of state-sponsored privatization programs. Long-term leases involve a government selling an asset to the private sector and then leasing it back.

Contracting-out. A government contracts with private for-profit or non-profit entities or another government (or government agency) to provide a public good or service. Contracting-out is the most common form of municipal privatization in the United States.

Franchise Concessions. The government awards exclusive or nonexclusive rights to private firms to provide a public good or service in a particular locale.

Incentives. Governments use incentives to encourage the delivery of public goods and services by the private sector. For example, a government may change zoning laws or provide zoning waivers to encourage the construction of low-income public housing.

Internal Markets. Government agencies or departments are encouraged to purchase various goods or services from either in-house or outside providers. In-house providers are thereby forced to compete with outside providers.

Managed Competition. A government continues to provide a public good or service, but competes with one or more contractors who also provide the same public good or service.

Management Contracts. The operation of a publicly-owned facility, e.g., an airport, arena, or convention center, is contracted out to a private firm.

Public-Private Partnerships (PPPs). The government finances, manages, and risk shares with the private sector to produce and/or provide a public good or service.

Self-Help. By encouraging individuals and community groups to participate in an activity for their own benefit, the government reduces the amount of government production that would otherwise be required.

Subsidies. Governments may provide financial or in-kind contributions to private organizations or individuals to encourage the delivery of public goods and services. For example, the government may provide space rent-free for a private-run senior citizen recreational center.

User fees. The government charges for services provided by the public sector.

Volunteers. Many governments regularly receive free help from individual citizens in producing and delivering various public goods and services. For example, in many smaller, rural municipalities, fire protection is regularly provided by volunteers.

Vouchers. The government distributes vouchers with a specified value that can used to purchase specific goods or services from qualified private providers.

In addition to the various forms privatizations take, there are several widely-held conceptions of privatization. As Walzer and Johnson write, privatization, "invariably means transferring responsibility for public services from government to the private sector in some fashion. The private sector can include nonprofit organizations, volunteers, and other public groups."[10] While this conception underpins most understandings of privatization that prevail in the public domain today in the United States, the many others that pervade public discourse deserve brief comment.

Upon its arrival on the national policy agenda in the early 1980s, the privatization issue became increasingly politicized. It was in this context, that the entire notion of privatization became linked (for many on the Left) to Right-led attacks on organized labor. In the 1990s, many (especially those on the Left) believed that national and state-led initiatives to reform welfare represented thinly-veiled attempts to rollback the welfare state and introduce market-oriented processes into the public sphere. Such initiatives often included various privatization components. For example, many welfare-to-work initiatives involved contracting-out formerly publicly-administered welfare functions to private sector firms, both for- and non-profit. As the number of municipalities privatizing what are commonly referred to as soft services (e.g., health and human services) has grown in recent years, the notion that privatization is linked to the gradual dismantling of the welfare state has been furthered.

The concept of privatization has also been attached to the idea of decentralization. That the public sector is too centralized and/or removed from its "clients" has long constituted a chief criticism of its practices.[11] Such criticism has generally been contrasted with private sector practice. The decentralization assumed to prevail in the private sector, it is claimed, allows it to better manage physical and human resources.

During the late-1980s and 1990s, the privatization issue became increasingly relevant in the international context. Thus, the term privatization became closely tied to various World Bank- and IMF-backed denationalization and/or liberalization (so-called "structural adjustment") policies throughout the world.

1.2 NEW YORK CITY'S PRIVATIZATION EXPERIENCE DURING THE 1990S

The election of Rudolph Giuliani to the New York City mayoralty marked a turning point for New York City government. Promising to correct the perceived gross mismanagement and inefficiencies of New York City government, Giuliani made a strategic privatization program a centerpiece of his 1993 campaign. While privatization was not new to New York City government—many of the goods and services provided and/or administered by the city have long been provided via contract—Giuliani alleged that his privatization program would be specifically aimed at improving the overall performance of city agencies.[12] While the successes and failures of individual privatization efforts are still widely debated, it is undeniable that Giuliani delivered on his campaign promise. During the next eight years, Giuliani's administration implemented some sixty privatization initiatives.[13] These privatization efforts took several forms and included: contracting-out fleet management in the Parks & Recreation Department, and custodial work at public schools; franchising private ferries; divesting radio and television stations; crafting a public-private partnership for new school construction; and, privatizing the day-to-day production and management of Central Park.

According to the Mayor's Management Report (2001), a semi-annual report that assesses New York City government's fiscal performance, Giuliani's privatization initiatives resulted in significant cost savings, cost avoidance, increased revenue, better service quality, and greater responsiveness to the public.[14] Among other examples, the report cites: identifiable savings from contracts totaling $42 million annually, a thirty percent reduction in fleet maintenance costs in the Parks Department, $43 million in cost avoidance due to sales of city-owned apartment buildings, and $657 million via various divestments between 1994 and 2000. While such estimates are of course open to debate, it is undeniable that Giuliani's privatization program restructured the way New York City provides many goods and services.

This book analyzes one of the most high-profile privatizations New York City's government carried out during the 1990s—Central Park's. While New York City's government, the Central Park Conservancy (the contractor that produces Central Park), and the broader public have emphasized the privatization's institutional form—a combination of the PPP and contracting-out forms of privatization—this book examines its *class* form. By focusing on the class implications of Central Park's privatization, this book reconceptualizes the park's privatization as an ensemble of complex and contradictory class effects. The class analysis developed reveals that Central Park-like privatizations can *undermine* private sector rates of accumulation and support *non-capitalist* producers. The former finding casts a shadow over the municipal privatization discourse's central theoretical efficiency and cost propositions. The latter finding highlights the limitations of the discursive and theoretical *association* between privatization and capitalism.

This association has long been central to the municipal privatization discourse. Building upon the latter finding, the analysis also shows how privatizations—in both the municipal and global contexts—afford opportunities for pursuing class-based, progressive development policies. Because these opportunities involve the generation and/or support of *non-capitalist* enterprises, they open up theoretical and policy space for radically rethinking privatization processes.

The remainder of the book is structured as follows. Chapter Two reviews and critically assesses the evolution of the mainstream privatization discourse and its relationship to the public-choice and Walrasian economic traditions. These two theoretical traditions provided the groundwork upon which the municipal privatization movement in the United States, inaugurated amid the 1970s fiscal crisis, was built. The efficiency and cost propositions that flow from these traditions—and which have served to rationalize the municipal privatization initiatives implemented across the United States since the 1970s—are shown to rely on an implausible reductionist logic that heavily circumscribes analytical conceptions of municipal privatization processes. In particular, the failure to recognize the class dimensions of municipal privatization is viewed as a consequence of this logic and the analytical circumscription it produces.

Chapter Three sets out the theoretical framework upon which the book's class approach to privatization is built. Two key concepts underlie this approach: the class process and an overdeterminist ontology. The joint deployment of these concepts allows the mainstream privatization discourse's efficiency focus and closely-related reductionist ontology to be displaced. It thereby allows the park's privatization to be recast as an ensemble of complex and contradictory class effects.

Chapters Four and Five, which comprise the book's centerpiece, present a class analysis of Central Park's privatization. The beginning point for the central argument is that the privatization *commodified* Central Park and that the Central Park Conservancy (CPC)—the non-profit organization that produces the park—operates as a *capitalist* enterprise. The ensuing analysis demonstrates that the CPC produces the park at a loss each year and must find alternative means in order to reproduce itself qua capitalist. Chapter Five explicates the complex class effects and implications that flow from the CPC's efforts to accomplish this. Foremost among these regards the fact that in its efforts to produce the park and reproduce itself qua capitalist enterprise, the CPC supports several *non-capitalist* producers.

Chapter Six extends the insights developed in Chapter Five and represents a critical engagement with the political Left in the United States over the issue of municipal privatization. In particular, I argue that once the class dimension of municipal privatization is recognized it becomes possible to reconceptualize municipal privatizations as avenues by which progressive, class-based policies can be pursued. Non-capitalist enterprise formation lies at the center of these policies.

The book's final chapter considers the privatization of state-owned enterprises and thereby extends the analysis developed in Chapter Six. Paralleling Chapter Six's argument, I argue that privatizations of state-owned enterprises provide opportunities for pursuing non-capitalist enterprise formation. As in the municipal context, I argue that the use of these types of privatizations as vehicles for non-capitalist enterprise formation would support efforts to construct and implement more progressive development paradigms.

Chapter Two
The Evolution of the Municipal Privatization Discourse

Two closely related analogies have been particularly influential to the evolution of the municipal privatization discourse.[1] Both were developed during the 1950–1970 period. The first analogy, derived from the public-choice theoretic tradition, is one drawn between the government bureaucrat (specifically, a government agency director) and *Homo economicus*. The second, derived from the Walrasian economics tradition, is one drawn between a government unit (agency) and the industrial firm. These two analogies provided a framework that helped shape perceptions of, discourses on, and solutions to the urban fiscal crisis that erupted across the United States in the 1970s. The following section outlines the basic contours of these two analogies. After this, a brief historical sketch of the 1970s urban fiscal crisis is presented. It was largely out of this crisis milieu that a practical demand for a theory of privatization (one based on these two analogies and theoretical traditions) forcefully emerged.[2] A discussion of the municipal privatization discourse's evolution, in both its mainstream and heterodox variants, follows.

2.1 THE DEVELOPMENT OF A THEORY OF PRIVATIZATION

Many of the original theoretical underpinnings of the theory of privatization that informs the modern discourse on the subject can be traced back to Milton Friedman's, *Capitalism and freedom*.[3] There, Friedman advanced several key themes. First, he developed an important analogy between government and private monopoly. Second, Friedman characterized all government regulation as anti-consumer; regulation was ultimately a ploy used by big business to erect substantial barriers to entry and thereby stifle competition. Finally, he made a critical distinction between government *responsibility* and government *provision*. By using its tax powers, he argued, governments could safely evade free rider problems and thereby leave the provision of many public goods and services to the private sector. In the two decades following the publication of Friedman's seminal work, these themes were elaborated on and extended by a number of analysts working across an array of academic disciplines. Especially important, however, were the works of William Niskanen, Gordon Tullock, Anthony Downs, and James Buchanan[4]

The Budget-Maximizing Bureaucrat. While there was a vast literature on bureaucracy produced during the 1950–1970 period, William Niskanen's, *Bureaucracy and Representative Government*, was among the most influential works. Niskanen's book provided the definitive theoretical rationale for why bureaucratic behavior begets inefficiency. As Mueller notes, Niskanen's work was "the first systematic effort to study bureaucracy within a public choice framework."[5] Niskanen's theory of the supply of public goods and services by government agencies (or, bureaus) rested on three assumptions. The supply of public goods and services was a function of: (1) a bureau's own characteristics, (2) its relationship to its environment and, (3) its maximand. Niskanen conceptualized a bureau as a non-profit organization financed by either a budget appropriation and/or a grant from its sponsor, e.g., a mayor. He assumed that a bureau's environment was dominated by its relationship with its sponsor, and that its head tried to maximize his total budget. Importantly, the bureau head's salary, perquisites, reputation, power, patronage, and his bureau's output were assumed to be positive monotonic functions of total budget. The belief that the bureau head tried to maximize his budget was thus analogous to the principle of maximization of utility by the individual or profit by the firm—principles central to the Walrasian (and neoclassical) economics tradition.

In addition to the assumption of maximizing behavior, Niskanen provided a theoretical basis for ensuring that maximization succeeded. The reasoning rested on the theory of bilateral monopoly: the bureau offers an output (to its sponsor) in exchange for its budget. This suggests that bureau output is indeterminate. However, "relative incentives and available information under most conditions, give the bureau the overwhelming monopoly power," argued Niskanen.[6] The asymmetry of the bilateral monopoly situation was due to two things. First, the sponsor lacked any profit motive and therefore lacked the incentive to use his potential power. Second, the sponsor lacked information regarding the bureau's production process. As a result, the bureau head was in a position to exploit his monopoly power, whereas, the sponsor was not. The result was oversupply by the bureau.

As Blais and Dion note, the idea that bureaucrats attempt to budget-maximize was not new.[7] It appeared in Tullock's and Downs' work.

However, in those works it had appeared as but one among many ideas. For Niskanen, it comprised the central hypothesis. Niskanen's original model was later amended to suggest that bureau heads act to maximize discretionary budgets rather than total budgets.[8] Among other things, this amendment meant the model predicted inefficiency rather than oversupply. Niskanen's model continued to undergo subsequent alterations as the literature on bureaucratic behavior evolved. However, the model's key message—that budget-maximizing behavior lay at the heart of bureaucratic inefficiency and/or oversupply—became widely accepted, especially by public choice theorists and Niskanen's fellow mainstream economists.

The idea that public sector bureaucrats were analogous to *Homo economicus* held important implications. As Tullock argued, it provided a ready-made answer to the question of why the public sector appeared to expand ad infinitum. Buchanan, meanwhile, argued that the idea provided a rationale for the importance of interest-group politics. Stigler elaborated the idea's implications as they applied to government regulation, arguing that government regulators would ultimately be bought off by the industries they were supposed to oversee—a result of the diffuse costs and concentrated benefits associated with the regulatory problem.[9]

The Government Unit as Industrial Firm: The Tiebout Hypothesis. Responding to the work of others in the nascent research area of public finance theory, Charles Tiebout's seminal 1956 essay, "A Pure Theory of Local Expenditures," sought to characterize local governments as firm-like.[10] As it is particularly relevant to the current discussion, Tiebout's opening remarks are especially noteworthy. He wrote:

> "One of the more important recent developments in the area of "applied economic theory" has been the work of Musgrave and Samuelson in public finance theory. The two writers agree on what is probably the major point under investigation, namely, that no "market type" solution exists to determine the level of expenditures on public goods. Seemingly, we are faced with the problem of having a rather large portion of our national income allocated in a "non-optimal" way when compared to the private sector. This discussion will show that the Musgrave-Samuelson analysis, which is valid for federal expenditures, need not apply to local expenditures."[11]

According to Tiebout, the local governments comprising large regional and/or metropolitan areas could be thought of as offering various packages of services to "consumer-voters" that would move to the community that best satisfied their preferences, i.e., they would, "vote with their feet."

Thus, Tiebout's work suggested that local governments shared common characteristics with industrial firms—and therefore provided a solution to Musgrave's and Samuelson's original problematic. Each local government produced particular products (goods and services), enjoyed different economies of scale, serviced "consumers-voters" and acted under various constraints. The result was a novel and powerful conceptualization of the system of municipal government. As Sonenblum, Kirlin, and Ries state:

> "the system's participants (producers, consumers, and financiers of public services) [seek] to achieve for themselves some kind of optimization which, in principle if not in content, is analogous to the profit or utility optimization of firms and households in the private economy. And the extent to which optimization is achieved measures the efficiency or performance of the system."[12]

Thus, competition between local governments, Tiebout hypothesized, similar to the benefits it assured in the private sector (under certain conditions), would provide for a maximization of personal choice, responsiveness and, above all, efficiency in the public realm.

The Two Analogies: Theoretical Implications and Prescription. The importance of these two analogies to the evolution of the theory of privatization can not be overstated. By applying the theory of rationality that had long informed economic theorizing to the behavior of the public bureaucrat, the first analogy provided a coherent and relatively simple argument that served to erode a public confidence and trust in government officials that had largely endured since the New Deal era.[13] The public's long distrust of big business (which had reached its zenith during the Progressive era) was shown to be just as applicable to big government. Indeed, such distrust of government was central to Friedman's overarching theme—the inherent conflict between government and individual freedom. The additional implication that budget-maximizing behavior on the part of bureaucrats resulted in inefficiency and/or oversupply in the public sector constituted an even more damning indictment of the entire institution of government.[14]

The second analogy, embodied in Tiebout's hypothesis, between local government and an industrial firm, held important implications *once it was brought together with the first analogy.* Specifically, if one could conceptualize local governments (or, government agencies) as industrial firms, then once it had been established that existing government units (or, institutions) were inherently inefficient due to budget-maximizing behavior and their monopoly-like status, a particular set of prescriptions emerged. The radical restructuring of local government comprised the centerpiece of this prescription set. Soon enough, the events that began to unfold in the mid-1970s provided an atmosphere in which those theoretical prescriptions would be carried out in practice.

2.2 A THEORY COMES OF AGE: THE 1970s WATERSHED AND URBAN FISCAL CRISIS

The 1970s marked the official ending point of the so-called Golden Age of US politico-economic hegemony, a period that began in the aftermath of the second world war. The confluence of international geopolitical and economic events that occurred during that decade, most notably the OPEC oil shock, increased economic competition from abroad (which severely imperiled US corporate-sector profitability), and a recession longer than any since the Great Depression, set in motion a chain of events that brought forth a fundamental restructuring of the global capitalist system, the US position therein, and the social contract that underlay the generally widespread prosperity the nation had enjoyed during the two previous decades. Concomitant with these developments, the nation's large urban areas increasingly became key focal points. This attention on the nation's cities was not new of course. In various ways, the Civil Rights Movement, the federal government's War on Poverty, and its urban renewal efforts, all of which dated to the 1950s and 1960s, had done much to catapult cities into the public limelight and onto the national agenda. However, beginning in the 1970s, this previously-generated interest in cities began to fuse with the broader political-economic events playing out on the national and international levels. Above all, it became increasingly apparent that the crisis facing US capitalism during the 1970s impinged in numerous ways on cities across the nation, and especially their governments' fiscal health. By the mid-1970s, with many cities and states facing severe fiscal crises, and some even contemplating bankruptcy, this fact became all too obvious. The"urban crisis,"once a term loaded with racial overtones, increasingly came to be understood as a catchall phrase referring to the number of pathologies thought to afflict the urban environment, its inhabitants, and the administration of its government. It was out of this crisis milieu that a practical demand (one largely emanating from local public administrators under serious fiscal duress and those charged with helping them) for a theory of privatization (whose theoretical underpinning had been developed over the course of the two proceeding decades) emerged.

The severity and urgency of the fiscal crises facing cities across the nation increasingly prompted national attention. The Advisory Commission on Intergovernmental Relations (ACIR), focusing on what it called the, "incredible and seemingly insoluble array of financial difficulties" facing urban governments, cited a number of problems facing cities including: outmoded capital facilities, declining tax bases, soaring demand for public services, debt ceilings, and taxpayer rebellions.[15] The "general inability to make the revenue sources stretch to fit the expenditures mandated by the state and demanded by the people" had reached, in the commission's view, emergency proportions. As the crisis deepened, many municipalities implemented austerity measures including severe municipal job cutbacks. A national survey in 1975 by the Joint Economic Committee found state and local governments eliminating some 140,000 jobs, raising taxes by $3.6 billion, cutting services by $3.3 billion, and canceling or deferring some $1 billion in construction projects.[16]

Likely due to its size and function as the nation's media capital, New York City's mid-1970s *de facto* bankruptcy came to symbolize the depth and severity of the fiscal crisis cascading across the country. Between 1969 and 1976, New York City lost 588,000 jobs—a 15.5% decline. It lost 50,000 public-sector jobs in 1975 alone. New York's experience was hardly unique. Major job losses were recorded in Chicago, Detroit, St. Louis, Philadelphia, and New Orleans, to name but a few. Above all, massive job declines translated into lost tax revenues. Reflecting this fact, many cities' accumulated deficit-to-revenue ratios rose dramatically. In 1971, this ratio equaled -9.2% in New York, –6.1% in Philadelphia, and –3.7% in Detroit. Five years later, these ratios had risen to -31.1%, -10.2%, and –5.6%, respectively.[17]

As fiscal crises swept the country during the mid- to late-1970s, city after city began to search for remedies. A wide variety of programs and reforms were initiated. Cutting public-sector jobs and reducing or shedding various municipal services were more often than not generally central to such efforts. At the same time, other solutions were soon put forth. Chief among these were various privatization schemes. As suggested, the theoretical underpinnings and rationales for such efforts had been set out by economists and public-choice theorists during the two preceding decades. The two key analogies that had been carefully elaborated provided a ready-made analysis of the fiscal crisis facing many cities. More importantly, the theories from which the analogies had been derived provided a solution: local government needed to be radically overhauled. Above all, this came to mean that the competitive environment thought to guide the behavior of the typical industrial firm— and that presumably promoted efficiency and cost-minimization—had to somehow be injected into or replicated within the public sector.

While the intensity and magnitude of the fiscal constraints under which local officials were forced to operate under during this period often obviated the need for empirical demonstrations and verifications of various privatization schemes' efficiency and cost propositions, two studies trumpeting privatization's virtues proved particularly influential during this period.[18] The first, by Roger Ahlbrandt, dealt with Scottsdale, Arizona's contracting-out for fire services with the Rural-Metropolitan Fire Protection Company (Rural), a private concern.[19] Ahlbrandt showed that Rural was providing the municipality fire services at just over half of what it would have cost it to provide such services itself. Ahlbrandt wrote:

> "Contracting for the provision of a public good or service may enable the producer to attain a scale of operation commensurate with production efficiencies. To the degree the costs savings are passed along to the consumer, the demand articulation of the community will benefit. Furthermore, to the extent that contracting induces competition on the supply side, cost savings in addition to those resulting from scale economies may result. A bureaucratic producer, maximizing a complex set of goals and objective, may not be motivated to utilize the least cost production techniques, whereas a competitive firm can only be inefficient up to the point of potential entry into the market."[20]

The second study, by E.S. Savas, compared the costs of public and private garbage collection in the New York metro area.[21] He concluded that, "it costs the city more than twice as much as the private sector to collect a ton of garbage . . . " Savas cited three factors that were responsible for the, "extravagant costs of public service": overmanning, overpaying, and underworking. These factors, he suggested, were the consequence of the, "essentially monopolistic position of the city" and argued, "The remedy for this condition, competition, is self-evident. . . . ." The lasting influence of the two previous decades' research (which had elaborated the two analogies that provided the foundations of the theory of privatization that became practice amid the urban fiscal crises in the late 1970s) on these early privatization studies should be noted. Indeed, Ahlbrandt duly noted that, "The theory of bureaucracy presented in this paper relies heavily upon the work of Downs (1967), Niskanen (1971), and Tullock (1965)."[22]

A significant body of literature subsequently developed around the privatization issue during the latter part of the 1970s.[23] Taking its methodological cues from Ahlbrandt's and Savas' work, much of this literature was devoted to evaluating and comparing the costs and efficiency of public- and private-sector production of various goods and services. Many of these studies compared contracting-out with private-sector production. Among others, these studies examined bus service, cleaning services, electric power, heath care, and water utilities.[24] Likely due to Savas' early work on the subject, there were several studies that analyzed the differences between public- and private-sector refuse collection. In many cases, these studies found that public production was more costly and/or less efficient than private production. However, this was far from a universal finding, and the cost and efficiency differentials allegedly found often varied widely across studies comparing the same service.

2.3 THE REAGAN YEARS

The privatization literature continued to blossom in the aftermath of Reagan's rise to the presidency. The official arrival of privatization on the national agenda furthered the academic and local-level interest on the topic while stoking new interest in other quarters, especially among policy think tanks. Not surprisingly, as Henig argues, the topic became increasingly politicized as, "privatization as economic theory became privatization as political strategy."[25] While Reagan did not run on a privatization platform, his administration soon realized that the privatization theme could be successfully appropriated to carry out more traditional anti-government goals.[26] Thus, the administration spun privatization not as a rejection of the goals associated with the welfare state, but rather as an adoption of private means to pursue public goals (including efficiency.) The President's Private Sector Survey on Cost Control, issued by the Grace Commission, defined privatization as an option, "allowing Government to *provide* services without *producing* them."[27] This political strategy was most forcefully advanced by Stuart Butler at the Heritage Foundation.[28] Butler's central message was that the welfare state's resilience was largely attributable to the structure of the costs and benefits associated with it. Thus, Butler and others within the administration saw privatization primarily as a means by which to reshape the interest-group environment. As Greiner and Peterson suggest,

> "One contention central to the Reagan critique of government [held] that the public sector is an inefficient, ineffective provider of services. From this it follows that budget cutting has virtues that transcend the political goal of reducing taxpayer burdens, the objective usually invoked to justify spending cuts. According to the Reagan analysis, one can reduce government waste simply by reducing the magnitude of public expenditures. Moreover, fiscal stringency may prompt the public sector to reorganize its service delivery along more imaginative and more efficient lines. It may even persuade the public sector to retire from service responsibilities better performed by the private sector."[29]

The idea of using privatization as a means to reshape interest-group politics led The Office of Personnel Management, for example, to propose a Federal Employee Direct Corporate Ownership Plan (Fed CO-OP), which would create new employee-owned independent companies that would compete for government contracts.[30]

In academic quarters (especially economics and public administration departments), much of the focus of privatization research remained on evaluating the differential impact of various privatization schemes, especially contracting-out, on efficiency and costs.[31] In addition to case studies, these empirical studies often used common econometric techniques.[32] Among the most common forms were bi- or multivariate statistical analysis of a cross-section of governments. Once various socio-economic indicators and quality were controlled, inferences regarding contracting's effect on efficiency, costs, and total municipal expenditures were drawn. Longitudinal studies were also widely employed. In a critical reexamination of reviews of many of these studies of local service contracting, Boyne writes:

> "Reviews of the evidence on local service contracting have generally concluded that it does produce the results that public choice theory predicts. For example, Stein claims that "research on contracting for individual goods and services has consistently found this mode of service arrangement to be more efficient than direct service provision and production. Similarly, Kiewiet concludes that virtually every study that has ever compared the operations of public bureaus with those of private firms providing identical services has found data to support the inefficiency hypothesis."[33]

The terrain of the privatization literature did expand during the 1980s, moving beyond studies aimed at assessing the cost and efficiency dimensions of the subject. As a result, the objects of the discourse broadened considerably over the course of the decade. To name but a few, research foci and questions included: what public goods or services were most fit for privatization or contracting-out; how should the contracting process be structured; what elements enable effective contract monitoring; how should public managers best respond to union resistance; what factors motivate the privatization or contracting-out decision; and, what impact does local government functional responsibility have on local expenditures.[34] Thus, to a considerable extent these new research questions represented a marked shift in the academic research program on privatization. In short, much of the literature that dates from this period in the 1980s ceased interrogating the privatization *concept* per se. Thus, a broad swath of the academic and policy research on privatization was redirected toward *managing* privatization initiatives.

As different privatization schemes were put into place and/or tested over the course of the 1980s (most at the local level), public administrators as well as many academic theorists came increasingly to view privatization as merely representing an "alternative delivery" option for the provision of public goods and services. Needless to say, this perception was not universal. There were significant union-led efforts aimed at blocking municipal privatization efforts.

While the success and/or extent of Reagan's privatization efforts at the federal level and the subsequent results at the state and local levels remain debated and, despite continuing argument over the empirical evidence surrounding its cost and efficiency implications, privatization's arrival onto the national agenda during 1980s guaranteed it a place among the major public policy issues of the last part of the twentieth century. The topic's continued import to the nation's public policy discourse was ensured when Clinton was elected, as privatization became central to the new administration's effort to "reinvent" government during the 1990s.

2.4 THE 1990s: REINVENTING GOVERNMENT

David Osborne's and Ted Gaebler's, *Reinventing Government: How the Entrepreneurial Spirit is Transforming the Public Sector,* published in early 1993, played a central role in shaping the discourse on and policy approach toward privatization during the 1990s.[35] The book's meteoric rise onto the nation's bestseller list shortly after its publication, its numerous (and, generally positive) reviews in leading periodicals and newspapers, and the Clinton and Gore endorsement it received—Clinton called the book "the blueprint"—firmly secured the book's place among the decade's leading works on privatization. Citing Peter Drucker—the preeminent management guru—as their chief intellectual inspiration, Osborne and Gaebler argued that government must be radically transformed in such a way as to allow it to incorporate the virtues of entrepreneurialism. This transformation or reinvention, they suggested, involved shifting the focus from the hackneyed question of *what* government should do to *how* they operate. The failure of government to date they claimed was, "one of means, not ends."[36]

While Osborne's and Gaebler's book centered around ten principle themes (each comprising a separate chapter) the chapter entitled, "Competitive Government: Injecting Competition into Service Delivery" comprised the book's most succinct statement on privatization (and, more specifically, on the contracting-out form of privatization). Interestingly, Osborne and

Gaebler write, "Competition will not solve all our problems. But perhaps more than any other concept in this book, it holds the key that will unlock the bureaucratic gridlock that hamstrings so many public agencies."[37] They cited four key advantages of competition: (1) it results in greater efficiency; (2) it forces public (and private) monopolies to respond to the needs of customers; (3) it rewards innovation (whereas monopoly stifles it); and, (4) it boosts the morale and work ethic of public employees.

Osborne's and Gaebler's book consistently cited much of the early literature that had laid down the theory of privatization's theoretical underpinnings. For instance, they frequently cited Niskanen, Savas, and Butler. While the book contained many messages, the core message concerned public sector bureaucracy and inefficiency. Indeed, this idea underlay the book's overarching theme:

> "even entrepreneurial public service providers are less adept at: performing complex tasks, replicating the success of other organizations, delivering services that require rapid adjustment to change, delivering services to very diverse populations, and delivering services that become obsolete quickly. Bureaucratic government organizations fall short on many other counts. . . . They have trouble, for instance, with tasks that require flexibility, rapid change, customer responsiveness, and extensive customization of services. The *private sector* is almost the opposite. . . . When tasks are economic in nature, or when they require an investment orientation, the private sector is far more effective than either the public sector or the third sector.[38]

Subsequent to Osborne's and Gaebler's book there was a veritable tidal wave of academic literature on privatization produced during the 1990s. Not surprisingly, this body of literature continued to widen the discourse's terrain. On one hand, this academic impulse reflected the growth of various privatization initiatives—such initiatives began to appear in an ever-wider array of arenas and industries, and on more and more government levels. On the other, it reflected "privatization's" ever-evolving and expanding meaning. New research questions were posed, further expanding the discourse's menu of objects. Among others, these included privatization's impact on: employee job satisfaction and well-being; the structure of the mental health system; alcohol sales and consumption; gender issues and property rights; professional ethics in health care; access to health care; broadcast media and news reporting; public sector unions and collective bargaining; labor market fragmentation; public employment levels; and, industrial-relations institutions and outcomes.[39] The increasing breadth of research questions explored meant that an increasing number of academic disciplines became involved in the discourse. Contributions to the literature from psychology, psychiatry, urban studies, geography, medicine, law, sociology, to name but a few, became increasingly common.

While academic research continued to broaden the terrain of the discourse during the 1990s, a vast non-academic literature also mounted. In many cases, this research was carried out by government comptrollers and auditors, management consultants, policy think tanks, and labor unions. Not surprisingly, a significant portion of this literature represented reversion back to the discourse's original hegemonic concept, namely, the efficiency/cost calculus. As historical data and documentation on various local privatization initiatives was built up such studies became increasingly common.[40] Public administrators and officials as well as those brought in to structure and manage such efforts (e.g., management consultants, which came to play an important role in the implementation of many local privatization initiatives during the decade) sought vindication of their own efforts, while others still contemplating such efforts sought verification of the discourse's core efficiency and/or cost savings hypotheses. Opponents (especially public-sector unions), meanwhile, either contested the efficiency and cost findings or found case studies highlighting the shortcomings of specific privatizations. Indeed, much of the non-academic literature and discourse produced during this period reverberated exclusively around the issue of efficiency and costs. For every study documenting the efficiency gains and/or cost savings yielded by a privatization initiative, one trumpeting the failures of some other privatization program was produced.

The proliferation of municipal privatization initiatives during the 1990s prompted considerable popular media coverage. Articles in major city newspapers provided on-going documentation and coverage of the privatization movement as it swept across city after city, including: Phoenix, San Diego, Charlotte, Cleveland, and Milwaukee, to name but a few. Indianapolis' alleged successful early-1990s privatization program, launched under the administration of Stephen Goldsmith, was among the most highly-publicized and widely-heralded large urban privatization programs of the 1990s. Goldsmith subsequently published a book, *The Twenty-First Century City,* setting out the broad principles underlying his approach to privatizing Indianapolis during the 1990s. Competition, or "making a market," in Goldsmith's terms, was among these core principles. In fact, Goldsmith notes, in the process of describing his administration's first privatization initiative—which involved billing city sewer users—privatization *per se* was not the key to his program's success. Rather,

"The key issue, we soon discovered, was not whether tasks were performed by public or private institutions. A private monopoly, like the water company, might be less bureaucratic and more efficient than a government monopoly. But without the spur of competition, the difference in what we could expect in price and service [via privatization] would be distinctly unrevolutionary."[41]

Similar books were written by other "visionary" mayors that led privatization programs during the decade, including Milwaukee's Democratic mayor, John Norquist.[42] In most cases, these from-the-trenches publications were written for popular audiences and were often financially supported, endorsed, and broadly marketed by some of the country's leading Right-leaning policy think tanks including, the Manhattan and Cato Institutes. The popular media coverage such publications received generally highlighted one major conclusion: successful privatizations injected competition into the public sector, which translated into increased efficiency and/or reduced taxpayer costs.

Privatization's relevance in the international context also increased dramatically during the 1990s. To a considerable extent, this reflected the events of 1989 and the so-called subsequent transitions toward market-oriented economies by many countries in the former Eastern Bloc. While privatization in this context often referred to divestitures of state-owned assets and/or various denationalization programs, its subsequent diversification and application across a broad range of industries and sectors in countries across the world yielded still more research questions. Most of these research questions were taken up by academicians. To name but a few, questions included: privatization's relationship to growth, its geographical dimensions, its impact on small enterprise formation, its effect on rural industry, and its impact in the context of public housing.[43]

2.5 THE HETERODOX TERRAIN OF THE PRIVATIZATION DISCOURSE: THE 1970S AND EARLY 1980S

To a considerable extent, the differences between early mainstream and heterodox approaches to the privatization discourse can be traced to each camp's perceptions of the urban fiscal crises of the 1970s. Most contributors to the mainstream literature and discourse recognized that the urban crises comprised a host of disparate yet related problems. Writing in 1974, Rogers and Hawley suggested that the dimensions of the urban crisis were many and included: the concentration of poverty in the inner city; a severe gap between municipal revenues and costs; runaway cost inflation of public services with salary increases generally not tied to productivity; public service union strikes and breakdowns; decaying housing, schools, and other physical plant and equipment; increasing crime, delinquency, and drug addiction; intensified conflicts among citizen groups for scarce services, housing, and neighborhood control, often along racial, ethnic, and religious lines; and, an accompanying lack of hope or expectation by many citizens and city officials that they can do anything.[44] After acknowledging that the burden of social problems could not be traced solely or even primarily to the failures of urban management, they continued:

> "Nevertheless, it is generally true that the machinery of city govern-
> ments has been inadequate and inflexible in the face of these new and
> continuing challenges. Too many city agencies at best functioned in a
> caretaker capacity, unable and unwilling to deal with change and try-
> ing instead to keep going and to conserve what was there. Too few
> city governments have had the managerial capability to plan, set goals,
> develop cost-effective programs, monitor and evaluate them, develop
> control systems that permitted a constant appraisal of employee perfor-
> mance and accountability, and become more responsive to changing cli-
> ent needs. In many cases, city, county, and state agencies have become
> extreme examples of static, traditional bureaucracies. Moreover, agen-
> cies responsible for urban problem-solving are increasingly fragmented
> both from one another and internally, further hampering their capacity
> to adapt and to deliver services.[45]

Thus, despite subtle differences among mainstream diagnoses of the urban crisis (and its fiscal dimension), many shared the belief that the malfunction and inefficiency of municipal government was central to the issue. The fact that the theoretical underpinnings for such a belief had been elaborated in detail over the two previous decades facilitated this idea's dissemination across academic disciplines as well as broad segments of the population.[46] Indeed, it was this perception of gross mismanagement (and assumed cor-ruption) that underlay Ford's announcement in October of 1975, in the midst of New York City's de facto bankruptcy, that he would veto any Fed-eral bailout of New York City. Ford's words prompted the most famous headline ever run by a New York City newspaper, as the Daily News, the following day, summed up the president's views across its front page: "FORD TO CITY: DROP DEAD."[47]

In contrast to this mainstream perception of the urban fiscal crisis, those working from Marxian or heterodox perspectives generally held dra-matically different views of the situation. For many Marxists and others on the Left, the urban fiscal crisis of the 1970s represented a grand indictment of the capitalist system. Far from seeing the urban malaise as an indictment of big government and the welfare state—as many in the mainstream did—those on the Left more often than not interpreted it as some type of Marxian crisis. Among the most important and influential works in this vein was James O'Connor's, *The Fiscal Crisis of the State*.[48]

O'Connor's analysis of fiscal crisis rested on the idea that the capitalist state was required to fulfill two basic functions. First, it was required to maintain or create the conditions in which profitable capital accumulation is possible—its *accumulation* function. Second, the state had to maintain or create the conditions for social harmony—its *legitimization* function. More often than not, these two functions were contradictory. O'Connor's Marxian analysis argued that, "the growth of the state sector and state spending [functioned] increasingly as the basis for the growth of the monopoly sector and total production."[49] He argued that while the state socialized more and more capital costs, the social surplus continued to be appropriated privately. Thus, "The socialization of costs and the private appropriation of profits creates a fiscal crisis, or 'structural gap' between state expenditures and state revenues. The result is a tendency for state expenditures to increase more rapidly than the means of financing them."[50]

O'Connor further argued that the fiscal crisis was exacerbated by the private sector's appropriation of state power for particularistic ends. Because private sector interest groups often wielded considerably more power on the local level than on the national level, the fiscal crisis on the local level was particularly acute. Furthermore, local government officials, unlike Federal ones, were forced to operate under considerable constraints, especially the specter of middle-class exodus from the city center.

O'Connor's work provided the touchstone for a body of literature that evolved during the 1970s and early 1980s that was dedicated to exploring the causes and effects of the urban and fiscal crises through the lens of Marxian crisis theory. Above all, this body of literature attempted to tie the public sector's breakdown to the political economy of capitalism. Thus, in various ways this body of research viewed urban fiscal crisis as the "twin" of a more general crisis of capital accumulation.[51]

Another important body of Left-oriented research, one related to the Marxian crisis literature, focused on social or class conflict. In many respects, as Gottdiener suggests, this body of research arose out of interest in an earlier form of the urban crisis—specifically, the race-based crisis of the 1960s. Rather than focusing on the systemic disorganization inherent in the political economy of capitalism, as the Marxian crisis literature did, this body of research suggested that modernity had resulted in fundamental social changes. Crises qua class conflict were thus interpreted as the result of the fact that existing political institutions were no longer capable of channeling and/or controlling social conflict in this new fundamentally altered social existence.[52]

Reacting to the growing importance of middle-class tax revolts, other analysts working from Left perspectives interpreted the struggle over taxes as but a reflection of the struggle over profits (capital) and wages (labor.) Indeed, as fiscal crisis around the country deepened, issues of the so-called middle-class tax revolt came to occupy a central place on the policy agenda.[53]

Another important strand of Left thought tied the fiscal and urban crises to Marx's uneven development thesis. William Tabb was among the most prominent Marxists to advance this line of research. According to Tabb, the heart of the urban fiscal crisis could be traced to the migration of capital and subsequently jobs, especially manufacturing jobs. This was particularly true of the Northeastern region of the United States and other older industrial centers (e.g., the Midwest), which saw their manufacturing bases decline precipitously during the 1970s. The so-called "rise of the sun-belt cities," was the flip side of the movement of capital out of higher-cost, older industrial regions.[54] This migration of capital and the crisis it helped produce was, according to Tabb, "caused by decisions based on private profit calculations and the failure of society through political processes to place social needs ahead of the imperatives of the market."[55] The urban fiscal crisis was but a reflection, "of an underlying contradiction between interests of private capital and society's citizen, both in their roles as tax-payers and workers."[56]

There was an important consequence of the crisis thematic's centrality within the heterodox discourse of the 1970s, however. Namely, it worked, to a considerable extent, to deflect attention away from the early privatization efforts taking shape at the local level. While such local efforts did not go completely unrecognized by those working from Left and hetero-dox perspectives—indeed, recognition of these efforts' efficacy in mediating crisis comprised a key part of Left-oriented criticism aimed at O'Connor's original thesis—they did not receive explicit theoretical attention.

2.6 RETRENCHMENT AND THE HETERODOX DISCOURSE OF THE 1980s

The urban fiscal crisis of the 1970s and the subsequent rise of Reagan to the presidency and his administration's decidedly anti-urban policy agenda meant that many local governments across the country were forced to undertake radical restructuring. Subsequent tax revolts and/or revenue limitations (e.g., Proposition 2 ½ in Massachusetts and Proposition 13 in California) exacerbated the fiscal situations of local governments further. Although local officials' predominant response to this new fiscal reality was often straightforward cost-cutting and/or service reduction, a number of localities launched various privatization initiatives. For example, in the context of discussing the local effects of Proposition 2 ½ in Massachusetts, Greiner and Peterson state:

> "These responses included initiation or expansion of such alternative service-delivery arrangements as contracts with private service providers, imposition of fees and charges, greater reliance on private funding and private contributions, greater use of volunteers, and requirements that the public itself bear greater responsibility for service delivery."[57]

As the 1980s proceeded, such initiatives at the local level became increasingly commonplace. Moreover, the idea that budget cutting had virtues that transcended the political goal of reducing tax-payer burdens—most importantly, that the waste and inefficiency of government could be reduced simply by reducing government expenditures and thereby forcing restructuring—had been central to the Reagan administration's policy stance toward the urban fiscal crisis.[58]

Despite the extent of local government restructuring (which increasingly involved various privatization schemes) that took place during the early 1980s, there was no clearly defined response outlined by Left-leaning academics. As Gottdiener writes, this fact was also reflected at the grassroots level: "The political environment once nurturing local insurgency has largely disappeared. Several factors are now at work that have enabled crisis restructuring and austerity to proceed with remarkable quiescence and social control rather than effective organized protest."[59]

Of course, there was not a wholesale cessation of all Left- and labor-based activity against such reform efforts. There was union-led resistance on the ground. AFSCME, in particular, was extremely active on the ground. Beyond AFSCME, think tanks, such as the Economic Policy Institute, produced reports discussing the limits to privatization.[60] As Ronald Moe notes, these reports were usually oriented toward protecting the role and functions of the civil service and/or disputing the cost and/or efficiency claims of privatization initiatives in particular locales.[61] Outside labor and think-tank quarters, there was some exploration of privatization initiatives legal and Constitutional dimensions, as some saw privatization schemes as representing a threat to constitutional rights.[62] Others, generally from legal, public administration, and political science perspectives, questioned privatization initiatives' effects on the publicness and/or ethos of public services and institutions.[63] There were also investigations of privatizations' and contracting-out's effects on the quality of and access to public goods and services.[64]

Heterodox and Marxian economists, however, devoted relatively little attention to the privatization movement that was mounting at the local level. This is especially noteworthy in light of their considerable contributions to the crisis-oriented literature and the subsequent government reform movement during the mid- to late-1970s. In short, the actual local government restructuring process *itself*—in particular, as it related to privatization—received little theoretical investigation by economists working from Marxian and heterodox perspectives. Given the historical importance of the distinction between productive and unproductive labor within the Marxian tradition (and this distinction's obvious relevance in the privatization context), this neglect is especially puzzling. Again, this is not to say that the issue of privatization was completely absent from these analysts' work during the 1980s. However, as was the case during the mid- to late-1970s, much of the Marxian and heterodox literature emanating from economics programs during this period was directed elsewhere—namely, toward the broader theme of deindustrialization. As Gottdiener suggests, this discourse attempted to, "identify proximate causes of crisis, such as job loss, and often took them to be fundamental determinants, and then combined them with concepts from Marxian crisis theory and nonspecified signifiers of structural analysis. The result was a loosely defined discourse on urban decline and restructuring in general."

Among the most important contributions in this vein was Barry Bluestone's and Bennett Harrison's, *The Deindustrialization of America*.[65] Similar to many other Left-oriented works of this period, Bluestone's and Harrison's work focused on exploring the forces that underlay the massive restructuring (they believed was occurring) of the national economy. They wrote:

> "Underlying the high rates of unemployment, sluggish growth in the domestic economy, and the failure to successfully compete in the international market is the deindustrialization of America. By *deindustrialization* is meant a widespread, systematic disinvestment in the nation's basic productive capacity. Controversial as it may be, the essential problem with the U.S. economy can be traced to the way capital—in forms of financial resources and of real plant and equipment—has been diverted from productive investment in our basic national industries into unproductive speculation, mergers and acquisitions, and foreign

investment. Left behind are shuttered factories, displaced workers, and a newly emerging group of ghost towns."[66]

While Bluestone's and Harrison's work and others working in the context of deindustrialization often drew on particular local case studies, the overarching concern with the national economic context of deindustrialization meant that the actual restructuring processes taking place at the local government level—which included various privatization initiatives—rarely received explicit theoretical or empirical attention from heterodox economists.

2.7 THE MID-TO-LATE 1980s: ENTREPRENEURIAL GOVERNMENT

Following the national recovery from the early-1980's twin recessions, many older urban areas—despite Reagan's anti-urban agenda—began to recover. Boston's and San Francisco's high-technology transformations were two of the most commonly cited instances of such turnarounds.[67] Central to many of these turnarounds were changes in the nature of local urban governance structures—ones that had grown out of the reform and restructuring movements of the late-1970s and 1980s. From a Left perspective, David Harvey's work on this theme proved particularly influential.

In his essay, "From Managerialism to Entrepreneurialism," Harvey traced the evolution of the 1980's reorientation of local urban "governance," a term, he argued, that means much more than urban government per se.[68] While a managerial form of urban governance was characteristic of the 1960s and acted predominantly as a stabilizer, according to Harvey, the entrepreneurial form that blossomed during the 1980s was designed to facilitate capitalist development. Harvey argued that this new entrepreneurialism comprised three elements.[69] The public-private partnership (in which, "a traditional local boosterism is integrated with the use of local governmental powers to try and attract external sources of funding, new direct investments, or new employment sources . . .") constituted the centerpiece of this new form of urban governance.[70] This public-private partnership was entrepreneurial (this comprised the second element) "precisely because it is speculative in execution and design and therefore dogged by all the difficulties and dangers which attach to speculative as opposed to rationally planned and coordinated development."[71] Finally, this entrepreneurial form of urban governance focused on, "the political economy of place rather than territory."[72] By this, Harvey meant that local government officials became much more concerned with constructing places (urban environments) amenable to capitalist development. Such efforts included things like the construction of new civic centers and the implementation of retraining schemes—things aimed at enhancing a particular place's quality-of-life and its attractiveness to capital. Such efforts, Harvey suggested, often had effects (e.g., lowering wages) that transcended a particular locale. This focus, he maintained, contrasted with the managerial form of urban governance which focused on various social and economic programs designed to improve the living and working conditions within a particular place.

The upshot of the foregoing discussion is this: despite instances of recognition by those working from Marxian and heterodox perspectives of privatization's role in the local government restructuring of the 1980s, little theoretical attention was directed toward exploring the privatization concept itself. This was particularly true of heterodox economists. To the extent privatization was treated at all by these analysts, it was generally treated within larger discussions constructed around more traditional Marxian (and Left) themes, including: uneven development; deindustrialization; and, the role of government and its relation to capitalist development.

2.8 THE 1990s: NEOLIBERALISM AND GLOBALIZATION

As previously noted, privatization's role within the "reinventing government" framework adopted by the Clinton administration secured its continuing importance on the national policy agenda during the 1990s. As the decade unfolded, the heterodox terrain of the privatization discourse became increasingly focused on constructing theoretical responses to the rise of Neoliberalism around the world.[73] In this context, the meaning of privatization was different from the one that had predominated during the 1970s and 1980s. In particular, the concept became linked to various efforts by nations to denationalize and/or liberalize their economies and capital markets. In many cases, the World Bank and IMF mandated such reforms as conditions for "structural adjustment" loans. Left theoretical interest in privatization, thus, became increasingly wedded to the Neoliberal development and globalization discourses. One by-product of this shift of meaning was that whatever little interest in privatization at the local government level had existed waned still further. At the same time, however, privatization's prevalence on the local government level increased dramatically.

Thus, similar to the late-1970s and 1980s, the issue of privatization (and, especially municipal privatization) was, during much of the 1990s, often but a subplot in a much grander Marxian and heterodox discourse. Whereas "crisis" and "deindustrialization" held the Marxian and heterodox center-stage during the 1970s and 1980s, Neoliberalism and/or globalization increasingly came to occupy it during much of the 1990s. The privatization movement of course was a common thread that ran through all three period-based Marxian and heterodox metanarratives. Yet, despite this, no theoretical work, grounded in a Marxian political economy, undertook a comprehensive study of privatization at the municipal level. This book is an attempt to redresses this lacuna.

2.9 CRITIQUING THE DISCOURSE: ASSESSING METHODOLOGY AND CONTENT

While the foregoing discussion sketched the evolution of the privatization discourse in both its mainstream and heterodox contexts, the remainder of this chapter critiques the discourse. This critique sets the stage for introducing (in the next chapter) the class-based approach to privatization this book develops and uses to analyze one of the most high-profile municipal privatizations of the 1990s—the privatization of New York City's Central Park. Two separate, though related, lines of argument comprise the critique. The first concerns the ontological logic that underlies the discourse on municipal privatization. The second concerns the discourse's content.

The Ontological Logic of the Discourse. Every discourse includes an understanding of cause and effect, or deploys an ontological logic. This understanding governs the way a discourse's contributors relate the social phenomena about which they theorize to other objects in the social totality. This logic may or may not be explicitly recognized and/or acknowledged by those employing it. Similar to many social scientific discourses, the one on municipal privatization has been dominated by essentialist or reductionist notions of causality. Such approaches to causality assume that all social phenomena can be understood through a cause and effect framework. Analysts using this framework view their central task as exploring the causal nexus of relationships surrounding the social phenomenon under investigation, e.g., a particular privatization process. Regardless of the analytical tools used, some cause(s) is (are) determined to be more important, significant, or essential in explaining and/or conceptualizing the phenomenon than others.[74] In this sense, any particular social phenomenon is assumed to be reducible to an underlying essence (or, cause(s)). Additionally, the social phenomenon is generally conceptualized as yielding some particular effect(s). As with its causes, one (or, some subset) of the phenomenon's theorized effects is assumed to be more important, significant, or essential than all others. This approach to causality (or, ontological logic) pervades the municipal privatization discourse.

For both the public choice and Walrasian theoretic traditions, efficiency is understood to be a result or an effect. More specifically, in the context of the Walrasian general equilibrium framework, both allocative and productive efficiency *result,* provided a particular set of conditions, ones characterizing the environment within which firms and consumers operate, are met. Once realized, these conditions ensure a "perfectly competitive" environment. The theory of rationality underlying the Walrasian superstructure ensures that this environment's agents behave in a particular manner—each seeks to maximize utility or profit. The market or price mechanism—the vehicle through which choice (or, preference) is mediated in the theory—produces the information necessary to guide the behavioral responses of all agents operating in the environment. Agents' behavior thus reflects the environmental constraints under which it is enacted and thereby produces rational, efficient outcomes. The presence of a competitive environment is thus essential to the efficiency conclusions that flow from the Walrasian general equilibrium framework. The inefficiency held to characterize the production of municipal goods and services is thus (it is assumed) a reflection of the absence of the conditions necessary for a competitive environment.

Above all, municipal privatizations are meant to replicate or generate a (more) competitive environment. How exactly are they conceptualized as accomplishing this? In the context of the theory of privatization that underlies the municipal privatization discourse, the theoretical importance imputed to the locational transfer of production invoked by a privatization process—viz., the production of public goods or services will no longer takes place *inside* the public sector but *in* the private sector—derives from the fact that this transfer (it is assumed) will alter the environment within which the production of public goods and services takes place. While these alterations are many and varied, the theory underlying the municipal privatization discourse focuses on two: the managerial process (reflecting the discourse's public-choice strand), and the competitive process (reflecting the discourse's Tiebout strand). By changing the managerial and/or competitive processes associated with the production of public goods and services, privatizations *produce* the conditions necessary for a (more) competitive environment. It follows that privatizations (to the extent they successfully produce or replicate these conditions) will (according to theory) increase the efficiency of public good and service production.

In this way, municipal privatizations are *reduced* to an underlying essence, one comprising the managerial and/or competitive processes associated with the production of public goods and services. More specifically, the essence of privatization processes is conceptualized as comprising the *changes* they imply in one or both these processes. For example, the privatization of a public good or service via contracting-out will (via competitive bidding) alter the environment within which the production of the good or service occurs (i.e., competitive forces will be brought to bear on its production). Alternatively, the privatization of a public good or service via managed competition will alter the constraints under which the municipal agency head responsible for the production of the public good or service acts (i.e., the head will no longer operate under monopoly constraints).[75] Further, and more importantly, privatizations are conceptualized as driving or causing efficiency gains. From the public administrator's perspective, such gains should translate into cost savings. (See Figure 2.1)

As noted, a significant part of the contributions to the municipal privatization discourse's early stages (especially as it played out during the late 1970s and 1980s), were dedicated to empirically verifying the causal linkages theorized between various privatization initiatives and efficiency and/or cost outcomes.[76] Indeed, despite differences in the specific research questions explored, the discourse's terrain quickly became littered with case studies and econometric analyses exploring and/or contesting the causal linkages between privatization initiatives (often contracting-out) and their efficiency and/or cost implications.

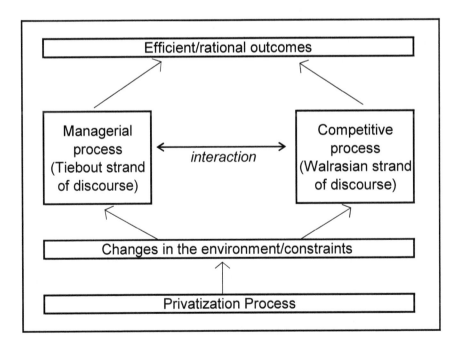

Figure 2.1 Conceptualizing Privatization Processes

The second stage of the discourse, developed over the latter part of the 1980s and 1990s, saw an explosion of new research questions related to privatization. For instance, these studies explored privatizations' effect(s) on: employee job satisfaction and well-being; the structure of the mental health system; alcohol sales and consumption; gender issues and property rights; professional ethics in health care; access to health care; broadcast media and news reporting; public sector unions and collective bargaining; labor market fragmentation; public employment levels; and, industrial relations institutions and outcomes.[77] Despite the novelty of specific questions under exploration, the ontological logic underlying such analyses remained decidedly reductionist. Privatization initiatives were foremost conceptualized as occupying the first position of a starkly reductionist ontological chain.

Despite obvious differences in the policy conclusions drawn, Left-oriented contributions to the discourse's second stage shared the reductionist ontological logic that underwrote mainstream contributions. Thus, while privatization proponents presented arguments causally linking privatization with the various outcomes they supported, contributors from the Left (generally privatization opponents) either contested these causal linkages or connected privatizations to outcomes or results they did not support.

The Content of the Privatization Discourse: The Absence of Class and the Absence of Class as Process. The second line of critique, which is closely related to the first, concerns the privatization discourse's content. Specifically, the hegemony of reductionist and/or essentialist notions of causality in the discourse have meant that privatization initiatives under analytical investigation have invariably been placed in a causal role, viz., privatization x increases efficiency, reduces costs or public employment levels, etc. The by-product of this reductionist ontology has been that most contributions to the discourse have worked to shift theoretical focus *away from* the privatization process *itself*. Beyond opening remarks regarding what a privatization means or entails in a specific research context (e.g., contracting, managed competition, etc.), most analysts have devoted little theoretical attention to the actual privatization process itself. Keen to say something about privatization—whether good or bad—contributors to the discourse have skipped theoretical investigation of the actual privatization process (taking its *presumed* essence (changes in the competitive and/or managerial processes) as given), and focused exclusively on its presumed consequences. Put otherwise, privatization processes have invariably become but a dummy or shift variable in a discourse dominated by reductionist understandings of causality. The result has been that the discourse has invariably moved too quickly from privatization *to* the epiphenomena it is theorized to have caused or affected. Questions regarding what changes are involved *in the production process itself*—changes that are necessarily implied once the production of a public good or service is performed by a non-public employee instead of a public one—have gone unasked and unexplored.

This book argues that the change in production arrangements invoked by a privatization process involves more than changes in the competitive and/or managerial processes associated with the production of public goods and services. Specifically, the public sector worker stands *economically in a different relation* compared to his private sector counterpart. Whereas the public employee's wage derives from *tax revenue,* the private employee's derives from *capital.* The failure to theoretically recognize this important difference and the implications that flow from it—and thereby to interrogate the privatization concept *itself*—reflects the absence of any *class content* in the municipal privatization discourse. As the ensuing chapter explains, this book represents an attempt to inject class content into the municipal privatization discourse. This allows privatization processes to be freed from the causal positions they occupy within reductionist ontological frameworks, and reconceptualized as *ensembles* of complex and contradictory class processes. Before setting out the theoretical framework that guides this attempt, some final comments regarding class and the privatization discourse are warranted.

It is not surprising that the mainstream privatization discourse is largely void of class considerations; class is generally not considered a valid theoretical category within many mainstream disciplines (including economics). Alternatively, one might expect to find some type of class dimension in the Marxian and heterodox discourse on privatization. Two points can be made regarding this expectation.

First, as elaborated, there has been little Marxian and/or heterodox work that treats privatization explicitly. When privatization has surfaced in Marxian and heterodox analysis, it has tended to be treated within larger metanarratives, e.g., crisis theory (1970s), entrepreneurial government (1980s and 1990s), and Neoliberalism (1990s). For many Marxists and heterodox analysts, the 1970s fiscal crisis, the ensuing government restructuring movement (which inaugurated the municipal privatization movement and eventually yielded the entrepreneurial government movement), and the subsequent attack on the welfare state set in motion on the national level by Reagan, were seen as prime examples of the on-going great historical class conflict between capital and labor. [78] In various ways, heterodox commentary interpreted the 1970s crisis milieu, and the subsequent 1980s and 1990s government restructuring movement as ones in which the state apparatus—local, state, or federal government—mediated the class conflict inherent in the capitalist system. This mediation or social harmonization role assigned to the state was, for instance, epitomized in O'Connor's legitimization function. Thus, while the *concept* of privatization arose in this body of literature (which was undoubtedly heavily infused with class content) it was rarely the center of analytical attention.

Second, a class dimension has been incorporated in some heterodox work that treats privatization explicitly. This class dimension enters via this work's interest in privatizations' effects on distributional equity and access to public goods and services.[79] This work has highlighted the declines in quantity and/or quality of public goods and services that particular groups—construed in broad socio-economic or class terms—experience following particular forms of privatization (usually contracting-out or voucher schemes). Such analyses have discovered that private producers of public goods and services often "skim" or serve the "best" or least-costly citizen-clients, while providing either no services or goods to others, or far inferior ones.

Two comments can be made regarding this body of heterodox work and its incorporation of class in the privatization context. First, similar to traditional Marxian analysis, this body of work conceives class as a referent. Whereas in traditional Marxian analysis the two great classes comprise capital and labor, the heterodox work on privatization generally conceives class in broad socioeconomic terms, e.g., groups delineated along racial, ethnic, or income lines.[80] Recognition of this particular approach to class (in the privatization context) is important in the current context precisely because there are alternative approaches to class. In particular, the approach that guides the remainder of this book conceptualizes class *as a process*. Hence, class is understood as an adjective (not a noun) designating a specific economic process—one that involves the production, appropriation, and distribution of surplus labor. As the ensuing chapter explains, this approach to class produces a decidedly different type of analysis of municipal privatization than those heterodox analyses that conceive class as a referent.

Second, the body of heterodox work that incorporates class into its analysis of privatization does so because of its interest in saying something regarding the *consequences* of privatization, e.g., its distributional and equity effects. Indeed, in this sense, this work (as noted) shares the ontology of the mainstream privatization discourse. This work does not, however, incorporate class in its basic conceptualization of privatization processes. Instead, it conceives these processes in the same manner in which most mainstream analysts do: the essence of privatization processes lies in the changes they imply in the competitive and managerial processes associated with the production of public goods and services. As a result, analytical effort is directed toward qualitatively and/or quantitatively describing and/or assessing the epiphenomena (changes in distribution and equity) the privatization act under investigation is *assumed to have caused.* Thus, the class implications (which relate to the fact that a public good or service will no longer be produced by public sector workers) of the privatization process *itself* (as opposed to its presumed consequences) are not examined.

The class analytic approach toward municipal privatization developed in the remainder of the book *begins* by recognizing the class implications involved in any municipal privatization process. The following chapter discusses these implications and explains why recognition of them comprises *but the starting point* for a class analytic approach to municipal privatization.

Chapter Three
A Class Approach to Municipal Privatization

This chapter explains what a class analytic approach to municipal privatization entails. It begins by sketching the Marxian class theory that underlies the approach. This sketch introduces the two concepts—the class process and overdetermination—that structure the approach. The aim of the discussion is to provide a framework and vocabulary that facilitate comprehension of the class analysis of Central Park's privatization developed in the next chapter. In addition to explaining the approach's implications, the discussion also compares it to the mainstream approaches whose evolution was traced in Chapter Two. The chapter's appendix extends the discussion of implications by addressing the issue of post-privatization wage outcomes.

3.1 THE CLASS PROCESS, CLASSES, AND THE SUBSUMED CLASS PROCESS

The focal point of the Marxian class theory that underlies a class analytic approach to municipal privatization is a particular economic process—the class process. A class process involves the production and appropriation of *surplus labor*.[1] For example, workers in a productive enterprise perform an amount of labor necessary to produce the goods and services their standard of living requires, i.e., they perform necessary labor. Thus, the goods or services produced during the portion of the day in which workers perform necessary labor are conceived as those they use to reproduce their own capacity to labor, i.e., they consume these goods or services as their standard of living. In most societies, however, workers perform labor beyond that which is necessary, i.e., they perform surplus labor. The goods and services produced during the portion of the day in which workers perform surplus labor may be kept by the workers (individually or collectively), or they may be "received" by others who did not directly participate in their production.

Because Marx theorized that surplus labor was embodied in the goods and services it produced, the receipt of goods or services produced during the portion of the day in which workers perform surplus labor can also be viewed as a receipt of surplus labor. The receipt of surplus labor (by anyone) is referred to as appropriation.

Marx recognized that the surplus labor produced in different types of societies was appropriated in different ways. That is to say, there were different means by which surplus labor was "extracted" from those who produce it. For example, in feudal society, the surplus labor performed by serfs often took the form of in-kind feudal rent that was periodically delivered to feudal lords. Because he theorized surplus labor as the creation of "unpaid value" in a capitalist commodity-producing society, Marx argued that the surplus labor produced in a capitalist society takes the form of surplus value. As noted, surplus value is conceived to be embodied within the goods and services capitalist wage-workers produce. Because wage-workers' employers "receive" the goods or services their employees produce, they are said to appropriate surplus value.

The different forms surplus labor takes (which reflect the different ways in which it is extracted from productive workers) serve as a basis for differentiating class processes. Thus, slave, communist, independent, feudal, or capitalist class processes may be differentiated on the basis of the form that the surplus labor they give rise to takes. These different types of class processes also serve as a means of periodizing the various types of social formations that have existed across history. Marx referred to primitive communist, slave, feudal, capitalist, and communist social formations. While all these social formations include (included) several types of class processes, the periodization or differentiation of any one concerns the prevalence of the class processes it hosted. In this way, the prevalence of a particular class process, say, the feudal class process, can be used as a basis for designating a particular social formation's (e.g., feudalism's) historical periodization as well as its theoretical specificity.

The specification of a class process as the production and appropriation of surplus labor leads to a particular interpretation of *classes*. Specifically, anyone who participates in a class process occupies a class position. For example, in a capitalist class process, wage-workers (who perform surplus labor) and those who appropriate that labor (capitalists) occupy class positions. Thus, there are two class positions associated with any class process: surplus labor performer (e.g., wage-workers) and surplus labor appropriator (e.g., capitalist). As will be explained momentarily, other individuals will also likely receive distributed portions of surplus labor. Such individuals occupy another class position. The upshot is that within Marxian class theory *classes* designate an individual's or entity's relationship *to surplus labor,* i.e., the individual *produces* surplus labor, *appropriates* it, *distributes* it, or *receives* a portion of it. It follows that individuals can occupy multiple class positions and may therefore belong to more than one class. For instance, an individual may occupy the class position of surplus labor performer in one site in society (say, in a capitalist commodity-producing enterprise), and simultaneously occupy a class position of surplus labor appropriator in another (say, in his household). This understanding of classes is thus very different from those in which classes designate particular groups of persons based on such criteria as income, wages, or socioeconomic status.

While the production and appropriation of surplus labor comprise the class process, the *subsumed* class process refers to the *distribution* of appropriated and realized surplus labor (regardless of the form it takes, e.g., in-kind feudal rent, surplus value, etc). Subsumed class distributions are made to individuals or entities that provide the many conditions that allow the *fundamental* class process (the production and appropriation of surplus labor) to occur. For example, a capitalist enterprise often makes subsumed class distributions (i.e., distributes a portion of appropriated and realized surplus value) to: the landlord that provides him with access to a certain parcel of land or a particular building; a banker that provides him with money capital; the state which provides him various services such as police and fire protection, paved streets, public transportation, etc. These subsumed class distributions (or, cuts of surplus value) take the form of rent, interest, and taxes, respectively. Individuals and entities that receive cuts of a capitalist's surplus value comprise a class and are referred to as subsumed class recipients.

3.2 OVERDETERMINATION

The Marxian class theory that underlies a class approach to municipal privatization conceptualizes the social totality as a constellation of densely interconnected processes (e.g., economic, political, cultural, and, natural ones).[2] Particular configurations of processes yield social relationships, which, in turn, constitute social sites, e.g., productive enterprises and households. These sites are thus constituted by a host of relationships which are themselves comprised of bundles of economic, political, cultural, and natural processes. Any site in society is nothing but a diverse and ever-changing bundle of processes. This conceptualization imparts an understanding of ceaseless movement or change to the social totality and the sites within it.

While all of the processes comprising a site exert their own effects upon the site, no one process is considered any more or less important than any other. More specifically, while the class process is a constituent part of an enterprise, it is not considered any more or less important that any other process that helps constitute the enterprise, e.g., its political processes. Thus, all of the processes that comprise a site *overdetermine* it. It follows that the processes comprising any site not only overdetermine that site, but simultaneously overdetermine each other. This implies, for example, that the fundamental and subsumed class processes that help constitute an enterprise not only overdetermine one another but also overdetermine (and are overdetermined by) all of the other processes constituting the enterprise.

Overdetermination implies more than mutual effectivity or causation, e.g., two or more independent processes mutually influencing one another. Instead, the crux of the concept is *constitutivity*—an idea that renders problematic the independence notion upon which the idea of mutual effectivity or causation rests. The concept therefore entails a distinct approach to and understanding of causality: no one process may be understood to be the unique effect of one or some subset of other processes. And, no one process, or subset of processes, may be deemed the unique cause(s) of any other process. This approach to and understanding of causality is referred to as an antiessentialist or antireductionist social theory or ontology. Unlike essentialist and reductionist social theories (like those that pervade the municipal privatization discourse), an antiessentialist ontology holds that no one process or site in the social totality can be conceptualized or explained by reducing it to some essential (or, set of) process(es) or cause(s).

The concept of *contradiction* is intimately connected to and bound up with the concept of overdetermination and the associated conceptualization of the social totality. As stated, the processes that comprise the social totality mutually constitute or overdetermine one another along with the sites they comprise. And, "because each distinct social process is the site constituted by the interaction of all other social processes, each contains "within itself" the very different and conflicting qualities, influences, moments, and directions of all those other social processes that constitute it."[3] In this sense, every process (and subsequently the social sites that processes constitute) contains or embodies all of the contradictions and complexities arising out of or associated with all of the other process that overdetermine its very existence. In short, all change is understood to be but an expression of the contradictions inherent in the constitutivity of all processes and the social sites they comprise.

Now that the concepts of class process and overdetermination have been introduced, the remainder of the chapter explains how their deployment underwrites a class approach to municipal privatization.

3.3 THE IMPLICATIONS OF A CLASS APPROACH TO MUNICIPAL PRIVATIZATION

As explained in Chapter One, municipal privatizations take a variety of institutional forms. Despite this fact, they involve the partial or complete transfer of the production of a public good or service to a private entity—in most cases, to a for- or non-profit entity. For this reason, they are often understood and described conceptually in locational terms, viz., production will no longer takes place *inside* the public sector but *in* the private sector. In the context of the theory of privatization that underlies the existing municipal privatization discourse (elaborated upon in Chapter Two), the theoretical importance imputed to this locational transfer derives from the fact that it is held to result in substantive changes in the environment within which the production of public goods or services takes place. More specifically, privatization processes *comprise* (i.e., are reduced conceptually to) changes in the managerial and/or competitive processes associated with the production of a public good or service. By inducing changes in one or both of these processes, privatization processes (according to theory) should yield efficiency gains and cost savings.

Changes in the managerial and competitive processes are not the primary focus of a class analytic approach toward municipal privatization. Instead, analytical focus is placed on the *class changes* induced by privatization. Specifically, the transfer of a public good or service to a private entity via a privatization process means it is no longer produced as a mere "use-value." A public park, for example, is consumed by the public and is therefore useful, i.e., it has use-value. It does not generally have "exchange value" however, i.e., it is not produced as a commodity for the purpose of exchange. Municipal workers generally produce parks. Because these workers' labor does not yield an exchangeable commodity, and because these workers exchange their labor-power against revenue (they receive a wage from the municipality out of collected tax revenues) not capital, the production of a public park, like municipal goods and services in general, *does not involve a class process as no surplus is produced.*[4]

Once a public good or service is privatized it becomes an object of exchange (a commodity), i.e., it represents *both* a use-value and an exchange value. Regardless of the institutional form the privatization takes, an exchange process occurs between the municipality undertaking the privatization and the private entity that will henceforth produce the public good or service. From a Marxian class perspective, this means the public good or service will be produced under starkly different social relations. In particular, the good's or service's production will now *require a class process whereas before it did not*. Recognition of this fact is important for two reasons.

First, any class process must be *reproduced* by the organization or enterprise that hosts it, i.e., the entity or enterprise must continually make efforts to reproduce its class process if it is going to continue to exist. Such efforts will necessarily impinge in complex and contradictory ways upon many other individuals and entities in the locale in which the privatization occurs. As the class analysis of Central Park's privatization reveals, efforts to reproduce a class process constitute an organization's subsumed class and nonclass processes. (Nonclass processes are ones that do not involve the production, appropriation, and distribution of surplus labor.) Analyzing an organization's (one that comes to produce a public good or service via a privatization process) subsumed class and nonclass processes considerably widens the field of "effects" that can be related to the privatization process. Thus, a privatization process *itself* can be reconceptualized as an ensemble of complex and overdetermined class and nonclass processes.

The theoretical differences between a class analytic approach to municipal privatization and most mainstream approaches are thus stark. A class analytic approach's recognition of the class implications of a privatization process not only considerably widens the field of effects that can be related to it, but necessarily places the organization that comes to produce the public good or service following its privatization at the center of analytical attention: the approach aims to explicate the complex effects that flow from such an organization's efforts to reproduce its class process. It is *through* such explication that the privatization process *itself* is analyzed (or, related to the larger social environment in which it occurs). In contrast, in the mainstream privatization discourse, analytical attention is usually directed away from these organizations and instead placed on an outcome variable (e.g., efficiency, municipality expenditures, public sector wages or employment, service quality and quantity, etc.) *assumed* to be affected somehow by the privatization. Thus, mainstream conceptions of municipal privatization tend to be structured around the outcomes presumed to flow from them. Because of this, the organizations involved in privatization processes tend to be of little theoretical or empirical interest. At moments when they do become objects of interest it is often due to prior interest in some outcome variable. Actual explicit theoretical and/or empirical investigation of these organizations is rare.

The mainstream discourse's neglect of the organizations central to municipal privatizations is largely attributable to the Walrasian and neo-classical economics traditions' approach toward the enterprise. More specifically, given the assumptions that a municipal privatization generates or replicates a (more) competitive production environment, and that the organization involved in the process is a for-profit one, the usual profit-maximization assumption largely short-circuits any further theoretical or empirical interest in the organization. On the other hand, if the organization involved in the privatization process is a non-profit or public-private partnership, it is assumed that its mission (one understood in contradistinction to that of a profit-maximizing entity) largely works to obviate any additional theoretical or empirical investigation of it.

To reiterate, recognition of the class dimension of a privatization process represents the *beginning point* for a class analytic approach to municipal privatization. Once the class dimension is recognized, the approach aims to explicate how the private organization (that will produce the good or service following its privatization) reproduces its class process. This is accomplished by analyzing the organization's subsumed and nonclass processes. This analysis allows the municipal privatization to be analytically related to the broader social environment (in particular, the many social agents and entities that operate within that environment) within which it was carried out. The approach thus involves an important shift in ontological orientation—one that involves embracing the concept of overdetermination, i.e., an anti-essentialist or non-reductionist social theory. The following remark by David Harvey encapsulates this orientation: "The Marxian theory thus starts with the proposition that everything relates to everything else in society and that a particular object of enquiry must necessarily internalize a relation to the totality of which it is a part. The focus of the enquiry is, then, on the relations of the epistemological object to the totality."[5]

Thus, implicit in the approach's ontological orientation is the idea that, "the act of changing how municipal public goods or services are produced will change virtually every aspect of the social totality in which such a change occurs."[6] Such an act will impinge not only on managerial and competitive processes, but also on all processes that comprise the social environment within which the privatization is carried out. Given this ontological orientation, a class analytic approach to municipal privatization uses the class process concept in order to bring a, "specific kind of order to the infinity of complexly interacting processes that a municipal privatization act will impinge upon."[7] The fact that a public good or service will, following its privatization, require a class process, and that this class process, in turn, will require efforts to ensure its reproduction, is shown, as a class analysis of a municipal privatization proceeds, to impinge upon a host of entities (e.g., capitalist enterprises, non-capitalist producers, and the municipality involved) in complex and contradictory ways.

The implications of this shift in ontological orientation should not be underestimated. Instead of *assuming* a privatization process occupies the *causal* position in a deterministic logic chain (viz., privatization >> increased competition/altered managerial environment >> increased efficiency), which "assumes necessity in the form of determinate relationships between privatization acts and outcomes," a class analytic approach "produces necessity as an effect of analysis." As a result, "causation/determination becomes a specific discursive effect rather than a pre-analytical ascription of ontological privilege."[8] That is to say, a specific notion of causation/determination is implicit in the theoretical concept specified as the class process. By analyzing an organization that lies at the center of a municipal privatization process (using the class process concept as a conceptual organizing device), a class analysis of a municipal privatization process recasts the process as an ensemble of contradictory class and nonclass processes (effects). The explication of these contradictions and interactions constitutes the objective of a class analytic approach to municipal privatization.

Additionally, by embracing an overdeterminist ontology, a class analytic approach to municipal privatization displaces the traditional privatization discourse's reductionist ontology and closely-related focus on efficiency. The point of a class analytic approach to municipal privatization is to examine one particular process—the class process—and how it impinges upon and reacts to the many other processes that constitute the social environment within which the privatization occurs. The mainstream discourse's general fixation on the efficiency outcomes of municipal privatizations (or, a very narrowly circumscribed set of similar outcome variables) has meant that these other processes are regularly discounted and/or ignored.

The second reason that recognition of the class dimension of municipal privatizations is important concerns the *type* of class processes most municipal privatizations have tended to create or support. The majority of municipal privatizations implemented in the United States over the past quarter-century or so have tended to create or support *capitalist* class processes. In other words, post-privatization, municipal public goods or services represent capitalist commodities containing surplus value. This means that the goods or services a democratically-elected body has decided to provide its citizens will henceforth be produced via a class process that will yield a surplus from which a profit may be derived. This class process, however, *excludes* those whose labor produced the surplus (productive workers) from participating in its appropriation and distribution. This exclusion means capitalist class processes are inherently *undemocratic*. The undemocratic nature of capitalist class processes provides the basis for the claim that they are *exploitative*. [9] Privatizations—be they ones carried out on the municipal level or on some other government level—are of interest to class theorists because they have tended to generate new or support existing undemocratic (hence, exploitative) class processes.

One final question must be addressed before the class analysis of Central Park's privatization is presented. Namely, why do some municipal privatization processes *create* class processes, while others merely *support* existing ones? The answer to this question reflects the need (from a class analytic perspective) to carefully specify the relationship between a privatization process, the *origins* of the class process that will yield the public good or service following its privatization, and the *type* of class process (e.g., capitalist, feudal, or communist) the privatization entails.

There are three possibilities regarding the relationship between a privatization process and the origin of the class process it involves. First, as Figure 3.1 shows (page 46), a municipal privatization process may involve the creation of an entirely new enterprise or organization. The creation of public authorities and public-private partnerships—quasi-independent entities established to oversee, manage, produce, and, perhaps most importantly, finance various public goods and services—in the municipal and county contexts in the United States are representative examples. In such privatizations, the creation of a new enterprise or organization would simultaneously create a class process. Second, a municipal privatization process might transfer the production of a public good or service to an existing organization that did not (prior to the privatization) host a class process. In this case, the privatization would *create* a class process within an existing organization. Third, a municipal privatization might simply transfer the production of a public good or service to an existing enterprise that already hosts a class process. Unlike the first two cases, such a privatization would *not* involve the creation of a new class process but would support an existing one.

In order to head off potential confusion that might arise from the foregoing discussion, one point should be reiterated. Specifically, regardless of the precise institutional form a municipal privatization process takes (e.g., a contract, a franchise, an asset sale, etc.), it involves the transfer of the production of a public good or service to a private entity. The subsequent production of that good or service by the entity will involve a class process whereas before the privatization the good's or service's production did not. Whether or not the privatization process also creates the class process (class origin forms one and two in Figure 3.1) or supports an existing class process (class origin three in Figure 3.1) is a separate issue.

These three class origin forms have tended to characterize the majority of municipal privatizations carried out in the United States during the past three decades. While the first form has become increasingly important over the past decade or so, the third has tended to be the most common. As demonstrated in the next chapter, Central Park's privatization was emblematic of the second form, i.e., the park's privatization created a class process within an organization that did not (prior to the parks' privatization) host a class process.

Two final points should be made in connection with the above discussion (and Figure 3.1). First, it should be recognized that the first two class origin forms leave open the question as to the actual *type* of class process that is created via the privatization. Second, other types of privatization process—specifically, those involving the divestiture of state-owned enterprises—necessitate consideration of two additional class origin forms. In particular, the privatization of state-owned enterprise can maintain a state-owned enterprise's class process. Alternatively, such a privatization could *transform* the enterprise's class process. As shown in Chapter Six, a class-structural privatization involving a state-owned enterprise has important policy implications.

APPENDIX: POST-PRIVATIZATION WAGE OUTCOMES

The issue of municipal privatization processes' impact on wages and benefits has long occupied a prominent place within the discourse. The issue has been a central concern among labor advocates (especially labor unions) and heterodox theorists. As discussed in Chapter Two, expected cost savings often underlie privatization efforts at the municipal level in the United States. Privatization advocates argue that the wage "premiums" often enjoyed by public sector workers (vis-à-vis their private sector counterparts) represent a potential source of cost savings that municipalities should exploit. It is often assumed that these premiums reflect the higher rates of unionization that tend to prevail in the public sector. Union resistance to privatization efforts at the municipal level, most notably by the American Federation of State, County, and Municipal Employees (AFSCME), has been (and continues to be) fierce and well documented.

The wage issue's prominence within the discourse mandates commentary. In particular, articulating how a class analytic approach to municipal privatization differs from those that focus on the wage issue is important. At the same time, explaining how the wage issue would be accommodated within a class analytic approach is also important.

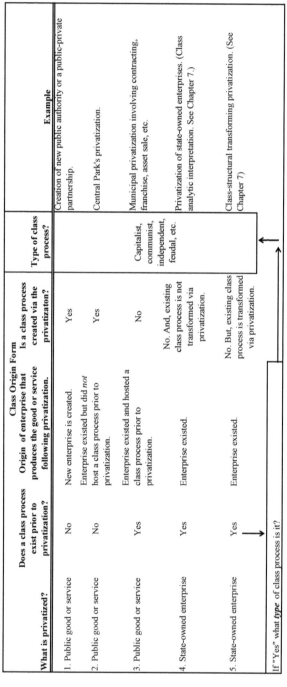

What is privatized?	Does a class process exist prior to privatization?	Class Origin Form	Is a class process created via the privatizaton?	Type of class process?	Example
		Origin of enterprise that produces the good or service following privatization.			
1. Public good or service	No	New enterprise is created.	Yes		Creation of new public authority or a public-private partnership.
2. Public good or service	No	Enterprise existed but did *not* host a class process prior to privatization.	Yes		Central Park's privatization.
3. Public good or service	Yes	Enterprise existed and hosted a class process prior to privatization.	No	Capitalist, communist, independent, feudal, etc.	Municipal privatization involving contracting, franchise, asset sale, etc.
4. State-owned enterprise	Yes	Enterprise existed.	No. And, existing class process is not transformed via privatization.		Privatization of state-owned enterprises. (Class analytic interpretation. See Chapter 7.)
5. State-owned enterprise	Yes	Enterprise existed.	No. But, existing class process is transformed via privatization.		Class-structural transforming privatization. (See Chapter 7)

If "Yes" what *type* of class process is it?

Figure 3.1: The Class Origin Form and Class Type of Privatization

THE LITERATURE ON LABOR'S POST-PRIVATIZATION WAGE OUTCOME

Despite significant empirical investigations of the cost savings issue surrounding municipal privatization, there are surprisingly few empirical analyses that compare pre- vs. post-privatization wage outcomes. In part, this reflects the difficultly of obtaining the relevant wage data. In many cases, analysts interested in the wage question have conjoined alleged findings of reduced costs of private production of public goods and services with: 1) the idea that public sector workers enjoy wage premiums and, 2) the idea that labor costs account for a significant share of total costs, to infer that findings of reduced total costs are attributable to labor cost savings.

The majority of the literature's insight on the wage outcome question is drawn from a handful of studies carried out during the 1980s. The National Commission on Employment Policy (NCEP) produced a comprehensive report in 1989 that analyzed the effects of privatization on city and county employees.[10] The study, encompassing thirty-four separate privatization acts, involved tracking the employment and wage status of more than 2,000 workers. It found that private contractors who came to produce a public good or service following its privatization hired more than half of the affected public sector workers. Twenty-four percent of the workers were transferred to other government jobs; sever percent retired; and, three percent were laid off. The study also concluded that there were more instances in which affected workers' wages *increased* than decreased after privatization. The study did note differences in benefits, however; government benefits were often more generous than those provided by private sector enterprises.

A U.S. Department of Housing and Urban Development study in 1984, which compared wage levels for eight services in twenty California cities—half of which produced the service in-house, and half which relied upon private enterprises for production—revealed little difference in the wage levels between the two sectors.[11] Comparable benefit levels were also found.

More recently, several analysts have attempted to shed light on the wage question via regression techniques. Such analyses involve estimating the earnings differentials between public and private sector workers, union and non-union workers, and the intersections of these cohorts. In this context, findings of earnings differentials between these (four) cohorts are interpreted as a means of gauging the potential labor costs savings that municipal privatization initiatives could realize.

Two recent studies that have employed these types of approaches are Hoover and Peoples and Wang.[12] Based on earnings equations regressions that use pooled data drawn from the Current Population Survey for the period 1983 to 1996, Hoover and Peoples estimate that unionized sanitation workers in the public sector received weekly earnings that were: 14.9 percent higher than their non-union counterparts in the public sector; 9.2 percent higher than non-union workers in the private sector; and, 11 percent higher than unionized private sector workers. Hoover and Peoples also document the differences between the rates of employer-provided pension and health care benefits that exist between public and private and union and non-union sanitation workers. For instance, whereas ninety-seven percent of unionized public sector sanitation workers have an employer-provided pension plan, just sixty-two percent of their non-union private sector counterparts do. The rates for these same two groups for employer-provided health care are 93.5 percent and eighty-five percent, respectively. As a consequence of these differences in benefits, the authors note that despite the earnings differentials (cited above), "the largest overall labor savings is likely to arise from using nonunion workers in the private sector."[13]

By combining two widely used government surveys (the Current Population Survey and the Census of Governments), Wang constructs a dataset that allows him to derive a geographical-based continuous privatization variable that can be incorporated into a traditional earnings equations regression framework. Wang's analysis provides estimates of the changes in wage outcomes (for workers in fourteen different industries) associated with an increase in the probability of privatization.[14] Wang concludes: "Our results show that in most industries earnings for both union and nonunion public workers will shrink when the probability of privatization increases."[15]

There has been more extensive investigation of the pre- versus post-privatization wage and benefits issue outside the U.S. municipal context. Much of this work was conducted in the late 1980s and early 1990s in the U.K., reflecting the country's extensive experience with the privatization of nationalized concerns and sectors under Thatcher. The findings emanating from that body of research have proven mixed on the wage question. According to Pendleton,

> "Anecdotal evidence collected by the Trades Union Congress on companies privatized in the early years of the Thatcher Government uncovered some unfavorable developments for workers, such as the consolidation of bonuses on unfavorable terms for British Shipbuilder's Yarrow yard and the reluctance of purchases of British Transport Hotels to maintain existing pay levels and institutions; but there was no evidence of a generalized downward movement in either rate of pay or total pay."[16]

Pendleton goes on to cite a study of pay in the public and private sectors and privatized companies between 1979 and 1988 by Bishop and Kay, which found that the average level of pay increased most in the privatized companies.[17] He also cites Haskel's and Szymanski's comparative study of fourteen public sector firms (four of which were privatized during the study period) and the economy as a whole, which found that the growth in wages during the 1980s was very similar in the two groups.[18] Moreover, no clear differences between the privatized and public sector firms were found.

An important issue raised in this U.K. body of research concerns the difficultly of separating out the influences of ownership changes from competition (or, compulsory competitive tendering (CCT), which was an important component of the U.K. privatization experience under Thatcher) on post-privatization changes in workers' pay and benefits. The hypothesis that competition not the change in ownership is the primary driver of the cost savings that flow from privatization has spawned additional research effort aimed at more precisely sourcing the cost savings and explaining how they relate to CCT.

As Pendleton notes, these research efforts have turned up evidence of contractors securing competitive advantages via reductions in pay and benefits of the public employees transferred to them. He cites several case studies of CCT. Collings found that CCT worked to cut workers' bonuses, resulting in a pay cut for some of around twenty-five percent.[19] He also found evidence of reductions in working time aimed at lowering employers' national insurance contributions. Davis' and Walsh's survey of CCT in forty local authorities found that only seven percent of successful contractors reduced basic pay and less than fifteen percent abolished the bonus system or cut holiday entitlements.[20] Pendleton interprets such surveys as offering evidence that, "reductions in the cost of service provision may be secured primarily by reforms to working practices and work intensification rather than adjustments to pay and benefits."

The upshot of this brief survey of research on the post-privatization wage question is this: one who approaches privatization with a principal concern with labor's wage outcome confronts ambiguous evidence (wages and benefits may rise, fall, or remain unchanged following privatization). Any particular privatization might prove beneficial or detrimental for public sector workers on wage and benefit grounds. Thus, one might reasonably stake out an infinite number of policy, political, and/or moral positions on particular municipal privatization acts on those grounds.

From a class perspective, the wage question is entirely recast. There are two substantive issues. First, the very different ontological framework that undergirds a class analytic approach to municipal privatization—premised on the concept of overdetermination—explicitly recognizes that changes in labor's post-privatization wage will be complexly overdetermined by a host of different processes. This idea flows directly from the recognition that any privatization will impinge not only on managerial and competitive processes, but also on all processes comprising the social totality, including political, cultural, and natural ones. All of these processes will impinge upon the wage outcome. Indeed, the apparent ambiguous evidence on the post-privatization wage issue lends support to this notion.

Further, recognition of the overdetermined nature of the post-privatization wage outcome forces an analyst to choose an "entry point" prior to investigating the wage issue. This choice allows the analyst to bring a specific type of order to the wage question. A class analyst selects the class process as his entry point. It is only after the class process has been selected as an entry point that the issue of an increase or decrease in labor's post-privatization wage can be interpreted and analyzed. Put otherwise, from a class perspective such wage changes become intelligible only once the wage category has been class contextualized.[21]

The second and perhaps more important issue regarding the post-privatization wage outcome question is that, from a class perspective, wage outcomes are not the primary focal point. Instead, as explained, a class theorist approaches the analysis of a privatization process with a principle interest in its class implications. Thus, a class theorist's political position on any privatization process will not hinge on the wage outcomes observed following the privatization (which, as explained, will necessarily be complexly overdetermined not only by the privatization process but many other social processes). Rather, his position will be based on the *type* of class process the privatization creates or supports.

More specifically, if a municipal privatization process generates a new *exploitative* class process (class origin forms one or two in Figure 3.1) or supports an existing one (class origin form three in Figure 3.1) it is viewed negatively on the grounds that the public good or service privatized will be produced via an undemocratic class process. Thus, it is entirely possible that a class theorist would support a municipal privatization in which productive workers' post-privatization wage was observed to decline, but which simultaneously allowed them to participate in appropriating and distributing the surplus they produced in the course of producing the public good or service. This support would reflect the fact that the production of the public good or service would involve a democratic (hence, non-exploitative) class process. By way of contrast, one who approaches municipal privatization with a principle concern for workers' post-privatization wage must be ready to acknowledge that she would (ostensibly) support a privatization process in which productive workers' post-privatization wage was observed to increase, but that generated a new or supported an existing exploitative class process. Put otherwise, a wage-oriented approach toward municipal privatization either: 1) fails to recognize and/or consider the class dimension of privatization, or 2) if it does recognize and/or consider the class dimension, elects to elevate the wage issue above the class issue. A class analytic approach to municipal privatization elevates the class issue above the wage issue.

One final point should be underscored. Specifically, the foregoing discussion does not imply that a wage-led approach to municipal privatization is inferior to a class analytic one. Rather, they are but two different approaches that can used to structure an analysis of municipal privatization. The interest in developing a class analytic approach to municipal privatization derives from the fact that it has not yet been pursued within the municipal privatization discourse.

Chapter Four

A Class Analysis of Central Park's Privatization

This chapter constructs a class analysis of Central Park's privatization. The first part of the chapter sketches the historical backdrop to the park's privatization. A class analytic interpretation of the park's privatization is then presented. This interpretation holds that the privatization process *commodified* the park. A class analysis of the organization that produces Central Park qua commodity (the Central Park Conservancy (CPC)) comprises the chapter's final section. This analysis reveals that the CPC produces the park via a *capitalist* class process. Thus, Central Park, one of the nation's most famous and treasured public goods, is, I argue, a capitalist commodity. The implications of this finding are developed in Chapter Five.

4.1 THE HISTORICAL BACKDROP TO CENTRAL PARK'S PRIVATIZATION

The Golden Age of U.S. capitalism came to an abrupt end in the 1970s, as a confluence of international geopolitical and economic events helped spark a recession that lasted longer than any since the Great Depression. A fundamental restructuring of the global capitalist system and the U.S. position therein ensued. As the decade wore on, it became increasingly apparent that these developments further added to the already intense pressures and contradictions (ones that had been ignited during the 1960s) emanating from the nation's largest urban centers. Above all, it became abundantly clear that these pressures and contradictions impinged acutely on these centers' governments' fiscal health.

Owing to its size and function as the nation's media capital, New York City's 1970's experience and well-known 1975 *de facto* bankruptcy came to symbolize the depth and severity of the urban fiscal crisis that cascaded across the country during the 1970s. Between 1969 and 1976, New

York City lost 588,000 jobs—a startling 15.5% decline. Its manufacturing sector shed 285,000 jobs, a decline of 35%, over the same period. The city lost 50,000 public-sector jobs in 1976 alone. As employment opportunities shrank, the city's population plummeted, declining 10.4% (a loss of over 800,000 persons) during the 1970s. Despite the associated decline in its labor force, the city's unemployment rate rose from under five percent in 1970 to twelve percent by mid-1975, before receding to 8.5 percent in late 1979.

The city's fiscal crisis hit its park system particularly hard. Under the severe austerity program the city was forced to adopt following its bankruptcy, the Parks Department's (Park's) budget declined $40 million between 1974 and 1980, a sixty percent cut in real terms.[1] The number of full-time permanent park workers dropped from a late-1960s peak of nearly 6,100 to about 4,800 in the early 1970s and then declined to 2,600 by 1979. Between fiscal years 1975 and 1976 Park's capital budget was reduced to $5 million from $24 million. Not surprisingly, the quality of the city's parks deteriorated dramatically. As Rosenzweig and Blackmar note, "By 1982 a state study estimated that the city's parks had almost $3 billion in deferred maintenance needs."[2]

Along with the city's other parks, Central Park's maintenance funds and staffing were cut during the 1970's fiscal crisis. In fact, Central Park may have lost as much as forty-four percent of its full-time workforce during the decade.[3] Reflecting its neglect and deterioration, New York State Senator Daniel Patrick Moynihan threatened then-Parks commissioner Gordon Davis with a federal takeover of Central Park unless something was done about what he dubbed the "national disgrace."

As Rosenzweig and Blackmar document, there had been a pronounced shift in both the meaning and use of Central Park during the 1960s.[4] In many ways, this shift was a reflection of the period's political and cultural movements, which worked to considerably broaden the types of activities that took place within the park, as it increasingly played host to regularly and often large cultural and political events, e.g., anti-war rallies. These developments meant that the city's fiscal crunch (and concomitant implications for its parks) came on the heels of a period during which the demand for Central Park had grown dramatically. These broader cultural and political trends, moreover, coincided with policy decisions to increase park spending on programs rather than maintenance and/or capital improvements.[5] Both of these factors implied that Central Park was already in need of significant rehabilitation prior to the fiscal crisis' onset.[6]

The Emergence of the Central Park Conservancy. In 1979, Davis appointed Elizabeth Barlow Rogers, a park activist and author of books and articles on parks and Olmstead, Central Park administrator. Outraged by the park's condition, Rogers had previously begun efforts to raise private monies for the park's restoration, as well as recruit volunteers to do maintenance and horticulture in the park. Davis asked Rogers to raise her own salary as administrator. In December 1980, New York City Mayor Koch officially recognized the formation of the fledgling Central Park Conservancy (CPC), which replaced Roger's own Central Park Task Force, a group of concerned park citizens, along with another private fund-raising group, the Central Park Community Fund. In an enthusiastic editorial, The New York Times heralded the formation of the CPC as signaling a unique partnership agreement between the city and the private group.

The Conservancy's board of trustees comprised thirty-some private citizens, many of whom were executives of major corporations located in the city. There were also six public trustees, three appointed by the Mayor, and three city officials that served ex officio. Rogers served as both the Conservancy's chief executive officer as well as the Central Park administrator. The administrator was appointed by the mayor and reported to the Park's commissioner, but was (and continues to be) paid by the Conservancy. Under the unique power-sharing agreement struck between the city and the CPC, the Parks Commissioner retained official control over Central Park policy. While the Conservancy's ostensible mandate was fundraising and park steward, it eventually began to play a significant role in the park's operations. By 1990, the Conservancy was supplying half the park's annual operating budget, half the funds for its capital improvements, subsidizing half of the park's staff, and almost all of its recreational and cultural programming.[7]

Soon after the CPC's formal recognition, in February 1981, Davis issued a lengthy report declining Bulgarian artist Christo's request for a two-week permit to install an unprecedented twenty-five mile long exhibit consisting of apricot-colored fabric banners hung from metal frames throughout the park. Davis's report was more than a simple denial of a park permit, however. The report, backed by the CPC, set out Gordon's intentions to affect a shift in park policy. While acknowledging the good intentions of his predecessors, who had embraced policies that placed a high value on the park as a place for recreation, education, and cultural activities, Davis argued that limits on how the public used Central Park were long overdue.

Davis' change in park policy dovetailed with the Conservancy's overarching focus to restore the park during the 1980s. At the center of this restoration process laid the Conservancy's and Rogers' deep commitment to an Olmstedian ideology, which held the park as foremost, "a scenic retreat, a peaceful space that would act as an antidote to urban stress."[8] Guided by an extensive three-year study carried out during the early 1980s, the CPC embarked on an ambitious restoration plan during the decade.[9] The CPC also began efforts to program the park, inaugurating a host of exhibitions, music series, and educational programs. By the end of the 1980s, the CPC had raised more than $65 million for the park's restoration, a feat that was aided greatly by the city's economic and real estate booms during the decade. While the CPC's fundraising efforts were undoubtedly important to the park's widely acknowledged and trumpeted "rebirth" during the decade, it remained true that the city actually paid for nearly three-quarters of the park's improvements.[10]

The CPC's restorative program continued during the 1990s, fueled by a five-year capital campaign during 1987–1991 that raised $50 million. The CPC's influence over Central Park policy and usage grew in tandem with its fundraising success. This influence and the CPC's focus on restoration also led to growing differences with various public groups' visions of the park's proper usage. Moreover, the city's severe early 1990's recession, which resulted in deep cuts in the Parks' Department budget, forced a reluctant CPC to redirect its privately-raised funds away from restoration toward subsidizing the park's maintenance personnel. These events not only worked to further the CPC's influence over the park (and, thereby exacerbate its relationship with many park users), but also heightened the city's reliance on the CPC.

Despite these realities, the city and the CPC continued to jointly operate Central Park under a rather loose agreement. In 1993, this agreement was transformed into a memorandum of understanding (MOU). This MOU established policies and procedures of mutual concern regarding the park and its operations. It did not require either party to obligate funds and did not create a legally binding commitment between the two parties. The agreement between the CPC and the city soon morphed again, however, under the mayoralty of Rudolph Giuliani.

The Mayoralty of Rudolph Giuliani. As noted in Chapter One, Rudolph Giuliani's mayoralship marked a turning point for New York City government, as he made privatization a centerpiece of his two administrations. While privatization was hardly new to New York City government, Giuliani's privatization program was specifically aimed at eliminating the inefficiencies he presumed characterized vast swaths of the city's government. Giuliani's administration implemented sixty privatization initiatives. Among the most high-profile and widely-heralded of these was the formal privatization of Central Park.

The Privatization of Central Park. Until early 1998, the aforementioned MOU governed the relationship between the CPC and the city. In

February of 1998, Giuliani fundamentally changed this relationship by entering into a renewable eight-year contract with the CPC. Under the contract, the CPC was obligated to perform "responsibilities associated with maintaining and repairing Central Park for the benefit of the public, including the provision of programs and activities that will increase public interest in and awareness of Central Park."[11] The contract also specified the two parties' respective financial commitments to one another.

Beginning with the fiscal year that began July 1, 1997 (the first year of an eight-year contract), the CPC was obligated to raise and expend a minimum of $5 million annually with respect to maintenance, repairs, programming, landscaping, and the renovation and rehabilitation of existing facilities in Central Park.[12] In consideration of these services, the city paid the CPC $1 million in the contract's first year. In the second year of the contract, the city paid the CPC an amount equal to $1 million if the $5 million threshold was met in the prior fiscal year, and $0.50 for each additional dollar raised and expended by CPC in excess of $5 million (up to a maximum equal to an additional $1 million). The structure of the contract in the third year was identical to year two except that the city also agreed to pay the CPC an amount equal to fifty percent of annual net concession revenues generated in the park above $6 million (up to a maximum of an additional $1 million). The remaining years of the contract were similar save for an increase to $2 million in the maximum paid for concessions. The contract specified that if the CPC did not meet the $5 million threshold in any single year, the city would not pay the CPC.

Given the nature of the contract, it is clear that the park's privatization (unlike many municipal privatizations) was not designed to foster competition. The policy rationale for the park's privatization centered on the managerial process underlying its production. Indeed, in the run-up to the park's privatization, Central Park Conservancy trustee and benefactor, Richard Gilder, wrote, in an essay urging the city to turn the park's management over entirely to the Conservancy:

> "What most tips the scales in favor of a management contract should
> be beyond dispute: the Conservancy does a better job running Central
> Park than the Parks Department can. The Conservancy's great advan-
> tage comes in staffing. It hires and pays its horticulturists, groundskee-
> pers, and cleanup crews as any private employer would. If they do well,
> they advance. If they do poorly, they're fired. Conservancy staffers are
> flexible enough to do more than one task, so they can be assigned to
> whatever job needs doing most urgently. And most crucial perhaps, the

Conservancy is able to instill a real sense of pride in those who work for it; they come to think of Central Park as *their* park."[13]

4.2 A CLASS ANALYTIC INTERPRETATION OF CENTRAL PARK'S PRIVATIZATION

Similar to most municipal privatizations, Central Park's privatization transferred responsibility for the production of a public good to a private entity. As explained in Chapter Three, however, the park's privatization is important from a class perspective for a more specific reason. From the point at which the contract between the CPC and the City of New York was signed, Central Park—the 843 acres that comprise the nation's most famous urban space and which lie at the center of the world's financial capital—became a good that no longer constituted a mere use-value, but one that also comprised exchange value. Put otherwise, the privatization process commodified Central Park. The CPC became the sole producer and seller of (what will be referred to as) the Central Park commodity, while the City of New York became its sole buyer.[14] What is the importance of this privatization-cum-commodification?

As elaborated in Chapter Three, the interest in any municipal privatization (from a class analytic perspective) flows from the recognition that it generally involves important shifts in the social (class) relations that underlie the production of public goods and services. In particular, the production of public goods and services by municipal workers generally does not involve a class process. Given the definition of a class process set out previously—an economic process involving the production, appropriation, and distribution of surplus labor—the existence of (or, the ability to theoretical specify) a class process requires: 1) the performance of surplus labor and, 2) the use-value(s) this surplus labor produces must be an object of exchange.[15] While Central Park represented a use-value (jointly produced by New York City Department of Parks & Recreation workers and CPC staffers) prior to its privatization, it was not an object of exchange, and its production did not involve a class process. Following its privatization, it became an object of exchange. Thus, the production of Central Park came to involve a class process.

It should be underscored that the CPC existed (and, played an important role in the park's operation) prior to the park's privatization, but it did not host a class process. In other words, the park's privatization generated a class process within the CPC. This implies that Central Park's privatization was representative of the second class origin form specified in Chapter

Three: the park's privatization created a class process in an organization that had not previously hosted one.

Recognizing that the park's privatization commodified the park and created a new class process is the first step in the argument. This primary step leads to the question, "Under what type of social relations of production is Central Park qua commodity produced?" An alternative way of framing this question is, "What type of class process did the park's privatization create?" As detailed in Chapter Three, the specification of the type of class process underlying a production process turns on the form that the surplus labor performed takes. In the case of Central Park's production, this surplus labor takes the form of surplus value because the CPC advances capital (in the form of wages) in order to secure the productive labor power of its workforce.[16] This implies that the class process created via the park's privatization and which yields Central Park qua commodity is a capitalist one. Thus, Central Park is produced as a capitalist commodity.[17] Prior to the park's privatization, the City of New York advanced tax revenues (in the form of wages) in order to secure the labor power of the municipal workers that produced Central Park qua a use-value. As Marx argued, there is an important difference between the production of public goods and services funded out of tax revenues, and ones funded out of capital:

> "The highest development of capital exists when the general conditions of the process of social production are not paid out of deductions from the social revenue, the state's taxes—where revenue and not capital appears as the labor fund, and where the worker, although he is a free wage worker like any other, nevertheless stands economically in a different relation—but rather out of capital as capital."[18]

Central Park's privatization fundamentally changed the nature of the social relationship in which those who produce the park stand.[19] Because tax revenues were advanced as wages to municipal workers, and because no commodity was produced (only a use-value), no "valorization" or expansion of capital was possible prior to the park's privatization, i.e., no class process existed. Further, the lack of a class process signaled the absence of Marxian exploitation. Post-privatization, capital is advanced as wages to the CPC's productive workers and a commodity is produced, i.e., valorization or expansion of capital occurs—hence, a capitalist class process exists. This expansion of capital occurs via the productive labor process that gives rise to the Central Park commodity. This expansion of capital takes the form of surplus value. The existence of a capitalist class process implies that the productive workers employed by the CPC are exploited. As explained in Chapter Three, this means they are excluded from participating in appropriating and distributing the surplus value they produce in the course of producing the Central Park commodity.

While the issue of exploitation raised by the park's privatization prompts important ethical questions (which are taken up in more detail in Chapters Five and Six), recognition of the class dimension of the park's privatization places the issue of reproduction at center stage. As explained in Chapter Three, any class process must be reproduced by the organization hosting it, i.e., the organization must continually make efforts to reproduce its class process if it is going to continue to exist. Such efforts will necessarily impinge in complex and contradictory ways upon many other individuals and entities. In the case of Central Park's privatization, the park's privatization created a new capitalist class process inside the CPC. Like all capitalists, the CPC must make efforts to reproduce its class process—*one that owes it existence to the park's privatization.* An organization's efforts to reproduce its class process constitute its subsumed class and nonclass processes.

The remainder of this chapter (as well as the next) explores how the CPC reproduces its capitalist class process, and how its efforts to do this impinge upon various social agents within New York City. By way of this task, a class analysis of Central Park's privatization is developed. This class analysis considerably widens the field of effects that can be related to the park's privatization. Alternatively, the park's privatization is reconceptualized as an ensemble of complex and overdetermined class and nonclass processes. And, while every municipal privatization process is unique, several of the insights that flow from this class analysis have important implications for municipal privatizations more generally.

4.3 CONCEPTUALIZING THE CENTRAL PARK COMMODITY

As explained in Chapter Three, any site in society, be it a theoretical one (e.g., the state) or a physically existing one, like Central Park, is conceived as a particular constellation of economic, political, cultural, and natural processes from a class perspective. Thus, Central Park exists as an urban space constituted by a host of different processes. The Central Park commodity must be conceptualized differently, however. For class analytical purposes, this conceptualization must be directly related to the intent of the labor process that gives rise to the park as a commodity.

Central Park qua commodity comprises two dimensions. The first dimension regards the park's aesthetics, e.g., its trees, meadows, pathways, benches, flowerbeds, bridges, waterbodies, etc. The second dimension regards the set of educational, cultural, and recreational programs that take place within the park. These two dimensions jointly constitute Central Park as a produced commodity. This is the commodity that the CPC's labor process (described in the next section) is designed to produce, and that is specified in the contract between the CPC and the city.[20]

The foregoing class analytic interpretation of the park's privatization as well as the conceptualization of the Central Park commodity raises two important questions. First, who consumes the use-value associated with the Central Park commodity? Second, how can a non-profit organization be considered a capitalist commodity producer?

The Use-Value of the Central Park Commodity. As Marx explains in the opening section of *Capital*, a commodity contains both use-value and exchange value. The use-value of a commodity flows to its purchaser, e.g., the buyer of a commodity (say, a coat) consumes its use-value (warmth). The exchange value of the commodity represents the price the buyer pays in order to acquire its use-value. Similarly, New York City's purchase of the Central Park commodity provides it a use-value. What exactly is this use-value?

The use-value received by New York City from its purchase of the Central Park commodity from the CPC is similar to that which it receives from its production of public education. The Central Park commodity is useful, i.e., has use-value to New York City, because it, like public education, contributes significantly to the city's quality of life. Indeed, the so-called "new view" of urban parks, a body of urban park literature that emerged during the 1990s, highlights, catalogues, and empirically documents the many quality of life use-values urban parks provide communities.[21] Among others these include: contributions to child development, workforce development, physical and psychic health, and community development. This literature also emphasizes urban parks' contributions to social capital. Discussing this concept, Chris Walker writes:

> "In addition to their tangible contributions to youth development, employment opportunities, and public health, parks help build and strengthen ties among community residents by bringing people together, including those who are otherwise divided by race or class, and by helping them work together on common projects. These ties— often labeled "social capital"—represent subtle but important assets for a community."[22]

Walker goes on to note the positive role such social capital may play in crime reduction. Indeed, the idea that the modern urban park form provides alternative activities (e.g., alternatives to criminal behavior) for urban residents (especially urban youth) is commonplace in the modern urban park literature. As Cranz remarks, the idea that urban parks can play a role in shaping social behavior is age-old. Referring to the four forms the urban park has historically taken, she writes, "all four models share one major dynamic: each grew out of an effort to solve urban problems arising from the twin problems of industrialization and urbanization. Thus, all are deliberate mechanisms of social control."[23]

The connection between urban parks and social behavior, moreover, underscores the importance of the programmatic dimension of the modern urban park form—a dimension which, as argued, is a constituent part of the Central Park commodity. Specifically, because urban parks are produced spaces, ones that invite potentially diverse forms of social activity, the programmatic dimension of today's urban parks is critical because it helps dictate the types of social activities that occur within parks.[24] Indeed, the new view literature underscores the critical role programming plays in modern urban parks. Recognition of the programmatic dimension of the modern urban park by park stewards and administrators, urban planners, politicians, and social scientists is central to the notion that urban parks can make valuable quality-of-life contributions to municipalities.

Similar to public education, modern urban parks play constituent roles in overdetermining a municipality's quality of life. For a variety of reasons, both education and parks have generally been provided and produced by municipal governments. In providing and producing these goods and services, municipal governments capture a set of use-values that flow from the public's consumption of them.[25] This set of use-values is a constituent component of municipalities' quality of life.[26]

The Central Park Conservancy: Nonprofit Organization and Capitalist Commodity Producer. The class analytic interpretation of the park's privatization raises an obvious question concerning the relationship between an organization's legal status and its class structure. Specifically, the CPC is a 501 (c) (3) organization, a legal designation providing it tax-exempt status under the Internal Revenue Code. As is well known, such organizations are more commonly referred to as nonprofit organizations. Is it possible to square the CPC's legal status as a nonprofit organization with its specification here as a capitalist commodity producer?

An organization's legal status plays a constituent role in overdetermining its existence as a social site. As explained in Chapter Three, any social site is understood to be nothing but an ever-changing complex constellation of political, economic, cultural, and natural processes. However, there is no necessary connection between these myriad processes—including the political process that stamps an organization with a particular legal (tax) status—and the class process the organization hosts. While an organization's legal designation as a nonprofit or for-profit undoubtedly impinges upon its class process, it places no restrictions on that class process. Thus, just as a nonprofit enterprise may host a capitalist class process (a la the CPC), a for-profit enterprise may host a non-capitalist (e.g., a communist) class process.[27] From a class perspective, the critical difference between nonprofit and for-profit organizations concerns their respective conditions of existence. Thus, for example, unlike for-profit enterprises, nonprofits, due to their tax-exempt status, do not have to pay taxes, nor may they pay dividends.[28]

The notion that nonprofit organizations aren't substantively different from for-profit capitalist enterprises actually has a long legal history, as the jurisprudence surrounding the regulation of 501 (c) (3) organizations makes clear. This jurisprudence's origins reflect recognition—by Congress, the Treasury and, not least, for-profit organizations—that nonprofits' tax-exempt status can afford them an obvious advantage vis-à-vis for-profits. As early as 1948, parts of the for-profit sector began expressing outrage over universities use of their tax-exempt status to shelter business profits from taxation.[29] For example, a famous case from 1951 concerned the New York University Law School's (NYU) ownership of the Mueller Macaroni Company. At the time, NYU also held Howes Leather Company, American Limoges China, and the Ramsey Corporation. More recently, the heightened commercial activities, profits, handsome salaries, lush office towers, and billion-dollar investment portfolios of nonprofits have drawn increasing attention—both within the legal community as well as from other academic disciplines.[30]

4.4 THE CENTRAL PARK COMMODITY'S PRODUCTION

Similar to most capitalist commodities, the production of the Central Park commodity involves a number of processes. For example, the park's production includes: political processes pertaining to the distribution of managerial authority and oversight of the productive labor process as well as those related to the complex power-sharing agreement between the CPC's management and the city's Parks and Recreations Department; cultural processes related to productive laborers' acceptance of their specific roles in the labor process as well as their recognition and acceptance of managerial authority; and, natural processes like photosynthesis, rainfall and the existence of particular insects that impinge upon and regulate various elements of the productive labor process, e.g., how often lawns must be mowed, trees pruned, and certain parts of the park fumigated. While no one of these processes is more important than another, the focus here is on the class process. The following sections describe the *first moment* of the CPC's class process—the productive labor process. This process comprises the diverse set of productive activities the CPC's maintenance crew and programmatic staffers, which produce the Central Park commodity's aesthetic and programmatic dimensions, engage in.

Producing the Park's Aesthetic Dimension. The operational program that guides production of Central Park's aesthetic dimension, referred to internally in the CPC as "total quality management," partitions the park's 843 acres into forty-nine zones. Each zone is maintained by at least one zone gardener trained in horticulture. These gardeners are responsible for all aspects of the management and maintenance of their respective zones. In addition to their managerial positions, these gardeners aerate, mow, weed, plant, seed, clip shrubs, clear pathways, and rake leaves. [31] Gardeners are assisted in these labor activities by several specialized park-wide crews, including those dedicated to: the park's trees (of which there are 26,000), turf (300 acres of lawns are mowed to about a 2-inch level twice a week), benches (which number over 8,500), playgrounds (or which there are 21), graffiti removal, bridges, fountains, arches, monument and sculpture conservation, art bronzes, and restroom facilities. There are also crews dedicated to soil and water-body conservation, pathways, the park's extensive storm drain (pipe) system, lighting fixtures, and signage.

In carrying out this diverse set of activities, the CPC's gardeners and maintenance crews expend, in Marx's terms, brain, nerves, and muscles. In short, these gardeners and crews combine the expenditure of labor-power with various elements of fixed and circulating capital to produce the park's aesthetic dimension. In return for their labor power, the CPC advances these gardeners and crew members wages. These gardeners and crew members perform both necessary and surplus labor and thereby produce surplus value.

Producing the Park's Programmatic Dimension. The programmatic dimension of the Central Park commodity comprises a set of free recreational, educational, and cultural programs. This set of programs, produced by the CPC's programmatic staff includes (among others): youth summer programs, elementary/high school teacher training courses, elementary and high school field programs, woodlands and geography exhibits, horticultural workshops, musical concerts, guided walking tours, and lecture series. What does the production of these programs entail?

Production of the park's programmatic dimension combines the expenditure of the CPC's programmatic staff's own labor-power in a variety of labor activities—creating, designing, drafting, informing, calling, presenting, issuing, mailing, arranging, devising, purchasing, etc.—with different elements of constant capital, e.g., computers, telephones, printers, faxes, software, fiber optic cable lines, and silicon micro-processing chips. All of these activities combine to produce the programmatic dimension of the Central Park commodity—a diverse set of educational, recreational, and cultural activities and programs. Similar to the CPC's gardeners and maintenance crews, its programmatic staff combines its labor-power with various elements of fixed and circulating capital to produce the park's programmatic dimension. In return for their labor power, the CPC advances them wages. Thus, they perform both necessary and surplus labor and thereby produce surplus value.

The fact that the productive labor process that yields the Central Park commodity involves two conceptually distinct labor processes (gardening/maintenance and programming) poses no conceptual problem from a class perspective. Indeed, many capitalist commodities (e.g., automobiles) involve multiple labor processes that, despite their conceptual distinctiveness (e.g., design and manufacturing), are constituent components of a single production (class) process.

The Second Moment of the Class Process: Appropriation. The second moment of the CPC's fundamental class process involves appropriation of the surplus labor produced during the productive labor process. As noted, this surplus labor takes the form of surplus value reflecting the CPC's capitalist class process. As with other capitalist commodities, appropriation occurs immediately upon the park's production. In generally, for a typical capitalist enterprise, the board of directors appropriates the surplus (embodied in the produced commodity). In the case of the CPC, the Board of Trustees appropriates the surplus.

The Class Positions Associated with the CPC's Fundamental Class Process. As explained in Chapter Three, individuals are embedded in social relationships with one another as a consequence of their participation in class and nonclass processes. The fundamental class process gives rise to two class positions: surplus value producer and surplus value appropriator. Those whose labor produces the Central Park commodity—the CPC's gardeners, crew members, and program staff—occupy the fundamental class position of surplus value producer. Based on calculations from the CPC's 2000 Annual Report, of the approximately 250 persons employed by the CPC, about 190 (seventy-six percent) produce surplus value and hence occupy the fundamental class position of surplus value producer. Those who appropriate the surplus value produced by the CPC's productive workforce, namely the CPC's Board of Trustees (which comprises approximately sixty individuals) occupy the fundamental class position of surplus value appropriator.

The remainder of the chapter constructs a class analytic model of the CPC. This model provides the primary theoretical vehicle through which the implications of the park's privatization are explored in greater detail in Chapter Five. The model specifies the CPC's revenue and expenditure flows in class analytic terms, and introduces a conceptual device by which these flows may be linked. More specifically, the CPC's various revenues are received by its board of trustees. The board then allocates these revenues (via a management fund) to the organization's managers. The management team subsequently expends (or, in class analytic terms, distributes) these funds in order to reproduce the CPC's capitalist class process. This distributive process constitutes the CPC's subsumed class process as well as a variety of nonclass processes. As explained in Chapter Three, these distributions are made to the set of individuals and entities throughout New York City that provides the various conditions that allow the CPC to produce the park. The model thus conceptually connects the CPC's efforts to reproduce its capitalist class process to the larger social environment of New York City. Because this class process was created via the park's privatization, the model allows the field of effects that can identified and related to the park's privatization to be considerably broadened.

The model yields several closely related insights. First, it reveals that the exchange value (or, price) the CPC receives by selling the Central Park commodity to the city has never allowed it to cover the cost of producing the park. In class terms, this implies that the park's exchange value is less than its value. As it would for any capitalist, this situation represents a potential crisis for the CPC as it implies that the organization can not reproduce its class process by simply selling the commodity it produces. And yet, as is well known, the CPC has, by all measures, been incredibly successful. Indeed, its well-documented success in producing an urban park whose quality is largely unrivaled has served to undergird the widespread notion that the park's privatization represents an exemplary model of municipal privatization.

As the model demonstrates, the CPC's ability to successfully produce the Central Park commodity and reproduce its capitalist class process rests wholly on its ability to capture a set of revenues that are largely unrelated to the production and sale of its primary commodity. In class terms, this set comprises a host of subsumed class and nonclass revenues. In particular, the model reveals that the CPC captures significant fundraising and investment revenue. Subsequent analysis (developed in the next chapter) shows that the organization's ability to capture such revenues has a number of complex and surprising implications. First, in producing the park and reproducing its class process the CPC engages the services (and, thereby, supports) a number of individuals engaged in *non-capitalist* class processes. In other words, the CPC's ability to successfully reproduce its capitalist class process—or, equivalently, the success of Central Park's privatization—owes much to a host of non-capitalist class processes (or, enterprises). Second, the CPC's fundraising activities—which are central to its reproduction efforts—are shown to have potentially detrimental (and, heretofore, never acknowledged) effects on the city's non-profit and for-profit sectors. While the latter finding casts a long shadows over the mainstream privatization discourse's central theoretical efficiency and cost propositions, the former finding—which demonstrates the potential co-dependencies between capitalist and non-capitalist class processes—serves to highlight the limitations of mainstream interpretations (on both the left and the right) of municipal privatization processes that associate them with "capitalist" practices and the institutions presumed to constitute its essence.

4.5 A CLASS ANALYTIC MODEL OF THE CENTRAL PARK CONSERVANCY

The Cost Price and Exchange Value of the Central Park Commodity. As in all capitalist enterprises, the CPC's managers advance capital to purchase the productive labor-power of its gardeners, maintenance crews, and programmatic staffers. They also advance capital to purchase the various elements of constant capital (e.g., rakes, hammers, lawn mowers, seeds, concrete, nails, software, computers, printer paper, etc.) used by their productive workers.

Let V represent the magnitude of capital advanced by CPC managers to purchase productive labor-power, i.e., this capital takes the form of wages and/or salaries to gardeners, crew members and programmatic staffers who sell productive labor-power to the CPC.[32] V qua magnitude of capital corresponds to (or, represents) a specific quantum of value (or, abstract labor time).[33] Similarly, let C represent the magnitude of capital used to purchase constant capital. As with V, C qua magnitude of capital corresponds to a specific quantum of value (or, abstract labor time). Labor-power and means of production are combined via the productive labor process and yield the Central Park commodity and surplus value.

In order to quantify the value of the Central Park commodity, it is necessary to sum the respective contributions to that value each of the two elements that enter into the commodity's production process makes. The conditions of capitalist circulation dictate that the respective contributions to the Central Park commodity's value each of these elements makes cannot be treated identically.[34] The contribution to the Central Park commodity's value (more specifically, its magnitude) made by labor-power is the value of that labor-power denominated in units of abstract labor time. This value is represented by the magnitude of capital advanced for productive labor-power (V). The contribution made to the Central Park commodity's value by the means of production consumed in its production must be theorized differently.[35] The magnitude of capital advanced by CPC management for means of production (C) expresses in money form some quantum of abstract labor time. In particular, it expresses in money form the quantum of abstract labor time socially necessary for the reproduction of the means of production (commodities) purchased under conditions of capitalist circulation. This quantum does not generally correspond to the quantum of abstract labor time physically or technically embodied in the commodities, however. Thus, "the quantity of labor time in money form which each capitalist must actually advance to get his constant capital goods (their production prices) becomes a constituent part of the value of the output produced with those constant capital goods."[36] This implies that, in general, conditions of capitalist circulation play a role in value formation. They do so because they play a constituent role in overdetermining what is socially necessary for the reproduction of the constant capital goods used in production processes.

Given the above, the Central Park commodity's value (W) per year can be expressed as:

$$W = C + V + S \qquad (1)$$

S equals the magnitude of surplus value created by the CPC's productive workforce in the course of producing the Central Park commodity. C and V are defined as per above.[37] And, $C = C_1 + C_2$, where, C_1 represents outlays on capital equipment, and $C_2 = M$ (outlays on raw materials). A commodity's value is distinct from its cost price, however:

> "What the commodity costs the capitalist, and what it actually does cost to produce it, are two completely different quantities. . . . the cost price of the commodity necessarily appears to him as the actual cost of the commodity itself. If we call the cost price k, the formula C = c + v + s is transformed into the formula C = k + s, or commodity value = cost price + surplus value. . . . The capitalist cost of the commodity is measured by the expenditure of capital, whereas the actual cost of the commodity is measured by the expenditure of labor. . . . On the other hand, however, the cost price of the commodity is by no means

simply a category that exists only in capitalist bookkeeping. The independence that this portion of value acquires makes itself constantly felt in practice in the actual production of the commodity, as it must constantly be transformed back again into the form of productive capital by way of the circulation process, i.e., the cost price of the commodity must continuously buy back the elements of production consumed in its production."[38]

Thus, (1) can be rewritten as:

$$W = k + S \qquad (2)^{39}$$

The Central Park commodity's cost price $(k) = C_1 + Z$, where, Z = circulating capital = capital advanced for productive labor-power (V) plus capital advanced for raw materials $(M = C_2)$ consumed during the production of the Central Park commodity. Thus, $Z = V + M$. The value of the Central Park commodity is therefore the sum of its cost price (k) and the surplus value (S) embodied within it (or, equivalently, the surplus value produced during its production). Figure 4.1, which partitions the park's cost price into its three respective components $(C_1, V, \text{and } M)$, shows the Central Park commodity's cost price between 1998 and 2003. (The Appendix provides a detailed explanation of the procedure used to estimate the park's cost price.)

The Central Park commodity's value (denominated in abstract labor units) is distinct from its exchange value (sale price). It turns out, that the exchange value the CPC receives from the city for the Central Park commodity has never covered its cost price (k). In other words, *the CPC produces the Central Park commodity at a loss each year.* This can be expressed as:

$$EV_{CP} < k \qquad (3)$$

EV_{CP} represents the Central Park commodity's exchange value. Figure 4.2 shows the park's exchange value between 1998 and 2005.

It should be underscored that the CPC's fundraising affects the exchange value of the Central Park commodity. If the CPC raises (via its fundraising efforts) and expends less than $5 million in any fiscal year, the city receives the Central Park commodity for free. In such a case, the CPC would fail to realize the surplus value embedded in the Central Park commodity. This has never happened.

In class terms, equation three implies that the exchange value received by the CPC for the Central Park commodity is less than the park's value (W). This is readily apparent once equations two and three are combined:

$$EV_{CP} < W = k + S \qquad (4)$$

The situation represented by equation three or four would set in motion a host of complex and contradictory struggles and contradictions within any capitalist enterprise. In short, it signals a potential crisis as the surplus value realized by the sale of a commodity is insufficient to ensure reproduction of the capitalist class process that gave rise to it. In Marx's terms, the exchange value received for the commodity does not allow the elements of production consumed in its production to be "bought back." The CPC regularly confronts this situation. And, yet, as noted, the CPC has by all measures been incredibly successful. Indeed, its success has served to undergird the widespread notion that the park's privatization represents an exemplary model of municipal privatization. How has the CPC managed this success? Two activities that are largely unrelated to the actual physical production of the Central Park commodity have been central to the CPC's success: fundraising and investing.

The Central Park Conservancy's Fundraising Activities. Figure 4.3 shows the total dollar amount of fundraising contributions the CPC received between fiscal years 1992 and 2003. As can be seen, following the park's privatization, the CPC's fundraising revenue increased significantly. In the six-year period prior to the park's privatization (1992–1997), the

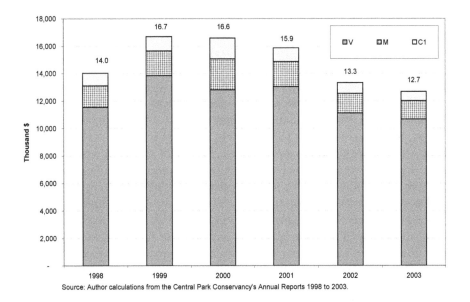

Source: Author calculations from the Central Park Conservancy's Annual Reports 1998 to 2003.

Figure 4.1 The Central Park Commodity's Cost Price by Capital Outlay, 1998 to 2003

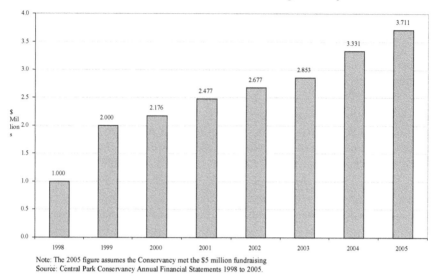

Note: The 2005 figure assumes the Conservancy met the $5 million fundraising
Source: Central Park Conservancy Annual Financial Statements 1998 to 2005.

Figure 4.2 The Central Park Commodity's Exchange Value, 1998 to 2005

CPC's fundraising revenue averaged $10.7 million annually. During the
first six years following the park's privatization (1998–2003), the CPC's
fundraising revenue jumped to $16.9 million annually. Among other rea-
sons, this increase reflected the fact that once the park was privatized fundraising became critically important to the CPC as it determined whether or
not the organization could sell the Central Park commodity to the city. Put
otherwise, fundraising became a key condition of existence for the CPC's
capitalist class process and its reproduction.

    While the CPC considers fundraising donations a single revenue
stream, class analytic accounting specifies these donations' origins. In other
words, who donates to the CPC and why? Such specification is important
from a class perspective because it allows the CPC's efforts to reproduce its
capitalist class process (which rely heavily on fundraising) to be conceptually (and, carefully) linked to many other individuals' and entities' class
and nonclass processes. Alternatively, it allows the CPC's capitalist class
process—*and thereby the park's privatization which created this class process*—to be related to the larger social environment in which the organization operates (or, equivalently, within which the privatization took place).

    The CPC receives significant donations from several New York City-
based capitalist enterprises. Such donations represent *subsumed class* revenue for the CPC because they are cuts of other capitalist enterprises' surplus
value. While capitalist enterprises regularly make such donations there are

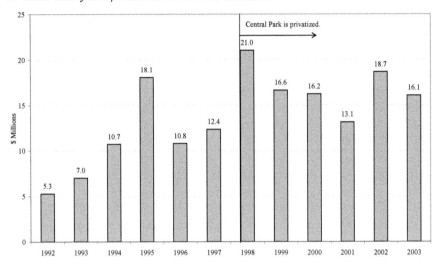

Source: Author's calculations from the Central Park Conservancy's Annual Reports and Financial Statements, 1992 to 2003.

Figure 4.3 Fundraising Donations Received by the Central Park Conservancy, 1992 to 2003

at least three reasons they do so. First, such donations play an important role in projecting particular public images, e.g., good corporate citizen. Crafting, nurturing, and maintaining such images are important to all capitalist enterprises' class processes. Second, donations provide tax benefits. These benefits help reduce another subsumed class distribution capitalist enterprises must make—namely, taxes to government entities. Fundraising donations may also, in specific cases, help fulfill regulatory mandates that require capitalists to invest in particular ways in the communities in which they operate.

The CPC also receives donations from non-capitalist enterprises. While non-capitalists' donations secure many of the same processes they secure for capitalist enterprises, they do not secure capitalist class processes because these organization's do not produce capitalist commodities. Thus, these types of donations represent *nonclass* revenue for the CPC.

Figure 4.4 shows a selected sample drawn from the hundreds of enterprises that made donations to the CPC during fiscal year 2000. The class analytic classification of a donation as either a subsumed class or nonclass revenue for the CPC depends upon whether or not a donor is a capitalist or non-capitalist enterprise. In many cases, this determination is straightforward. In other cases it is less clear. For instance, financial institutions often host capitalist class processes and also nonclass processes that generate significant subsumed class revenue. In such cases, the "balance among the processes generating an enterprise's revenues" may be used to determine its particular status and subsequently the classification of its donation to the CPC.[40]

In addition to the donations it receives from enterprises, the CPC also receives donations from private individuals. The rationales for private donations are many and likely include a variety of cultural, political, and tax considerations. In all cases, however, such donations represent nonclass revenue for the CPC, as they do not, in general, represent distributions of surplus value.[41] Finally, the CPC receives donations from two additional sources: private charitable philanthropic foundations and government entities. Such donations also represent nonclass revenue to the CPC.

The above discussion allows the following equation representing the CPC's fundraising revenue to be specified:

$$D = Y_{SC2} + Y_{NC2} \qquad (5)$$

D represents the CPC's total fundraising (donor) revenue. Y_{SC2} represents donations received from capitalist enterprises (subsumed class distributions), and Y_{NC2} represents donations received from non-capitalist enter-

Enterprise	Amount
Chanel, Inc.	$10,000-$24,999
Chase Manhattan Corporation	$25,000-$49,999
Chevron	$5,000-$9,999
Citigroup, Inc.	$100,000-$249,999
Consolidated Edison Co. of New York, Inc.	$25,000-$49,999
Ernst & Young LLP	> $100,000
IBM Corporation	$10,000-$24,999
J.P. Morgan	$25,000-$49,999
Marsh & McLennan Companies, Inc.	> $250,000
Nabisco, Inc.	$10,000-$24,999
News Corporation	$10,000-$24,999
Paramount Pictures	$10,000-$24,999
Saks Fifth Avenue	$5,000-$9,999
Time Warner Inc.	$100,000-$249,999
Xerox Corporation	$5,000-$9,999
Source: Central Park Conservancy Annual Report, 2000.	

Figure 4.4 Selected Fundraising Donations to the Central Park Conservancy, 2000

prises, individuals, philanthropic foundations, and government entities (all of which represent nonclass revenue for the CPC).

Fundraising and the Central Park Conservancy's Board of Trustees' Class and Nonclass Positions. Many processes overdetermine the success or failure of any nonprofit's fundraising operation. The CPC's sophisticated fundraising operation has played an undeniably large role in the success of Central Park's privatization. Not surprisingly, the CPC's fundraising success owes much to the makeup of its board. Many CPC board members are either high-ranking corporate executives and/or members of the city's elite philanthropic community. Thus, in addition to occupying a fundamental class appropriator position by virtue of their membership on the CPC's board, many board members simultaneously occupy other fundamental appropriator class and subsumed class positions in capitalist and non-capitalist enterprises.

The Central Park Conservancy's Investment Activities. In addition to fundraising, the CPC holds a large endowment investment portfolio. The CPC's board has authorized a policy designed to preserve the value of this portfolio in real terms and provide a predictable flow of funds to support the CPC's operations. According to the CPC's financial statements, its portfolio comprises several different asset classes: money market and mutual funds, master demand notes, U.S. Treasury bonds & notes, U.S. government agency bonds and notes, and common stocks. The dividend and interest payments the portfolio earns represent subsumed class or nonclass revenue (depending upon their class analytic origins) for the CPC. The capital gains (losses) the portfolio earns represent nonclass revenue for the CPC. Figure 4.5 shows the subsumed class and nonclass revenues that flowed to the CPC from its portfolio, as well as the portfolio's market value, at the end of each fiscal year between 1997 and 2003. To take but one year as an example, in 2001, the CPC's portfolio generated $9.6 million—equivalent to sixty-one percent of the Central Park commodity's cost price in the same year.

Importantly, the subsumed class and nonclass revenue the portfolio earns in any year is but a portion of the total endowment-related revenue available to the CPC for operations. Specifically, the endowment-derived revenue available to the CPC to fund operating activities in any given year is equal to five percent of a three-year moving average of the portfolio's fair market value (as of December 31 of the three previous years). Thus, in 2002, this meant that the portfolio could provide $14.6 million for the CPC's operating activities (or, more than enough to cover the park's cost price ($13.2 million) in that year).

Let E_t represent the endowment-derived revenue available to the CPC to fund operating activities in fiscal year t. Thus, E_t can be written as:

$$E_t = .05 \times 1/3(E^{MK}_{t-1} + E^{MK}_{t-2} + E^{MK}_{t-3}) \qquad (6)$$

where, E^{MK}_{t-n} is the portfolio's market value on December 31 in year t-n. Alternatively, E^{MK}_{t-n} may be written as:

$$E^{MK}_{t-n} = E^{MK}_{t-n-1} (1 + r) + A \qquad (7)$$

where r represents the portfolio's total annual rate of return, and A represents net injections (withdrawals) to the portfolio, which, for simplicity, are assumed to occur but once at the end of every fiscal year. While the class analytic origins of A can not be precisely identified, most of A derives from fundraising donations that donors or the board designate for long-term (portfolio) investment. Thus, A can be represented as some portion φ of total fundraising donations (D) received by the CPC in any fiscal year:

$$A = \varphi(Y_{SC2} + Y_{NC2}) = \varphi D \qquad (8)$$

The Central Park Conservancy's Class Analytic Revenue. The foregoing analysis indicates that the CPC has three primary revenue streams: the sale of the Central Park commodity, fundraising donations, and investment-related revenue. Thus, its total revenue (Y) can be expressed as:

$$Y = Y_{FC} + Y_{SC} + Y_{NC}, \qquad (9)$$

Y_{FC} represents revenue from the sale of the Central Park commodity to the city. Similar to the other two terms in equation nine Y_{FC} represents a certain

$ thousands			
	Subsumed Class or Nonclass Revenue	Nonclass Revenue	
Year	Interest & dividends, net of investment expenses	Net gain (loss) on sale of investments	Portfolio's FY-end Market Value
1997	$1,302	$1,276	$42,994
1998	$1,506	$1,690	$53,617
1999	$2,134	$13,836	$84,093
2000	$2,691	$14,937	$113,568
2001	$3,959	$5,654	$93,882
2002	$2,785	(9,452)	$89,933
2003	$3,343	(5,325)	$101,789
Source: Author's calculations from, "Statement of Activities," Central Park Conservancy's Annual Financial Statements.			

Figure 4.5 Class Analytic Revenue from the Central Park Conservancy's Investment Portfolio, 1997 to 2003

quantum of abstract labor time. As explained, the magnitude of this value revenue is a function of three things: a fixed $1 million payment made if the CPC successfully meets the $5 million fundraising target; a fundraising match equal to fifty percent of the total amount the CPC raises in excess of $5 million (this is capped at an additional $1 million); and, a concession share equal to fifty percent of annual net concession revenue generated in the park in excess of $6 million (this is capped at an additional $2 million). The magnitude of the EV_{CP} thus expresses in money form some quantum of abstract labor time, and thus represents (or, corresponds) to Y_{FC}, the value revenue the CPC receives by selling the Central Park commodity.[42]

Y_{SC} represents subsumed class revenue which includes: dividend and interest payments the flow from the portfolio's holdings of stock and bonds of capitalist enterprises (Y_{SC1}), and fundraising donations from capitalist enterprises (Y_{SC2}). Y_{SC} also includes revenue earned from the sale of various commodities (e.g., T-shirts, books, mugs, etc.) in gift shops located throughout the park as well as via an on-line retail store (Y_{SC3}).[43]

Y_{NC} represents nonclass revenue which includes: dividends and interest payments that flow from the CPC's portfolio's holdings of stock and bonds of non-capitalist enterprises (Y_{NC1}); donations from non-capitalist enterprises, individuals, private charitable foundations, and government entities (Y_{NC2}); special events revenue, including entrance and/or per plate fees to the CPC's annual gala fundraisers (Y_{NC3}); capital gains (losses) on the sale of financial assets held in the portfolio (Y_{NC4}); and, the value of volunteer labor-power (approximately 40,000 hours per annum) the CPC receives (Y_{NC5}).[44]

Gathering terms, equation nine can be rewritten as:

$$Y = Y_{FC} + Y_{SC1} + Y_{SC2} + Y_{SC3} + Y_{NC1} + Y_{NC2} + Y_{NC3} + Y_{NC4} + Y_{NC5} \quad (10)$$

Equation ten represents a complete class analytic specification of the CPC's revenue. Several points follow. First, it is clear that the revenue the CPC earns from the sale of the Central Park commodity need not cover its cost price (k). Thus, the aforementioned potential crisis stemming from the fact that the park's exchange value is less than its value is circumvented via the CPC's fundraising and investment activities. The (subsumed class and nonclass) revenues these activities yield allow the CPC to cover the park's cost price as well as secure all of the other processes that provide conditions of existence to its class process. Second, it should be clear that the elements on the right-hand side of equation nine not only overdetermine the CPC's total revenue, but also one another in complex and contradictory ways.[45] Finally, and most importantly, equation ten reveals that the CPC qua capitalist enterprise is constituted not only by its own internal fundamental, subsumed, and nonclass processes, but is also complexly constituted by (and, thus related to) a host of external subsumed class and nonclass processes. It is through the explication of but a few of the many implications that flow from this complex constitution that the remainder of the chapter (and, the ensuing chapter) seeks to reinterpret Central Park's privatization (and, by extension municipal privatization processes more generally) as an ensemble of contradictory class and nonclass processes. Before that explication is undertaken, the other side of the CPC's balance sheet—its expenditures—is set out.

The Central Park Conservancy's Expenditures. The CPC board allocates operating funds (F) to the CPC's managers. These funds can be specified as:

$$F = \alpha_1 SC_I + \alpha SCR + \beta NCR \qquad (11)$$

$\alpha_1 SC_I$ represents a subsumed class distribution the board makes to management out of the surplus value it realizes from the sale of the Central Park commodity. αSCR represents a portion of total subsumed class revenue the board receives via its positions as subsumed class recipient vis-à-vis other capitalist enterprises. And, βNCR represents a portion of total nonclass revenue the board receives from various individuals and institutions.

Alternatively, operating funds derived from the endowment (E) can be rewritten as:

$$E = \zeta_1(\alpha SCR + \beta NCR) \qquad (12)$$

And, those derived from fundraising donations can be rewritten as:

$$D = \zeta_2(\alpha SCR + \beta NCR) \qquad (13)$$

The $(\alpha SCR + \beta NCR)$ term of equation nine does not derive entirely from fundraising and investing, but includes other forms of revenues (O), including merchant revenue (Y_{SC3}), special events revenue (Y_{NC3}), realized capital gains from the portfolio (Y_{NC4}), and volunteer labor-power (Y_{NC5}). Thus, let:

$$O = \zeta_3(\alpha SCR + \beta NCR) \qquad (14)$$

And, let $(\zeta_1 + \zeta_2 + \zeta_3) = 1$. Making the requisite substitutions, equation eleven can be rewritten as:

$$F = \alpha_1 SC_I + E + D + O \qquad (15)$$

Equation fifteen associates the respective portions of management's operating funds with the subsumed class and nonclass processes from which they derive. More specifically, the CPC's fundamental class process yields surplus value, a portion of which is (following its appropriation and subsequent realization) distributed via the subsumed class process to management as $\alpha_1 SC_I$. The investing and fundraising activities the CPC engages in yield (subsumed class and nonclass) revenues which are subsequently distributed via a nonclass process to CPC managers qua E, D, and O.

Figure 4.6 provides a conceptual rendering of the relationship between the CPC's revenue and expenditures (or, alternatively represents the CPC's internal class analytic structure). First, the board receives the surplus value realized by the sale of the park, along with various other (subsumed and nonclass) revenues. It then allocates these revenues as operating funds (F) to managers. CPC managers advance part of F to acquire productive labor-power and means of production. This part of F constitutes k , the cost price of the Central Park commodity. Management expends the rest of F—namely, i, g, and m—to fund all of the organization's other nonclass processes, including fundraising and investing.[46] These expenditures, in turn, generate surplus value and other (subsumed class and nonclass) revenues.

The ensuing chapter uses this class analytic model of the CPC to analyze the implications that flow from its efforts to reproduce its capitalist class process. By way of this task, the park's privatization—*which created this capitalist class process*—is related to the larger social environment within which it was carried out. The result is a considerably more nuanced interpretation of the park's privatization than those that have heretofore been articulated.

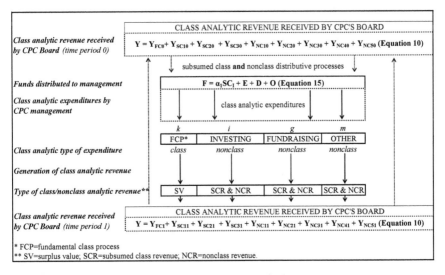

	CLASS ANALYTIC REVENUE RECEIVED BY CPC'S BOARD			
Class analytic revenue received by CPC Board (time period 0)	$Y = Y_{FC0} + Y_{SC10} + Y_{SC20} + Y_{SC30} + Y_{NC10} + Y_{NC20} + Y_{NC30} + Y_{NC40} + Y_{NC50}$ (Equation 10)			
	subsumed class **and** nonclass distributive processes			
Funds distributed to management	$F = \alpha_1 SC_I + E + D + O$ (Equation 15)			
Class analytic expenditures by CPC management	class analytic expenditures			
	k	*i*	*g*	*m*
	FCP*	INVESTING	FUNDRAISING	OTHER
Class analytic type of expenditure	*class*	*nonclass*	*nonclass*	*nonclass*
Generation of class analytic revenue				
*Type of class/nonclass analytic revenue**	SV	SCR & NCR	SCR & NCR	SCR & NCR
	CLASS ANALYTIC REVENUE RECEIVED BY CPC'S BOARD			
Class analytic revenue received by CPC Board (time period 1)	$Y = Y_{FC1} + Y_{SC11} + Y_{SC21} + Y_{SC31} + Y_{NC11} + Y_{NC21} + Y_{NC31} + Y_{NC41} + Y_{NC51}$ (Equation 10)			

* FCP=fundamental class process
** SV=surplus value; SCR=subsumed class revenue; NCR=nonclass revenue.

Figure 4.6 The Central Park Conservancy's Internal Class Structure

APPENDIX: ESTIMATING THE CENTRAL PARK COMMODITY'S COST PRICE

The CPC's *Schedule of Functional Expenses* for fiscal years 1998 to 2003 provides a means by which the Central Park commodity's cost price (k) can be estimated. A copy of this schedule for fiscal year 2001 is presented as Figure 4.7.[47]

The CPC's actual schedule of functional expenses is conveniently separated into two parts: "program services" and "supporting services." The section labeled program services (on the left-hand side of Figure 4.7) roughly corresponds to capital outlays directed toward the productive labor process (outlays on labor-power and means of production), while the section labeled support services (on the right-hand side of Figure 4.7) roughly corresponds to outlays used to secure the management function as well as the nonclass process of fundraising.

Estimating the Central Park commodity's cost price begins with estimating V, the magnitude of the capital advanced to purchase productive labor-power. This advance totaled $13.1 million in fiscal year 2001, $7.6 million of which was used to purchase the productive labor-power of the CPC's own gardeners, crew members, and program staff.[48] As indicated in Figure 4.7, the remaining $5.4 million was used to purchase *outside* contractor services. For simplicity, it is assumed that the entirety of this amount constituted the purchase of productive labor-power used in the productive labor process that yields the Central Park commodity. This is the equivalent of assuming that this outside labor-power is indistinguishable from the CPC's own gardeners'/crews'/program staff's.[49] The capital advanced for raw materials (M) consumed in the production of the park totaled $1.7 million. This represents the sum of the "total" column for the following categories: printing/publications, postage/shipping, transportation, equipment maintenance/rental, uniforms, occupancy, and miscellaneous.[50] Also included in this $1.7 million is one-half of the $2 million allocated to the category "materials, equipment, and supplies."[51] The sum of the outlays on V and M represent the total capital advanced for circulating capital, $Z = V + M = \$13.1$ million $+ \$1.7$ million $= \$14.8$ million. Finally, it is assumed that the other half of the $2 million allocated to the schedule's "materials, equipment, and supplies" category is used to purchase new capital equipment (e.g., lawn mowers, rakes, and computers) and replace worn out (depreciated) equipment.[52] These outlays thus represent C_1. Summing C_1 and Z yields the Central Park commodity's cost price (k) for fiscal year 2001: $k^{2001} = C_1 + Z = \$1$ million $+ \$14.8$ million $= \$15.8$ million. Similar calculations were carried out in order to derive cost price estimates for the remaining fiscal years between 1998 and 2003.

Year ended June 20, 2001 (dollars in thousands)

	Program Services — Design & Construction	Horticulture, Maintenance and Operations	Public Programs	Total	Cost Price Component (k)	Supporting Services — Fundraising	Management & General	Total	Total Expenses 2001
Salaries	745	5,197	1651	7,593	V	1,374	1,033	2,407	10,000
Payroll taxes and employee benefits	156	1,091	359	1,606		290	203	493	2,099
Total salaries and related expenses	901	6,288	2010	9,199		1,664	1,236	2,900	12,099
Contracted services:									
Construction, design, and related costs	3,854	110	12	3,976	V = 7,593 + 5,459 =	4		4	3,980
Consulting	127	63	228	418	$13,052	163	467	630	1,048
Mailings	0	-	4	4		383	2	385	389
Pruning	4	244	-	248		-	-	-	248
Other	84	336	393	813		150	171	321	1,134
Sum of Above	4,069	753	637	5,459	V				
Materials, equipment, and supplies	533	1,358	115	2,006	2,006 (0.5 X 2,006) to M	29	124	153	2,159
Printing and publications	8	3	169	180		454	61	515	695
Conferences, conventions, and meetings	2	13	26	41		26	25	51	92
Postage and shipping	5	4	26	35		279	14	293	328
Transportation	2	2	4	8	$M =$ sum of these	4	4	8	16
Equipment maintenance and rental	36	26	29	91	components (ex. ins	26	26	52	143
Uniforms	-	40	23	63	and cont. svs.) = 698	-	-	-	63
Insurance	10	71	30	111	+ 1,003	27	10	37	148
Occupancy	5	26	7	38		246	130	376	414
Miscellaneous	17	47	178	242		123	39	162	404
Contributed services	157	154	153	464	$1,003 = 0.5 X 2,006 = C_1$	44	44	88	552
Total expenses before depreciation and amortization	5,745	8,785	3,407	17,937		3,622	2,353	5,975	23,912
Depreciation and amortization	138	133	39	310	Depreciation of constant capital (C_1)	97	115	212	522
Total expenses 2001	5,883	8,918	3,446	18,247		3,719	2,468	6,187	24,434

Source: Central Park Conservancy, Inc., Financial Statements and Schedule (June 30, 2001 and 2000) with Independent Auditors' Report Thereon, KPMG, LLP. Schedule 1, p. 14

Figure 4.7 The Central Park Conservancy's Schedule of Functional Expenses, Fiscal Year 2001

Chapter Five
The Class Analytic Implications of Central Park's Privatization

Building on the class analytic model of the CPC developed in Chapter Four, this chapter develops three arguments. First, I demonstrate how a privatization like Central Park's can lower a municipality's capitalist sector's accumulation rate. Second, I discuss how a Central Park-like privatization can undermine a municipality's non-profit sector. These findings challenge the notion that the park's privatization represents an exemplary model of municipal privatization, and cast a shadow over the central theoretical efficiency and cost propositions that underlie the municipal privatization discourse.

The third argument highlights the class analytic diversity that surrounds the production of Central Park and the reproduction of the CPC's capitalist class process. Specifically, I show that the success of Central Park's privatization owes much to a host of *non-capitalist* commodity producers. By demonstrating the co-dependencies that exist between the CPC (a capitalist) and several non-capitalist producers, the analysis highlights the limitations of the discursive and theoretical association between privatization and capitalism (and/or the institutions and practices presumed to constitute its essence). This association (which pervades the municipal privatization discourse) is one that both the political Left and Right in the United States assume and/or adopt. The demonstration that non-capitalist producers play an important role in the park's production and the reproduction of the CPC's capitalist class process sets the stage for the development of a larger argument (developed in Chapter Six) that concerns the opportunities municipal privatizations afford for pursuing progressive, class-transformative public policies.

5.1 BEYOND EFFICIENCY AND COST

Reflecting the public-choice and neoclassical economics theoretic traditions that underlie it, efficiency and cost considerations have long occupied a central place in the municipal privatization discourse. The centrality of efficiency and cost considerations—especially as they have related to policy-making surrounding municipal privatizations—has had an important effect. Specifically, the high value placed on these considerations has meant that considerably less effort has been devoted to analyzing the broader effects municipal privatizations may have on the urban and/or metropolitan environments within which they occur.[1] This lack of effort is all the more surprising given recognition by some that the municipal privatization movement constitutes an important component of the urban restructuring movement that has swept the country over the past three decades, and which has generated a vast political-economy literature. Writing nearly twenty years ago, Wolch and Geiger wrote:

> "Although a great deal has been said about the politics of privatization and about the relative efficiency and equity of private vs. public service delivery, we still lack a clear understanding of how new configurations of service production (and in some instances, responsibility for service provision) have affected the basic economic structure of metropolitan regions."[2]

Despite the obviousness of the fact that municipal privatizations do not take place inside vacuums—but, rather are often (like Central Park's) carried out in complex urban milieus—Wolch's and Geiger's words remain largely true today.

Of course, the many distributional effects of privatization processes have not gone entirely unnoticed. As Vickers and Yarrow note, in discussing privatization processes more generally:

> "In discussing distribution issues [of privatization], it is useful to identify major groups which might be effected by privatization. Apart from political decision makers themselves, these include consumers, employees (including managers), new shareholders, taxpayers, suppliers of inputs other than labor, and suppliers of "privatization services" like financial institutions responsible for handling the sales, recipients of advertising revenues, consultants and lawyers."[3]

Vickers and Yarrow's comment aptly highlights the vast number of individuals and institutions in any geographic locale that may be affected by a single privatization process.

The class analytic model of the CPC developed in the preceding chapter provides a vehicle for explicating some of the larger distributional implications (effects) of Central Park's privatization. (As suggested previously, a class approach to municipal privatization considerably broadens the field of effects that can be related to any single privatization process.) In particular, the class analytic model of the CPC is used to develop three vignettes. Each vignette explicates a class analytic implication (or, effect) of Central Park's privatization, and thereby serves to ground one of the aforementioned arguments. And, while Central Park's privatization is obviously unique (as are all municipal privatizations), the arguments developed here are applicable to many municipal privatizations.

5.2 THE CENTRAL PARK CONSERVANCY'S FUNDRAISING AND THE CAPITALIST SECTOR

As explained in Chapter Two, a common proposition advanced by privatization proponents is that privatizations deliver fiscal benefits to municipalities and by extension their taxpayers. Cost savings are presumed to result either from private enterprises' superior management techniques and/or orientations and/or the constraints (competition) they face. As noted, the policy rational underlying Central Park's privatization rested on the CPC's alleged superior managerial competence (vis-à-vis the city's Parks Department's).

The following discussion constructs a stylized class analytic model to show that municipal privatization processes that involve turning the production of a public good or service over to a tax-exempt non-profit enterprise (as Central Park's did) can give rise to a host of contradictions—ones that cast doubt on the supposition that municipal privatization processes must of necessity prove beneficial to a municipality and its taxpayers. This model arises directly out of recognition of the importance that fundraising plays in the reproduction of the CPC's capitalist class process.

Assume that New York City's economy comprises two sectors, a for-profit one consisting of capitalist enterprises, and a non-profit one consisting of tax-exempt enterprises like the CPC that rely heavily on fundraising donations in order to reproduce their respective class processes.[4] For simplicity, let S represent the for-profit sector's total appropriated and realized surplus value. The for-profit sector's receipt of S requires a host of outlays or subsumed class distributions. These subsumed class distributions must be paid *out of* S.

Portions of S must be distributed to various parties that provided the for-profit sector's various conditions of existence—specifically, those that allowed it to produce, appropriate, and realize S. More specifically, portions of S must be distributed to: shareholders in the form of dividends (H), lenders of money capital in the form of interest payments (K), New York City in the form of taxes $(T)^5$, landlords in the form of rents (R), and merchants in the form of merchants' discounts (N). Finally, assume that the for-profit capitalist sector must also distribute a portion of S to the non-profit sector in the form of fundraising donations (D). Assume that the non-profit sector produces a composite quality-of-life commodity, which includes, among other things, the city's parks, cultural institutions, etc. Thus, the CPC's Central Park commodity would represent a constituent component of this composite quality-of-life commodity. Similar to all of the other subsumed class distributions the for-profit sector makes, the subsumed class distribution it makes to the non-profit sector (qua fundraising donations) for the quality-of-life commodity plays an important role in allowing it to appropriate and realize S. For instance, this quality-of-life commodity makes New York City an attractive place for labor to live and work.

Another part of S is allocated to the for-profit sector's managers. Call this M. Some portion of M, say β, is used by managers for accumulation purposes, i.e., for increases in capital (C) and labor (L). The remaining portion of S, namely, $(1-\beta)$, is directed toward all other for-profit sector internal operations (e.g., support staff and bureaucratic functions, etc.). The following equation can be used to represent the above discussion:

$$M = \beta M + (1-\beta)M = S - (H + K + O) \qquad (1)^6$$

where, $O = \sum T + R + N + D$. Equation one has the following interpretation: M represents the difference between the for-profit sector's appropriated and realized surplus value (S) and the sum of all subsumed class distributions $(H + K + O)$ it must make to various entities and agents that provide the conditions that allow the for-profit capitalist sector to appropriate and realize S.

Dividing equation one by $(C + L)$ yields:

$$\beta M/(C+L) = [S - [(1-\beta)M + (H + K + O)]]/(C+L) \qquad (2)$$

Let $\beta M/(C+L) = (\Delta C+\Delta L)/(C+L) = A$, the for-profit capitalist sector's rate of accumulation. $S/(C+L)$ represents the for-profit sector's value profit rate (þ). And, $[(1-\beta)M + (H + K + O)]/(C+L)$ represents the rate of subsumed class distributions (λ) the for-profit capitalist sector must make. Thus, $\lambda = f(H, K, M, T, R, N, D)$. Thus, equation two may be rewritten as:

$$A = \text{þ} - \lambda \qquad (3)$$

Equation three indicates that *given a for-profit sector value profit rate (þ)*, the for-profit capitalist sector's accumulation rate (A) is inversely related to the distributions rate (λ). For a given *þ*, a rise (fall) in λ will ceteris paribus decrease (increase) the for-profit sector's accumulation rate.

Equation three raises several intriguing issues. First, increases in D ceteris paribus increase the for-profit sector's distributions rate, i.e., $\delta\lambda/\delta D > 0$. Thus, to the extent municipal privatizations, like Central Park's, transfer the production of public goods and services to the non-profit sector, they, ceteris paribus, decrease the for-profit sector's accumulation rate (A). In effect, such a privatization increases the demand on the for-profit sector to fund the municipality's composite quality-of-life commodity that is produced by its non-profit sector, i.e., such a privatization translates into increases in D, a subsumed class payment the for-profit capitalist sector must make. Clearly, Central Park's privatization is emblematic of this type of dynamic. As explained in Chapter Four, the success of Central Park's privatization owes much to the CPC's ability to secure and increase donations from the city's for-profit capitalist sector.

An additional implication can be drawn from the above analysis if the reasonable assumption that New York City economy's rate of job growth (g) is positively related to the for-profit capitalist sector's accumulation rate (i.e., $\delta g/\delta A > 0$) is made. To the extent municipal privatizations increase the for-profit sector's cost of securing the quality-of-life commodity (via increases in its subsumed class distribution D), by transferring the production of public goods and services to the non-profit sector, they may work to slow for-profit sector accumulation and thereby the municipality's rate of private-sector job growth. Of course, increases in fundraising donations from the for-profit capitalist sector to the non-profit sector may translate into job growth in the non-profit sector. This could partially or completely offset slower job growth in the for-profit sector. In fact, non-profit sector employment in New York City grew by about twenty-five percent during the 1990s, whereas overall employment grew by only four percent. Importantly, average wages in the city's non-profit sector were approximately $33,000 in 2000, well below the citywide average of $49,000 and a New York City government average of $45,000.[7] This pattern of sectoral job growth, in conjunction with the wage differentials cited, not only holds important fiscal (tax revenue) implications for the city, but also suggests that the hypothesized relationship between A and λ warrants further scrutiny.

Clearly, the inverse relationship between the capitalist sector's rate of accumulation (A) and its distributions rate (λ) rests on the assumption that changes in λ and þ are related to one another in particular ways. Specifically, an inverse relationship between A and λ requires that $\delta þ/\delta\lambda < 1$. There is no reason to assume this condition holds or that the relationship between þ and λ is stable over time. Depending upon the way in which changes in λ and þ are related to one another, the capitalist sector's accumulation rate might rise or remain unchanged given an increase in privatization-induced donations. As the following examples show, there are several outcomes that might arise from a municipal privatization process like Central Park's, i.e., one whose success is in part *purchased* via increases in donations from the for-profit sector.

First, a rise in D might be entirely offset by some other component of λ. For example, assume that the capitalist sector recognizes that a privatization like Central Park's represents an increase in its distributions rate. Further, assume that the capitalist sector is intent on maintaining its existing accumulation rate. As a result, it might elect to begin lobbying for a reduction in taxes (T) it pays the city.[8] If such a campaign were successful, the reduction in taxes might entirely offset the privatization-induced rise in D. On the assumption that the rise in D and the reduction in T did not translate into any change in the sector's value profit rate, the sector's accumulation rate would remain unchanged. At the same time, such a scenario could mean that the fiscal benefits of the privatization were zero. Under such a scenario, one would have a municipal privatization process that spawned a subsumed class struggle—one between the municipality that undertook the privatization process and its own non-profit sector.

Alternatively, under the same assumptions, the for-profit sector might elect to attempt to offset the privatization-induced rise in D by lobbying for lower rents (R), another subsumed class distribution it must make. If such lobbying was successful, it would squeeze the city's commercial landlords—a group of individuals that occupy subsumed class positions vis-à-vis the city's for-profit capitalist sector. Commercial landlords could also, of course, elect to offset some of the rise in D by making donations to the non-profit sector themselves. While this might work to lessen the pressure the for-profit sector would otherwise put on landlords to reduce rents, it could also reduce landlord's incomes.

The above two examples make clear that a rise in D emanating from a municipal privatization process like Central Park's might be offset in a variety of ways, owing to the complex class analytic composition of λ, i.e., the for-profit sector's distributions rate. At the same time, a rise in D could also lead to changes in the for-profit capitalist sector's value profit rate. Assume once again that despite the rise in D, the for-profit capitalist sector is intent on maintaining its existing accumulation rate. In the absence of offsetting effects in its distributions rate (λ), like those just described, maintaining its accumulation rate would require the for-profit capitalist sector to increase its value profit rate ($\flat$). This it could do by either raising the rate of exploitation ($\varepsilon = S/V$), or lowering the organic composition of capital ($\kappa=C/V$). This is readily apparent once equation three is rewritten as:

$$A = þ - \lambda = \varepsilon/(\kappa+1) - \lambda \qquad (4)$$

Thus, the for-profit capitalist sector might elect to attempt to offset rises in D (again, increases in subsumed class distributions it must make as a result of a privatization process, like Central Park's) by instructing managers to raise productive workers' productivity—perhaps by demanding they work longer hours or more intensely. This increase in the rate of exploitation (reflected in a rise in þ) could serve to offset the rise in D. In this case, the municipal privatization process would induce a fundamental class struggle between for-profit sector capitalists and their productive workers. If one makes the additional assumption that the rise in D (consequent upon the privatization process) does provide the municipality's taxpayer "fiscal benefits"—perhaps by allowing the municipality to lower personal income taxes—one must simultaneously acknowledge that such benefits would be in part (under the scenario just described) the product of an increase in the rate of exploitation of the municipality's for-profit capitalist sector's productive workforce.[9] This possibility underscores the limitations of assuming that the "representative taxpayer" necessarily benefits from municipal privatization processes, and underscores the value of the class analytic approach toward such processes.

Clearly, the types of class analytic trade-offs highlighted in the above examples may or may not materialize. It is possible that a privatization-induced increase in D could increase the for-profit capitalist sector's value profit rate (and thereby, possibly, its accumulation rate). For example, increases in D may increase a municipality's quality of life. Indeed, the quality of the Central Park commodity has undoubtedly been raised post-privatization. An increased quality of life plays an important role in attracting workers to a municipality. Increases in a municipality's labor force may serve to lower the value of labor power.[10] Thus, it may be the case that a privatization-induced increase in for-profit capitalist sector donations today (which may lower its current accumulation rate) may serve to raise the sector's profit (and/or accumulation) rate in the future, if those donations increase the municipality's quality of life and thereby its labor force.[11]

It should also be acknowledged that the for-profit capitalist sector might be unwilling to meet the required increase in donations that stem from a municipal privatization process like Central Park's. Clearly, there are likely to be differences in the relative importance the for-profit capitalist sector assigns to the various subsumed class distributions it makes in order to reproduce its capitalist class processes. Thus, despite the fact that all subsumed class distributions play a constituent role in the overdetermination of the sector's efforts to reproduce its capitalist class processes, some subsumed class distributions, like charitable donations, are more discretionary than others. Thus, in the event that the for-profit capitalist sector was unwilling to meet a privatization-induced increase in D, the successful production (and reproduction) of the quality-of-life commodity would turn on the non-profit sector's ability to secure revenues from other sources. As detailed in Chapter Four, the CPC captures a wide variety of subsumed class and nonclass revenues. The effect of other entities or institutions (beside the city's for-profit capitalist sector) financing the privatization-induced increase in demand for donations would of course hold other implications. For example, if the city's merchant class elected to meet the increased demand for donations, it might simultaneously attempt to bargain for lower rents with the city's commercial landlords. Thus, here again, a municipal privatization process would generate a subsumed class struggle, one between the city's merchant and landlord classes.

The various class analytic effects described above derive from a highly stylized model. Clearly, only a small fraction of the city's for-profit capitalist enterprises contribute to the CPC and the many other non-profit enterprises that produce commodities that comprise the city's quality of life. Further, corporate donations are generally highly targeted, as they often provide donors important advertising and goodwill (both of which may boost demand for their commodities and thereby possibly increase their profits). Moreover, Central Park's privatization as well as New York City's for-profit corporate sector is undoubtedly unique. Such qualifications clearly limit the extent to which generalizations can be drawn from Central Park's privatization. Nevertheless, these types of class analytic effects can not be discounted. Just as there is nothing that guarantees their materialization, equally, there is nothing that precludes it. To the extent that the growth and use of public-private partnerships by municipalities suggests that Central Park-like privatizations are more common, recognition of and appreciation for such effects will become increasingly important for policy-makers. Equally, these types of effects necessarily represent challenges to the basic theoretical efficiency and cost propositions that have been central to the municipal privatization discourse.

5.3 THE CENTRAL PARK CONSERVANCY'S FUNDRAISING AND THE NON-PROFIT SECTOR

While the preceding discussion revealed how a Central Park-like privatization could impinge upon a municipality's for-private capitalist sector (and, thereby, in turn, impinge upon still other social agents and entities), it could also impinge upon the non-profit sector. Before discussing this issue some general comments on this sector (and, New York City's non-profit sector more particularly) are warranted.

Recognition of the importance of the non-profit sector (especially in large urban areas) has grown immeasurably over the past two decades. In part, this reflects the sector's growth: its revenues now account for ten percent of GNP, and its organizations own nearly ten percent of all property in the United States.[12] Perhaps more importantly, however, the particular tax benefits the sector enjoys, coupled with its growing commercialization have meant that its relationship with the for-profit sector, and the economy (and society) more broadly has become an object worthy of serious investigation. Indeed, as discussed previously, the tax benefits that many of the sectors' organizations enjoy long ago spawned a complex jurisprudence—one that remains largely unsettled and hotly debated today.

In the current context, the interest in the non-profit sector stems from the fact that its organizations are "understandable as alternative mechanisms for providing public-type [goods] and services."[13] Given this fact, it is perhaps not surprising that tax-exempt non-profit organizations like the CPC have become increasingly important in the context of municipal privatization. In many instances, these organizations' role in the production of municipal goods and services is understood as constituting public-private partnerships. Despite the growing importance of these types of organizations in the context of municipal privatization, there have been surprisingly few efforts to link the ever-burgeoning discourse on them to the municipal privatization discourse. Given that the urge to privatize on the municipal level is unlikely to abate any time soon, local governments' reliance on tax-exempt non-profit capitalist enterprises to produce public goods and services—as in the case of Central Park's privatization—is likely to increase. Thus, it becomes increasingly important for policy-makers to understand how these types of enterprises interact with the broader urban environment. As the following vignette demonstrates, municipal privatization initiatives that involve turning the production of a public good or service over to a tax-exempt non-profit capitalist enterprise prompt a host of important questions.

To the extent that municipal privatizations generate new or rely upon existing tax-exempt non-profit enterprises to produce municipal goods and services, they likely stimulate the non-profit sector's demand for fundraising donations. As shown in Chapter Four, fundraising is critical to the CPC's ability to reproduce its capitalist class process (or, equivalently, fundraising has been critical to the success of the park's privatization). As Figure

4.3 showed, the CPC significantly increased its fundraising-derived revenue following the park's privatization, as annual average donations jumped to $16.9 million during the first six years following the park's privatization, from $10.7 million in the six-year period prior to the park's privatization. The discussion that follows take this rise in the CPC's fundraising revenue as a backdrop and analyzes the implications of a privatization-induced growth in the non-profit sector's demand for fundraising donations. Before setting out this discussion, I briefly describe New York City's non-profit sector.

New York City's Non-Profit Sector. Similar to many large metropolitan areas, New York City boasts a large and diverse non-profit sector. The city has over 27,000 registered non-profit organizations, of which 9,078 file annual reports with the Internal Revenue Service (IRS).[14] These filing organizations expend $43 billion annually and employ an estimated 528,000 persons, or fourteen percent of New York City's resident employment base. Overall, the city's non-profit sector receives thirty percent of its revenues from fundraising contributions, while the average non-profit receives fifty-three percent of its revenues from contributions.[15] The reliance on contributions, moreover, varies widely across the sector's segments. For example, within the public benefit segment, contributions account for forty-six percent of revenues, whereas within the health segment they account for sixteen percent. The sources of contributions similarly vary across segments. Within the arts segment, direct contributions (which include corporate donations) account for seventy-eight percent of all contributions, whereas within the housing development segment direct contributions account for twenty-six percent of contributions. Clearly, fundraising contributions constitute a key condition of existence for the vast majority of the city's non-profit organizations.

The CPC's success at increasing its fundraising revenue (by $7 million annually) following the park's privatization has been noted, as has the fact that fifty-three percent of the average New York City non-profit organization's revenue derives from fundraising contributions. Moreover, the vast majority (seventy-six percent) of the city's non-profit organizations have annual operating expenditures below $1 million—a point that suggests that $7 million could support several non-profit organizations.[16] Clearly, it seems possible that the CPC's fundraising success (and, thus, by extension, the alleged success of Central Park's privatization) may have undermined other non-profits' ability to capture fundraising revenues. If this was the case, the park's privatization would have generated a crowding-out type effect within the nonprofit sector—one related to increased competition for fundraising donations. While this possibility can not be easily documented, the potential for municipal privatizations (that turn the production of public goods/services over to tax-exempt non-profit entities) to stimulate and/or exacerbate this type of competition has rarely, if ever, been acknowledged. This is especially noteworthy given the increasing use of non-profit organizations in municipal privatizations.

Competition among non-profit organizations for fundraising donations is not particularly well understood; there is relatively little academic research on the topic.[17] There are two studies that do, however, lend support to the above crowding-out hypothesis. Using a utility framework, Rose-Ackerman shows that competition for fundraising donations reduces the level of service provision relative to funds raised for all charities. She writes, "In the absence of entry barriers, the number of charities increases until the fundraising share [of receipts used for fundraising activities] of the marginal charity approaches one."[18] More recently, Cha and Neilson have argued that, "when more charities attempt to raise funds from the same pool of donors, the charities must work harder to get a given individual's donation."[19] As a result of this heightened competition for donations, the premium associated with the extra time, effort, or incentives a charity must provide to garner contributions increases. The increase in this premium, "causes dead weight loss, so that the total amount of charitable services provided falls after a new charity enters into the market."

Given evidence of a longer-term decline in the proportion of operating expenses that fundraising contributions represent within the non-profit sector, there is reason to believe that competition for donations has indeed become increasingly more intense.[20] To the extent municipal privatization processes like Central Park's have worked to increase the demand for donations within the non-profit sector, they have surely heightened this type of competition. The following discussion explicates some of the class analytic contradictions that might result as a consequence of heightened competition for fundraising donations among tax-exempt non-profit enterprises.[21]

Assume the CPC's significant post-privatization increase in fundraising revenue *did* undermine the ability of some other non-profit organization to secure fundraising revenue. Further, assume this non-profit organization sells a commodity to New York City—similar to the CPC. (In New York City, a large number of small non-profit enterprises produce human and social service commodities that they sell, often exclusively, under contract, to the city.) In the face of declining fundraising revenue, one action this non-profit could take would involve attempting to renegotiate a higher price for the commodity it sells to the city.[22] In many cases, the contracts for social and human service commodities are let via competitive bidding processes, and thus contractors frequently renegotiate prices with the city.

If this action was successful, it would clearly hold fiscal implications for the city.

In effect, heightened competition for fundraising donations within the non-profit sector constitutes a type of subsumed and/or nonclass struggle between the sector's enterprises. Municipal privatizations that rely on non-profit capitalist enterprises, like the CPC, to produce public goods and services could thus exacerbate such competition. Tougher competition for fundraising donations could force some non-profits to secure alternative revenues. Those that sell commodities to the city may well try to raise the exchange values of the commodities they sell the city in order to secure those revenues. In fact, there is evidence that declines in fundraising contributions lead some non-profits to rely more heavily on government sources of revenue.[23] Thus, to the extent municipal privatizations transfer the production of public goods or services to non-profit organizations—and, thereby stimulate competition for donations within the non-profit sector— they may imperil the viability of some non-profit organizations. Competition for fundraising donations will undoubtedly produce winners (like the CPC) and losers. Losers will either fade away (which could decrease the number of suppliers producing such commodities, and thereby put upward pressure on the exchange values of these commodities), or they may end up back on the government's doorstep seeking alternative forms of revenue, e.g., grants.

The significant presence of human and social services commodity producers in New York City, the city's extensive use of contracting in that field, and those organizations' heavy reliance on direct contributions (such contributions account for forty-two percent of all contributions among human services non-profit organizations) suggest that such a possibility is hardly remote. According to the City's *Executive Budget for Fiscal Year 2000,* the city was party to 18,656 contracts, totaling $4.9 billion. This represented nearly fourteen percent of the city's $35.3 billion FY 2000 budget. One quarter of the total amount contracted was due to contracts let by the City's Administration for Children's Services ($1.2 billion). The single largest category of contracts let by this city agency was for payments to children's charitable institutions ($665 million). These institutions provide services to children in a variety of foster care placements. Many of them, similar to the CPC, rely on donations in addition to their government contract revenue in order to reproduce their conditions of existence.

There is of course another action that a non-profit commodity producer might take when faced with heightened competition for fundraising donations. Namely, it could seek to capture entirely new revenue streams, perhaps by engaging in direct competition with for-profit enterprises.

Indeed, the growing commercialism of the non-profit sector has (as noted) become an increasing focus of academic and private sector attention over the past decade.[24] Such commercialism has been both a cause and an effect of the decline in the proportion of non-profit organizations' expenditures that donations comprise.[25] As the growth of the non-profit sector—in part fueled by the municipal privatization movement—increasingly constrains non-profit organizations' ability to reproduce their conditions of existence via fundraising donations, these organizations will be forced to find alternative revenue sources. In many cases, this hunt for new revenue brings non-profit commodity producers into direct competition with for-profit enterprises.

The CPC's decision to open an internet-based retail store provides a perfect example of how (expected) declines in fundraising revenue could lead to such behavior. Specifically, the CPC carried out several high-profile quality improvements to the Central Park commodity following the park's privatization. The CPC used these quality (capital) improvement campaigns as a fundraising device. The completion of many of these improvements means there are fewer in the offing, and, subsequently, that the CPC's success in the city's highly competitive arena for fundraising donations may be reduced in the future. Clearly, the CPC's apparent strategy to increase its merchant revenue will impinge upon some merchants in the city.

Competition Reconsidered. The two discussions just set out—concerning the potential class analytic effects (on the for-profit and non-profit sectors) that could flow from a Central Park-like privatization—produce a considerably richer understanding of competition than the one that pervades the municipal privatization discourse. This understanding of competition treats it as largely synonymous with the number of suppliers producing (or bidding for) a particular public good or service. The specific circumstances surrounding Central Park's privatization would lead most to conclude that it held no competitive implications; the CPC is the sole producer of the park and the city its sole purchaser. In contrast, from a class perspective, any municipal privatization process sets in motion a complex set of competitive forces (or, equivalently, class analytic effects). These forces comprise the host of complex class (subsumed as well as possibly fundamental) and nonclass struggles among the myriad social agents and entities that occupy various fundamental, subsumed, and nonclass positions vis-à-vis the organization the produces a public good or service following its privatization.

The foregoing discussion underscores the value of a class analytic approach to municipal privatization. The approach's recognition of the class dimension of municipal privatization requires detailed analysis of an organization that produces a public good and or service following its privatization. In particular, it analyzes how such an organization reproduces its class process. As shown, by reconceptualizing municipal privatizations as ensembles of complex and contradictory class and nonclass effects, such an analysis considerably broadens the field of effects that can be related to a municipal privatization. It thereby highlights the limitations of the chief theoretical efficiency and cost propositions that underlie the municipal privatization discourse. Such propositions do not take the types of class effects described above into account.

Finally, it must be acknowledged that the materialization of the types of class analytic effects described here will be overdetermined by a host of political and economic processes. Further, because Central Park's privatization as well as New York City's for-profit and non-profit sectors are undoubtedly unique in many ways generalizations must be carefully drawn. Nevertheless, these types of class analytic effects can not be entirely discounted. Just as there is nothing that guarantees their materialization, equally, there is nothing that precludes it. The larger purpose of the foregoing discussion has not been to claim that the park's privatization produced such effects. Rather, it has been to highlight the potentially rich assortment of effects that may arise out of Central Park-like privatization processes. Such effects have gone unrecognized within the municipal privatization discourse. To the extent Central Park-like privatizations are increasingly used by municipalities, greater recognition of and appreciation for their class analytic effects—and the policy questions they raise—seems warranted.

5.4 CENTRAL PARK'S PRIVATIZATION AND INDEPENDENT AND COMMUNIST PRODUCERS

While several factors have contributed to the CPC's success (and, thereby, the success of Central Park's privatization), including fundraising, the analysis developed in the rest of this chapter reveals that a collection of *non-capitalist* producers also play an important role in the CPC's success. This finding represents a challenge to the municipal privatization discourse because it highlights the limitations of the privatization-capitalism *association* that (as elaborated in Chapters Two and Three) has long permeated it. This association provides the chief theoretical and policy basis for the pro-privatization position of the political Right in the United States. As shown, however, the success of Central Park's privatization has as much to do with the CPC's fundraising efforts—a non-class process—as it does with the CPC's capitalist class process. At the same time, this association underwrites the anti-privatization position of the political Left in the United States, because it is taken to imply that municipal privatizations advance (above all else) the interests of "Capital."

Further, by revealing that municipal privatizations can support non-capitalist producers and enterprises, the analysis opens up theoretical and policy space for radically rethinking municipal privatization. In particular, it throws up the question of whether municipal privatizations represent avenues by which progressive, class-based policies might be pursued. Such a possibility holds important implications for those on the political Left in the United States. This possibility—the product of a class analytic approach to municipal privatization—has heretofore gone unrecognized. The broader implications (and, requirements) of this possibility are developed in Chapters Six and Seven.

Independent and Communist Producers in the Context of the Central Park Conservancy's Fundraising. As shown in Chapter Four, fundraising is vital to the CPC as it yields (subsumed class and nonclass) revenue streams that allow it to reproduce its capitalist class process. It turns out, that the CPC's fundraising activities depend upon (or, equivalently, support) many individuals engaged in *non-capitalist* class production processes. This group of individuals comprises several performers and artists. As the ensuing discussion demonstrates, these non-capitalist producers play an important role in the successful execution of the CPC's fundraising activities.

Figure 5.1 shows the CPC's fundraising expenditures between 1998 and 2003.[26] These expenditures increased steadily between 1998 (the first year of the park's privatization) and 2001, declined in 2002, and then rose to $3.8 million in 2003. Of the $3.8 million spent on fundraising in 2003, forty-seven percent ($1.8 million) represented development officers' salaries. The remaining fifty-three percent ($2 million) flowed to individuals and entities outside the CPC. What individuals and entities captured portions of these monies and what did they provide the CPC?

A portion of the CPC's fundraising expenditures destined for external entities is used to purchase the office supplies and equipment its development staff uses to carrying out its unproductive labor process. These purchases obviously nourish many enterprises' class processes, many of which are likely capitalist ones. Another portion of the CPC's fundraising expenditures is used to finance its annual set of major fundraising events. While the themes of these galas are diverse, they often include various types of musical, visual, and performance art. Such art and performances are standard fare at fundraising galas, as the individuals who attend them generally expect to be wined, dined, and entertained. Such art and performances play an important role in the success of these events. These events thus

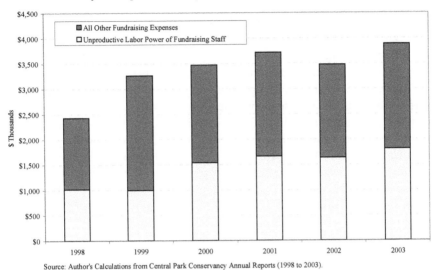

Source: Author's Calculations from Central Park Conservancy Annual Reports (1998 to 2003).

Figure 5.1 The Central Park Conservancy's Fundraising Expenditures, 1998 to 2003

often necessitate the purchase of various art and performance commodities. In many cases, these commodities are produced by individuals and groups engaged in non-capitalist (e.g., independent and communist) class processes. In this sense, the CPC's fundraising activities (which provide it revenues that allow it to reproduce its capitalist class process) are dependent upon (or, equivalently, support) non-capitalist commodity producers. The following section elaborates upon this idea.

A Central Park Conservancy Fundraising Gala Event. As part of its 2003 year-long celebration of Central Park's 150th birthday, the CPC commissioned a pyrotechnic show entitled *Light Cycle* produced by Chinese artist Cai Guo-Qiang. Cai is world renowned for his ambitious (and often politically motivated) pyrotechnic projects, which use gunpowder's constructive power and energy as an artistic and expressive medium.[27] (In 2002, Cai created a pyrotechnic rainbow over Manhattan's East River for the opening of the Museum of Modern Art in Queens, New York.) On the same night as Cai's show, which the CPC dubbed the denouement of its 150th anniversary celebration, the CPC simultaneously hosted *150 Dinners on the Park,* a major year-end fundraising gala. These dinners, attended by over 1,500 people, were held in homes, hotels, and clubs boasting views of Central Park and Cai's production, which used the park's Great Lawn as a staging area. The gala was widely touted as among the city's hottest fall-season charity events. Ticket prices for entrance to the dinners were $1,000 per plate. As explained in Chapter Four, the donations the CPC received in the course of the *Light Cycle/Dinners on the Park* gala event constituted subsumed class and nonclass revenue.

Consider the class implications of this event. Cai is an independent art producer. Specifically, he appropriates (and then distributes) his own surplus labor in the course of producing his pyrotechnic shows qua independent commodities. The CPC's commissioning of Cai's *Light Cycle* show represented the purchase of a commodity produced via an independent class process. Alternatively, the CPC's fundraising—which became a condition of existence of its capitalist class process following the park's privatization—provided a condition of existence for this independent producer and the non-capitalist class process he engages in. The CPC's commissioning of Cai's *Light Cycle* show allowed Cai to realize the surplus labor he produces in the course of producing his commodity. Cai's show (qua independent commodity) served as the centerpiece of the CPC's *Dinners on the Park* gala, and undoubtedly increased the philanthropic community's interest in the CPC's fundraising gala.

The Target Benchmarks Central Park program, conducted by the CPC in the course of the park's 150th anniversary celebration, represents another example of how the CPC's fundraising efforts depend upon (and, thereby, support) non-capitalist producers. This program (sponsored by retailer, Target) invited fifty-three eminent New York artists, architects, designers, and celebrities to use their creative talents to turn traditional Central Park benches into works of art. Each artist was provided a four-foot long unfinished wooden slat Central Park bench. After approximately six weeks, during which the benches were displayed in several prominent Chelsea galleries and on the CPC's website, the benches were auctioned off by Christies.

Similar to Cai's *Light Cycle* show, this CPC fundraiser provided a condition of existence to several independent art producers (most were well-known New York City-based artists). The CPC's commissioning of these artists' works of art allowed them to realize the surplus labor they appropriated from themselves via the independent class production processes they engaged (in which benches were transformed into works of art (qua independent commodities). The revenue the CPC received via Christies' auctioning of these works of art constituted subsumed class independent revenue.

The CPC's annual fundraising galas also support communist producers. As noted, these events regularly feature various performances, including musical ones. If the CPC hires a band to produce the entertainment component of a gala, and if the members of that bank collectively produce and appropriate their surplus labor, the CPC purchases a communist commodity. In cases in which a musical performance was produced by a solo artist, the CPC would purchase an independent commodity.

Given the fact that the cap on the price the city pays the CPC for the Central Park commodity ($4 million) was nearly reached in 2004 ($3.7 million), it seems likely that the CPC's efforts to reproduce its capitalist class process will become increasingly dependent upon subsumed class and non-class revenues in the future. This implies that the organization is likely to become increasingly dependent on fundraising revenue in the future. This, in turn, implies that it will become increasingly dependent on its annual fundraising galas, and, thereby, on the non-capitalist commodity producers that provide the performance and art commodities that play a constituent role in making those events successful. The larger implication of this possibility should not be missed. Namely, it implies that the future continued success of Central Park's privatization will increasingly depend (at least in part) on a host of non-capitalist commodity producers.

Independent and Communist Producers in the Context of the Production of the Central Park Commodity's Programmatic Dimension. As explained in Chapter Four, the Central Park commodity comprises two dimensions—an aesthetic one and a programmatic one. The latter is produced by the CPC's programmatic staff. In the course of producing the set of recreational, educational, and cultural programs that comprises this dimension of the Central Park commodity, the CPC's program staff must secure, arrange, and structure various inputs. One of the inputs programmatic staffers use in order to produce the park's programmatic dimension is highly specialized knowledge. For example, specialized knowledge and skill related to horticulture, botany, floral arrangement and design, photography, music, etc., represents a key input into the production of many of the programs that comprise the park's programmatic dimension. Such knowledge and skill is analogous to the various inputs the CPC's maintenance crew uses in producing the park's aesthetic dimension. Consideration of this aspect of the production of the Central Park's programmatic dimension prompts the following question: under what class conditions is such specialized knowledge qua input (into the production of the parks' programmatic dimension) produced? The following section elaborates on this question and considers its class implications.

Consider a particular collection of programs that help comprise the park's programmatic dimension. This set of programs represents a continuing education-like component of the programmatic dimension.[28] For example, these programs include workshops and classes on horticulture, floral arrangement, gardening, and photography. These classes are taught by individuals with specialized knowledge in these areas. In most cases, these individuals are not employees of the CPC. In particular, they are not involved in the CPC's productive labor process, which involves only its gardeners, maintenance crews, and programmatic staff. These individuals do not therefore produce surplus value for the CPC. Rather, these individuals are independent producers (engaged in independent class processes) who sell their commodities—specialized knowledge-cum-classes—to the CPC in the course of its production of the park's programmatic dimension. The exchange process that occurs between these independent producers and the CPC allow these producers to realize the surplus labor they produce and appropriate from themselves in the course of producing their various commodities.[29]

The above analysis is equally applicable to the many free, live musical performances held throughout Central Park each year. Such performances are constituent components of the park's programmatic dimension. Consider the following CPC promotional advertisement for a Sunday afternoon performance in the park by the group NAMA:

> "NAMA stands for New Amsterdam Music Association, a ten-piece Jazz ensemble comprised of veteran New York musicians. These musicians, many elder statesmen of the New York scene, bring literally lifetimes of experience to their warmly honest performances. The afternoon will consist of Jazz and Blues standards and is sure to keep the audience's toes tapping and hands clapping."

NAMA's performances are a regular part of the CPC's annual summer-long Harlem Meer Performance Festival. Similar to the CPC's fundraising galas, such performances feature a variety of musical bands and solo artists. If the bands (like NAMA) that produce these performances collectively produce these performances and appropriate their surplus labor, they participate in communist class production processes. The communist commodity they produce is purchased by the CPC as an input into its production of the park's programmatic dimension. *This suggests that a communist class production process plays a constituent role in the CPC's production of its capitalist commodity (Central Park).* In cases in which a solo artist produces such performances and appropriates her own surplus labor, an independent class process would be involved.

Central Park's other Independent and Communist Producers. While the foregoing discussion highlighted the existence and importance of several independent and communist producers and related and/or linked them to the production (in the case in which such producers and their commodities are constituent inputs into the production of the Central Park commodity's programmatic dimension) and reproduction (in the case in which such producers and their commodities play a role in the successful execution of the CPC's fundraising activities) of the Central Park commodity, the following section extends the discussion of these types of producers, but theorizes their location *outside* the CPC's production and reproduction processes. Thus, while these producers are not directly involved in the production or reproduction of the Central Park commodity, they operate and sell their commodities physically within (or, nearby) Central Park. This set of independent and communist producers includes: artists/artisans/musicians, horse-carriage operators, and street performers. The following section introduces these producers and elaborates on the complex class analytic relationships that exist between them, the CPC, and the park. Similar to the argument just constructed, the analysis demonstrates the potentially symbiotic relationships that exist between these non-capitalist producers and the CPC. It also highlights the ways in which these non-capitalists and the CPC undermine each another.

Central Park's Artisans. Any visitor to Central Park will not miss the many independent vendors that line the park's entrances and dot its boundary thoroughfares. The wares these vendors peddle are diverse and include, among other items: T-shirts, pretzels, crafts, paintings, sculptures, and portraits. From a class perspective, many of these vendors represent independent merchants. Others, are independent producers that locate within or near the park in order to sell their commodities to the park's patrons. Some of these independent producers sell original works of art or crafts. Others produce and sell hand-sketched "on-the-spot" portraits to passing tourists and other visitors to the park. These sales allow them to realize the surplus labor they produce and appropriate (from themselves) via independent class processes.

Central Park's Horse-Drawn Carriage Operators. Horse-drawn carriage rides have long been associated with Central Park. Indeed, the elaborately adorned carriages that meander through the park have long comprised an important part of the park's iconography. Approximately seventy horse carriage operator licenses were issued many years ago by New York City.[30] Today, roughly forty individuals own those licenses. While some license owners operate their own carriage-ride businesses, most rent their licenses to others. From a class perspective, most of the park's horse-carriage operators are self-employed independent producers. They produce a commodity, horse-drawn carriage rides through Central Park, that they sell to the public and thereby produce and appropriate their own surplus labor.

Most horse-carriage operators own their own capital: a horse-drawn carriage, one or more horses, and various tools and equipment used to maintain their capital stock. Many also rent stable space on Manhattan's Westside in order to store their horses and carriages. Operators' storage-rental payments are but one subsumed class distribution they make in order to reproduce the independent class process they are engaged in. The rent most operators pay to license owners (generally, a "gentlemen's agreement-type" percentage of revenue) represents another subsumed class payment they make. Some operators also rent their equipment and sublease their licenses to other operators on days they do not work.

Central Park's Street Performers, Musicians and Bands. Central Park regularly serves as host to a diverse collection of street performers, musicians, and bands. Any stroll through the park, especially during weekends, allows one to experience a rich assortment of impromptu, avant garde performances. The reasons these performers elect to play Central Park are of course diverse. Some perform in Central Park simply because they enjoy it. Others, however, perform with the intent of selling their performances to the public. Many of these latter performers may therefore be conceived as independent or communist producers who produce performance commodities via independent or communist class production processes.[31]

How the CPC and the Park's Independent and Communist Producers Complement Each Other. As explained in Chapter Four, the revenue the CPC receives from the city for the Central Park commodity is largely a function of the CPC's fundraising success and the concession revenue generated in the park. (Concession revenue increases the park's exchange value.) Since 2000 (the first year in which the CPC benefited from the park's concession revenue), the portion of the park's exchange value tied to concession revenue increased steadily, eventually reaching fifty-one percent in 2004. The concession revenue generated in the park derives from various sources: push-cart vendors, restaurants (the Loeb Boathouse and Tavern on the Green), snack-bars, bike, paddle-boat, and sailboat rentals, ice-skating, newsstands, and recreational facilities. Among other things, the steady increase in the value of these concessions since 1998 (the year the park was privatized) reflects a rise in park attendance. Indeed, visitorship to the park rose from an estimated twenty million people in 1999 to twenty-five million in 2002.[32] While this rise in visitorship reflected many things, the various qualitative improvements made to the park by the CPC (especially those related to its increased outlays on the park's programmatic dimension) undoubtedly played an important role. Whereas in the six-year period prior to the park's privatization, CPC *contributions* to the park's programming averaged $1.6 million, in the six-year period following privatization,

CPC *outlays* on the production of the Central Park commodity's programmatic dimension averaged $2.3 million—a 42% increase.[33]

On the assumption that the CPC's efforts to improve the quality of the Central Park commodity—efforts spanning both its aesthetic and programmatic dimensions—contributed to the rise in park attendance, and thereby the exchange value of its commodity, it seems reasonable to assume that those efforts increased the opportunities for independent and communist commodity producers to sell their commodities, and thereby realize the surplus labor they produce and appropriate from themselves via the respective class production processes they engage in. Clearly, the success or failure of these producers' efforts to reproduce their class processes is overdetermined by a host of processes. The ability to sell their commodities is clearly one of those processes. Thus, to the extent these producers benefit from an increased volume of foot-traffic through the park, the CPC's efforts (and incentives) to increase park attendance are likely beneficial to these producers.

While the CPC's efforts to reproduce its capitalist class process benefit the park's independent and communist producers (via the CPC's interest in increasing park patronage and thereby, ostensibly, the park's concessions revenues), the CPC also benefits from these producers and their commodities. These benefits derive from the complementarity that frequently exists between these producers' commodities and the Central Park commodity. In various ways, these non-capitalist producers and their commodities enhance the public's enjoyment of the Central Park commodity. While these complementarities are somewhat amorphous they are nevertheless articulable.

To a certain extent, the CPC recognizes the role that the park's independent and communist producers and their commodities play in enhancing the public's enjoyment of the park. For example, the CPC regularly promotes (in its brochures and on its website) horse-drawn sightseeing tours as among the recreational activities park patrons can pursue. Such promotion suggests the CPC is cognizant of the complementarity that exists between this particular independent commodity and its own. Consumers of horse-drawn tours through Central Park consume not only these tours, but these tours enhance their enjoyment of the Central Park commodity.[34] Moreover, it is possible that those who consume such tours end up spending additional money in the park (say, at a gift shop or on a concession) by virtue of the fact that they literally see more parts of the park as a result of their tours. In this sense, it is possible that increases in these independent commodity producers' sales may help increase revenue for the CPC.

Similar to horse-drawn carriage operators' commodities, the park's many other independent and communist producers' (artists/artisans, musicians, and street performers) commodities enhance the public's enjoyment of the park and therefore represent complements to the Central Park commodity. The following set of visitor remarks, culled from two websites designed to capture public feedback on Central Park, lends support to this notion:

> "I love Central Park because it is full of fun and laughter, beauty and action. We fly up from Florida, pack a soccer ball and my kids run and play forever on the grass. They play with the "local" kids at the playground and as I watch them, I realize we are all "one" when we laugh and enjoy life. In a big city like NYC, to have a sanctuary like Central Park, with the zoo, playgrounds, skaters, entertainers, and peaceful walking paths . . . .it is an oasis for us! We also picnic on the rocks, eat at Tavern on the Green, LOVE the Plaza, and FAO Schwartz nearby. A trip to NYC isn't complete without a walk in the Park, especially when the snow is falling and the dogs have their slippers on. We LOVE the Park and New York!"

> "Generally, after the Wildlife Center, we exit the park heading south on Wien Walk. This has the largest crowds of people walking in and out of the park. It in turn also has the most artists and street performers. Some of the artists are incredible. We could spend hours just watching them make a canvas come to life with the subject in front of them."

> "People watch. Don't laugh. The last time I was there I saw a group of ten Chinese brides and grooms getting their photos taken. I also saw Nathan Lane and Bette Midler filming a movie. Magicians, bagpipers, and stilt walkers are just a few of the other interesting people I watched."

> "But, if you just drive by [Central Park] and don't get out and walk around, then you've missed something really special. At the very least, take a ride around the park in the horse-drawn carriages. You can simply wander around and make your own discoveries like the playground for kids with water to wade in, artists drawing your face in cartoon style, teens rollerblading to music, and vendors selling hot pretzels from push carts. Every time we went, we had such fun. Central Parks was one of my favorite parts of New York City."

These comments raise an important point that deserves underscoring. Namely, the complementarity that exists between the Central Park commodity and the various commodities produced by the park's independent and communist producers does not require an exchange process (as is generally the case with complementary goods). For example, merely watching a Central Park artist produce his independent commodity—say, a hand-sketched on-the-spot portrait (one that some other park patron has elected to purchase)—might enhance a park patron's enjoyment of the Central Park commodity. Similarly, consumption of a park street-performer's virtuoso juggling performance (regardless of whether one elects to place money in the hat following the performance) likely enhances a park patron's enjoyment of the park. In this sense, the complementarity that exists between the park's independent and communist producers' commodities and the Central Park commodity might best be conceptualized as arising out of the constituent role such producers play in constituting the park's aura.

Despite the obvious lack of specificity the term aura invokes, its theoretical articulation in the current context is important. Specifically, the park's independent and communist producers and their respective commodities have what Walter Benjamin described as "auratic qualities."[35] These qualities enhance the Central Park commodity (both its aesthetic and programmatic dimensions) and play a constituent role in infusing it with a type of distinctiveness that often attaches to particular places like Central Park.[36] Describing the increasing importance of such distinction in the context of urban areas' cultural products industries, Allen Scott writes:

> "To take just one specific example, the film industry of Los Angeles—or more narrowly of Hollywood—draws on a complex web of local cultural assets that play a crucial role in imparting to the products of the industry their distinctive look and feel ( ); and, the same products in turn create images (real or imagined) of Los Angeles/Hollywood that then are assimilated back into the city's fund of cultural assets where they become available as inputs to new rounds of production. One consequence of these intricate relationships is that the reputation and authenticity of cultural products (qualities that often provide decisive competitive advantages in trade) are sometimes irrevocably tied to particular places. Think of Danish furniture, Florentine leather goods, Parisian *haute couture,* Thai silks, Champagne wines, London theatre, or, again, Hollywood films."[37]

In discussing the same idea, David Harvey writes:

"If claims to uniqueness, authenticity, particularity and specialty under-lie the ability to capture monopoly rents, then on what better ter-rain is it possible to make such claims than in the field of historically constituted cultural artifacts and practices and special environmen-tal characteristics (including, of course, the built, social and cultural environments)? . . . .The most obvious point of reference where this works is in contemporary tourism, but I think it would be a mistake to let the matter rest there. For what is at stake is the power of col-lective symbolic capital, of special marks of distinction that attach to some place, which have a significant drawing power upon the flows of capital more generally. . . . .The collective symbolic capital which attaches to names and places like Paris, Athens, New York, Rio de Janeiro, Berlin and Rome is of great import and gives such places great economic advantages relative to say, Baltimore, Liverpool, Essen, Lille and Glasgow."[38]

It is in this sense that Central Park can be conceptualized as a dis-tinct cultural product—one produced by the CPC via a capitalist class process. The argument here is that horse-carriage rides, avant garde street and musical performances, and artistic works—commodities produced via non-capitalist class processes—play an important role in constituting the iconography, authenticity, and particularity of Central Park qua capitalist commodity.[39]

How the CPC and the Park's Independent and Communist Producers Undermine Each Another. While the CPC and the park's independent and communist producers benefit one another, they may also undermine one another. This fact, of course, is but a reflection of the complex and contra-dictory relationships that necessarily characterize any set of class processes. The following remarks illustrate this point.

While the park's independent and communist producers benefit from the CPC's efforts to increase park attendance, there are likely limits to those benefits. For example, the CPC's role in increasing park attendance follow-ing the park's privatization may have not only contributed to the viability of the park's existing independent and communist producers, but may also have simultaneously worked to increase the number of these producers and thereby heightened competition among them. More intense competition may, in turn, have undermined the ability of some of these producers' to reproduce their class processes. [40]

Another example of the complexity of the relationship that exists between the CPC and the park's independent and communist producers came to light during the summer of 2004 when a protest group sought a permit to use Central Park's Great Lawn to hold a large protest over the Iraq War. New York City mayor Michael Bloomberg successfully denied the group a permit after an intense court battle.[41] As debate over the permit raged, the CPC, sensing the need to make its position on the issue clear, weighed in. In a statement posted on its website, the CPC explained why it sided with the administration. While acknowledging its support of First Amendment rights, the CPC wrote, "Our concern is that an event of this magnitude, with 250,000 people expected to attend, would severely damage not only the Great Lawn but also other areas of the Park."[42] The CPC went on to cite the history of Central Park's deterioration in the 1970s and early 1980s and its subsequent restoration, noting that the Great Lawn had been restored at a cost of $18.2 million.[43]

Thus, despite the fact that the protest would ostensibly have generated significant concession revenue (which would have directly benefited the CPC), it would also have likely translated into considerable clean-up and restoration expenditures for the CPC. Clearly, the protest would have proven beneficial to many of the park's independent and communist producers, as it would have brought thousands of protestors, spectators, tourists, and media personnel to the park.

Finally, as noted previously, the CPC recently launched an on-line retail store, suggesting that it has become more interested in securing merchant-related revenue. In part, this interest reflects the completion of several major capital improvements in the park. These improvements helped the CPC secure significant fundraising donations. With fewer such improvements in the offing, the CPC must secure alternative revenues. Such efforts may adversely affect the park's independent and communist producers. In particular, if future merchanting activity by the CPC becomes increasingly situated in the park, the commodities the CPC would sell would compete with those offered by the park's independent and communist producers. Such competition may undermine these producers' viability. Given the auratic qualities these producers and their commodities lend the park, the park's quality could suffer. This may adversely affect the CPC.

5.5 MUNICIPAL PRIVATIZATIONS AS ENSEMBLES

By highlighting the ways in which non-capitalist producers (and their commodities) complement the Central Park commodity, and explicating some of the complex relationships that exist between them and the CPC, the foregoing analysis serves to highlight the rich class analytic constitutivity of the CPC's capitalist class process and its reproduction. Two important implications flow from this analysis.

First, the demonstration that the reproduction of a capitalist class process *(specifically, one tied to a municipal privatization process like Central Park's)* can depend in part on non-capitalist producers forces those who promulgate the virtues of municipal privatization—based on the supposition that successful municipal privatizations derive primarily from their promotion of capitalist practices and/or institutions—to acknowledge that such success may be constituted by a complex set of class processes. This set may well include non-capitalist ones.

Second, the demonstration that the reproduction of a capitalist class process *(specifically, one tied to a municipal privatization process like Central Park's)* may depend in part on non-capitalist producers implies that that very dependence supports or enables such producers. This insight forces those who adopt anti-privatization positions—based on the supposition that such processes by definition (or, as is more generally the case, by association) advance solely the interests of "Capital"—to acknowledge that municipal privatizations may, by virtue of their complex class analytic constitutivity, support and/or enable non-capitalist producers. Thus, while municipal privatizations may be viewed negatively by those on the Left on the grounds that they often spawn or support capitalist enterprises, they may also *simultaneously* be viewed positively to the extent they support and/or enable non-capitalist class producers.

The foregoing analysis thus underscores the value of a class approach to municipal privatization. In particular, this approach moves beyond the usual pro- vs. anti-municipal privatization policy debate by recasting municipal privatization processes as ensembles of complex and contradictory class effects. The failure to recognize and appreciate these complexities (e.g., the potential co-dependencies that may exist between non-capitalist and capitalist producers) is a product of the discursive and theoretical association between privatization and capitalism that pervades the municipal privatization discourse, and which generally dictates the policy positions of its participants.

Finally, it should be clear that from a class perspective some municipal privatizations will be more preferable than others. As explained in Chapter Three, class theorists' interest in municipal privatizations stems from a concern with undemocratic (and, thereby) exploitative class processes. From a class perspective, municipal privatizations that spawn new or support and enable *non-capitalist* class processes (e.g., independent and communist ones) are more preferable than those that do not. These types of class processes allow the productive worker(s) engaged in them to appropriate and distribute their own surplus labor—hence, they are democratic.

The final point above prompts an obvious and intriguing question. Specifically, could a municipal privatization be designed to generate a non-capitalist enterprise? If so, what would the class implications be? Chapter Six pursues these questions. As it shows, their answers hold important policy implications—ones that are pertinent not only to the municipal privatization discourse, but also, to the broader global privatization discourse.

Chapter Six
Rethinking Municipal Privatization

> Aristotle once remarked that if only there were a fixed point in outer space, we could construct a lever to move the world. The remark tells us a great deal about the shortcomings of Aristotelian thought. Bourgeois social science is heir to the same shortcomings. It attempts to construct a view of the world from outside, to discover some fixed points (categories or concepts) on the basis of which an 'objective' understanding of the world may be fashioned. The bourgeois social scientist typically seeks to leave the world by way of an act of abstraction in order to understand it. The Marxist, by way of contrast, always seeks to construct an understanding of society from within rather than imagining some point without. The Marxist finds a whole bundle of levers for social change within the contradictory processes of social life and seeks to construct an understanding of the world by pushing hard upon the levers.
>
> David Harvey, Spaces of Capital

This chapter represents a critical engagement with the political Left in the United States over the issue of privatization.[1] I argue that once the class dimension of privatization is considered it becomes possible to reconceptualize privatization processes as vehicles by which progressive class-based development policies can be pursued.[2] I am well aware this argument will strike many on the Left as at best odd or naïve, and at worst dangerous and misguided. The primary motivation for the argument is (as explained in the book's opening chapter) this: it seems increasingly unlikely that the economic, political, and ideological forces that drive privatization initiatives will abate in the future. This suggests that the Left faces an insuperable task—pouring ever more resources into fighting more and more privatization initiatives with (at best) scattered successes. In light of this, the argument developed aims to chart a new class-based privatization strategy. This strategy centers upon (what I refer to as) democratic enterprise formation.

Privatization processes afford vehicles for forming such enterprises. Before explaining what these enterprises are and why they could and should be pursued via privatization processes, it will be useful to set the stage by reviewing the argument developed in the two preceding chapters.

The argument that Central Park's privatization spawned a capitalist class process provided the foundation upon which the model developed in the second part of Chapter Four was built. The analysis developed in Chapter Five used that model to explicate some of the complex and contradictory class effects the park's privatization (and, by extension, ones that could arise out of municipal privatizations more generally) gave rise to. The final remarks of Chapter Five raised an intriguing question. Namely, could a municipal privatization process be designed to create or support a non-capitalist enterprise? If so, what would the implications be? These are the questions this chapter addresses.

The chapter's argument can be summarized. I argue that municipal privatizations could be designed to generate non-capitalist enterprises. Alternatively, municipal privatizations need not necessarily generate new or support existing capitalist enterprises. Further, I argue that non-capitalist enterprises can coexist with competitive markets and private ownership, and can accommodate corporate-like managerial processes and organizational structures. In short, there is no necessary connection between these institutions, processes, and structures and enterprises' class structures. This argument has an important policy implication. Specifically, if such institutions, processes, and structures are held to be the keys to successful municipal privatizations (as generally argued by privatization proponents) and, if they can co-exist with and/or be accommodated by non-capitalist enterprises, then the issue of what particular class form a municipal privatization should take becomes a political question worthy of debate. That is, the question, "What particular class form should a municipal privatization process take?" warrants as careful scrutiny as that which regularly attends the question of what particular institutional form (e.g., public-private partnership, contract, franchise, internal market, managed competition, voucher system, user fee system, or enterprise (asset) sale) the process should take.

Removing municipal privatizations from the "capitalist" penumbra the Left has (understandably) assumed them to lie within, opens up theoretical and policy space for those theorizing about and/or politically engaged in municipal privatizations. In short, it opens the door for theorizing, and perhaps politically realizing, *progressive* municipal privatizations. Unfortunately, the specific class conditions that would yield such privatizations have not been met heretofore. The municipal privatizations that have been implemented across the United States during the past three decades have too often been anything but progressive.

6.1 NON-PROGRESSIVE MUNICIPAL PRIVATIZATIONS

Two conditions provided the basis for the argument that Central Park's privatization created a capitalist class process inside the CPC. First, the contract struck between the CPC and the city signaled that the two parties would engage in an annual exchange process. As explained, the contract sets out the conditions under which this exchange occurs. In particular, it specifies the commodity the CPC must produce—the Central Park commodity—and the conditions under which the city will purchase it. The contract also provides a basis for determining the exchange value of the Central Park commodity. This background provided the basis for the argument that the park's privatization commodified Central Park, i.e., transformed what was formerly a use-value (a public park) into a commodity constituting both a use-value and an exchange value. It also served as the basis for the specification of the existence of the CPC's fundamental class process, i.e., the positing of a commodity production process that yields (requires) surplus labor and an appropriative process in which that surplus labor is appropriated.

Second, because the surplus labor produced by the CPC's maintenance crews, gardeners, and programmatic staffers was determined to take the form of surplus value, the CPC's class process was deemed a capitalist one. This implies that the CPC's productive workers who produce the surplus value embodied within the Central Park commodity are *excluded* from participating in decisions over how the fruits of their labor (i.e., surplus value) will be used (or, distributed via the subsumed class process). This exclusion provides the basis for deeming the CPC's capitalist class process (and all other capitalist class processes) undemocratic. This undemocracy, in turn, provides the basis for deeming the CPC's capitalist class process (and all other capitalists' class processes) exploitative. On the basis of its creation of an undemocratic (and, hence, exploitative) class process inside the CPC, Central Park's privatization may be characterized as a *non-progressive* one.

As explained in Chapter Three, the class process tied to Central park's privatization represented but one class origin form. Specifically, the park's privatization *created* a class process within an organization that did not (prior to the privatization) host one. The class processes involved in other privatizations may originate in other ways. For example, a privatization that involves contracting-out the production of a public good or service to an existing capitalist enterprise would not involve the creation of a new class process but would simply support an existing one. More generally, any privatization process—regardless of whether it occurs on the municipal, county, state, or nation state levels—that creates a new or supports an existing class process that is undemocratic (and, hence, exploitative) is considered non-progressive from a class perspective.

If a privatization is deemed non-progressive, based on its generation of an exploitative class process or support of an existing exploitative class process, then a *necessary* condition for a *progressive* privatization is that it generate or support a non-exploitative class process. Because individuals engaged in independent and communist class processes appropriate and distribute their own surpluses, these types of class processes are democratic and thus non-exploitative.[3] Thus, a municipal privatization that generated a new or relied upon an existing independent or communist class process (enterprise) would satisfy this condition.

6.2 NON-CAPITALIST ENTERPRISES AND THEIR VIABILITY IN THE CONTEXT OF MUNICIPAL PRIVATIZATION

Independent Enterprises. While it is often the case that the production of a municipal good or service requires an enterprise comprising several individuals, there are some public goods or services that might be produced via independent class processes. (As explained in Chapter Four, independent class processes involve a single individual who appropriates and distributes her own surplus labor.) For example, consider municipal towing services, which are often produced by non-government entities. In many cases, local tow-truck operators contract with municipalities to tow illegally-parked cars. In the event a single individual operated her own tow-truck operation and thereby produced a towing service commodity for a municipality, she might do so via an independent class process. Note that the individual comprising such an independent enterprise would not need to own her own tow-truck, as the municipality could rent her a truck. She would then pay a rental fee (a subsumed class payment) to the city.[4]

Because the production of most municipal goods and services requires considerably more than one individual (which suggests that the potential for independent enterprises in the context of municipal privatization is limited), the remainder of this section explores the issues surrounding other types of non-capitalist enterprises in the context of municipal privatization processes—in particular, communist enterprises. The interest in these enterprises reflects the fact that the class processes they host (communist ones) satisfy the first necessary condition for a progressive municipal privatization—namely, that it generate a new or support an existing non-exploitative class process (enterprise).

Communist Enterprises. On the assumption that a municipal privatization could be structured to support an existing communist enterprise or generate a new communist enterprise (which seems more likely), it is worth setting out in greater detail how such an enterprise's class structure would differ from a capitalist enterprise's. In particular, the circumstances surrounding each enterprise's appropriative and distributive processes must be more clearly articulated.

Consider Figures 6.1 and 6.2 (pages 114 and 115) which provide a conceptual rendering of Central Park's actual privatization process and a revamped version of that process. Begin by considering Figure 6.1. Prior to its privatization, Central Park constituted a public good or use-value. This use-value was jointly produced by New York City's Parks and Recreation Department and the CPC. The production of the park qua use-value involved a complex set of organizational, technical, and managerial processes. These processes along with many other economic, political, natural, and cultural ones impinged upon the production of the park. The production of the park as a use-value did not involve a class process, however. As the figure shows, the park's privatization commodified the park and generated a capitalist (hence, exploitative) class process within the CPC. This implies the park's privatization was non-progressive.

Now consider Figure 6.2, which is identical to Figure 6.1 in all aspects but one. In particular, it depicts a hypothetical situation in which the park's privatization generates a communist class process inside the CPC. This communist class process would imply that the CPC's productive workers (its maintenance crews, gardeners, and programmatic staffers) collectively appropriate and distribute the surplus value they produce in the course of producing the Central Park commodity. Thus, the CPC's class process would be non-exploitative. This would satisfy a necessary condition for a progressive privatization, i.e., that it generate or support a non-exploitative class process (enterprise).

What would the realization of a communist class process within the CPC imply? Imagine an actual CPC board meeting. Similar to most capitalist enterprises' board meetings, the CPC's board uses such meetings to distribute the surplus value it appropriates. This distribution process constitutes the CPC's subsumed class process. As described in Chapter Four, the board distributes portions of surplus to the individuals and institutions that provide the conditions that allow the CPC to produce and realize surplus value. The CPC's productive workers are excluded from participating in the appropriative and distributive processes. By way of contrast, if the

CPC hosted a communist class process, its productive workers would participate in these processes. As Figure 6.2 shows, such a class-transformative change would not necessarily require any other change inside the CPC, e.g., to its productive and managerial processes and/or its organizational form.

Clearly, additional issues must be addressed regarding communist class processes (enterprises). For example, the question of whom else might participate (e.g., managers and support staff) along with the collective of productive workers in the appropriative and distributive processes must be addressed. Similarly, the question concerning the basis upon which the collective of workers participate in these processes remains open. Thus, while a municipal privatization process that spawned a communist enterprise would be preferable to a non-progressive one (from a class perspective), it would not quality as a *progressive* municipal privatization. To reiterate, the condition that a municipal privatization generate or support a non-exploitative class process is but a necessary condition for the realization of a progressive municipal privatization. Before elaborating on this point, the issues of whether a communist enterprise can coexist with competitive markets and private ownership, and whether it can accommodate "corporate-like" managerial processes and organizational forms must be addressed.

The Viability of Communist Enterprises in the Context of Municipal Privatization.

The theoretical proposition that a municipal privatization process could generate a communist enterprise represents but a starting point. More important is the question of whether or not such an enterprise would be viable. From a class perspective, the viability of communist enterprises would necessarily be complexly overdetermined by a host of interacting and contradictory processes. Indeed, just as the viability of capitalist enterprises has been intermittently enhanced and undermined repeatedly throughout the course of their history, so too, would communist enterprises' viability. This suggests that a more appropriate line of inquiry concerns communist enterprises' relationships with the institutional arrangements and processes, practices, and structures that generally prevail in the private sector. More specifically, could communist enterprises coexist with competitive markets and private ownership? And, could they accommodate corporate-like managerial processes and organizational forms? (Hereafter, I refer to these questions as the coexistence/accommodation issue.) If one is interested in elevating the question of the class form of municipal privatization processes in order to make it an object worthy of political debate, such questions must be addressed. If communist enterprises cannot coexist with and/or accommodate these institutions, processes, practices, and structures, the class form question will appear irrelevant to policy-makers.

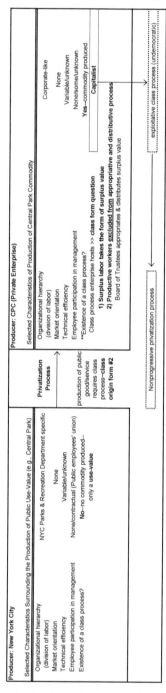

Figure 6.1 Central Park's Privatization: From Use-Value to Capitalist Class Process

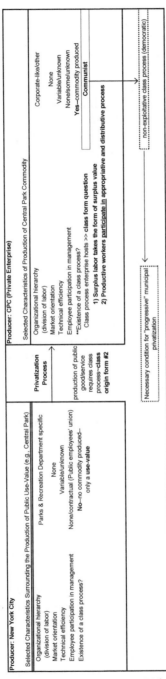

Figure 6.2 Central Park's Privatization: From Use-Value to Non-Capitalist Class Process

Communist Enterprises and Managerial Processes and Organizational Structures. As noted (and shown in Figure 6.2), a communist class process within the CPC would not necessarily require any alteration in its existing corporate-like managerial process or its organizational structure (division of labor). As explained in Chapter Three, an enterprise's managerial process is a political process. Political processes regulate and structure the ways in which power and authority are distributed and exercised within an enterprise. While an enterprise's managerial and class processes over-determine one another, they are nevertheless separable. That is to say, if the CPC exhibited a communist class structure, it might nevertheless retain its existing managerial process and organizational structure. This point is important because the presumption that the CPC's managerial process and corporate-like organizational structure are superior to the New York City Parks Department's was used to publicly rationalize the park's privatization. As CPC benefactor, Richard Gilder, wrote, arguing for the park's privatization, in 1997:

> "Though the Parks Department has many fine people in Central Park, they work under a bureaucratic, seniority-based union system. Rigid union job descriptions can create a ready excuse for leaving work undone. When scores of fish died of a mysterious ailment in the Rowboat Lake a few years back, Parks Department workers maintained—rightly, no doubt—that retrieving them wasn't in their contract."[5]

As elaborated in Chapter Two, the supposition that private sector managerial processes and organizational structures are superior to those within the public sector is held by privatization proponents to be one of the key factors that explain why municipal privatization processes yield efficiency gains.

The larger point of the foregoing discussion deserves underscoring. In particular, the theoretical distinction between an enterprise's class process and its managerial process implies that there might well be a host of different types of communist enterprises differentiated on the basis of their unique managerial processes. One can imagine a communist enterprise in which all managerial power was vested in the hands of a single individual.[6] Alternatively, one might imagine a communist enterprise in which managerial authority was structured more democratically. It seems likely that communist enterprises would accommodate some managerial processes more easily than others. Moreover, a communist enterprise's managerial processes, similar to capitalist enterprises,' will evolve and shift over time in response to various stimuli.

In like manner, a communist enterprise's organizational structure (or, internal division of labor) could vary widely. Thus, the transformation of the CPC's class structure into a communist one would not necessarily require any alternation in organizational structure. A communist enterprise might just as easily accommodate a highly hierarchical corporate-like organizational form as a "flat" one. As with its managerial process, a communist enterprise's organizational structure will evolve and shift over time.

Communist Enterprises and Competitive Markets. Like managerial processes and organizational structures, product market competition is generally considered a key factor in explaining why municipal privatization processes "succeed." Privatization proponents argue that competition ensures that the enterprises the come to produce municipal public goods and services following a privatization process are forced by the market (which, in the case of many municipal privatizations is constituted via a competitive bidding process) to cost minimize. Such behavior promotes efficiency and thereby ostensibly delivers municipalities fiscal benefits. Could communist enterprises coexist with this type of competition?

As explained in Chapter Four, Central Park's privatization did not involve product market competition; the CPC is the sole producer of the Central Park commodity. Because of this, Figure 6.3 (page 119) represents a hypothetical municipal privatization process in which the enterprises that come to produce a municipal good following a privatization process face competition. This example allows the relationship between an enterprise's class structure and market competition to be more closely examined.

Assume a municipality has elected to privatize waste collection via a competitive bidding process. Further, assume that the municipality has elected to award three separate contracts in order to ensure some type of competition between contractors. Assume also that the privatization is structured so that the best-performing enterprise in any given year is not required to rebid the following year, while the others must. The right-hand side of Figure 6.3 shows three hypothetical contract awardees. In particular, it shows two contractors (enterprises) that exhibit capitalist class structures and one that exhibits a communist class structure.

From a class perspective, the critical difference between the three enterprises is that the productive workers of enterprise 1 collectively appropriate and distribute the surplus value they produce in the course of producing a sanitation service commodity—whereas, the productive workers of enterprises 2 and 3 are excluded from those processes. Thus, enterprise 1 hosts a non-exploitative class structure, while enterprises 2 and 3 host exploitative class structures. Note also, that the communist enterprise is assumed to exhibit a managerial process and organizational structure that is identical to the capitalist enterprises.' The ensuing competition that would result from this hypothetical municipal privatization process would thus pit one communist enterprise against two capitalist enterprises. What the outcome of such competition would be is of course unknowable and would be a function of several factors. The larger point is to suggest that there is nothing inherent in a communist enterprise's class structure that would preclude its coexistence with a competitive marketplace. As with capitalist enterprises, communist enterprises' relationship with competitive markets would be expected to give rise to all sorts of complexities and contradictions. Just as a capitalist enterprise must constantly negotiate such complexities and contradictions, a communist enterprise would be forced to devise processes and systems, and undertake actions that would allow such contradictions to be overcome. In the event they were not it would perish, just as a capitalist enterprise would.

If communist enterprises could coexist with competitive markets, the question of how they might be expected to "behave" remains open. Specifically, as noted, one of the chief virtues of municipal privatization, according to its proponents, is that the introduction of competition into the production of public goods and services yields efficiency gains. Unlike government entities, private producers are forced by the competitive marketplace to wring inefficiencies out of their production and operational processes—those that do not often perish. Would a communist enterprise that came to produce a public good or service via a municipal privatization process, and which was exposed to a competitive marketplace behave as a capitalist enterprise would? Would it cost-minimize? The short answer is possibly. As Stephen Cullenberg writes, "simply because a firm is structured on the basis of collective appropriation does not imply necessarily any particular "business" behavior."[7] Thus, there is no reason to presume that a communist enterprise would necessarily be any less concerned than a capitalist one about productive efficiency. In fact, it seems possible that to the extent a communist enterprise might elect to pursue goals besides (or, in addition to) maximizing profit, it might care deeply about productive efficiency.[8]

Whatever goals a communist enterprise elected to pursue would have to be balanced, would involve risks, and would likely constantly shift and change—similar to the goals capitalist enterprises pursue. Moreover, it is undoubtedly true that a communist enterprise exposed to competitive market forces would have to take those forces into account when selecting its goals.

Producer: Municipality

Selected Characteristics Surrounding the Production of Public Use-Value

Organizational hierarchy (division of labor)	Municipal agency specific
Market orientation	None
Technical efficiency	Variable/unknown
Employee participation in m	None/contractual (Public employees' union)
Existence of a class process?	No—no commodity produced—only a **use-value**

Privatization Process

creation (support) of a class process

Producer: Private Enterprise #1

Selected Characteristics of Production of Municipal Sanitation Services

Organizational hierarchy (division of labor)	Corporate-like
Market orientation	Competition via contract'g process
Technical efficiency	Variable/unknown
Employee participation in manag.	None/some/unknown
Existence of a class process?	**Yes**
Class process enterprise hosts >> **class form question**	**Communist**

1) Surplus labor takes the form of surplus value
2) Productive workers participate in appropriative and distributive process

Producer: Private Enterprise #2

Selected Characteristics of Production of Municipal Sanitation Services

Organizational hierarchy (division of labor)	Corporate-like
Market orientation	Competition via contract'g process
Technical efficiency	Variable/unknown
Employee participation in management	None/some/unknown
Existence of a class process?	**Yes**
Class process enterprise hosts >> **class form question**	**Capitalist**

1) Surplus labor takes the form of surplus value
2) Productive workers excluded from appropriative and distributive process

Producer: Private Enterprise #3

Selected Characteristics of Production of Municipal Sanitation Services

Organizational hierarchy (division of labor)	Corporate-like
Market orientation	Competition via contract'g process
Technical efficiency	Variable/unknown
Employee participation in management	None/some/unknown
Existence of a class process?	**Yes**
Class process enterprise hosts >> **class form question**	**Capitalist**

1) Surplus labor takes the form of surplus value
2) Productive workers excluded from appropriative and distributive process

Figure 6.3 Municipal Privatization: From Use-Value to Competition between Capitalist and Non-Capitalist Producers

Thus, it is entirely possible a communist enterprise would pursue the goal of profit-maximization. Alternatively, it might elect to balance that goal with others. In either case, the class process of a communist enterprise would ensure that the goals it pursued would be decided upon via a democratic process.

Communist Enterprises and Labor Markets. It has already been established that communist enterprises could coexist with competitive commodity markets. Could they also coexist with labor markets? The answer is yes. As Resnick and Wolff explain, this would mean:

> "The collective [i.e., the enterprise's workers] buys each individual unit of labor power from its own members (much as it also buys tools, equipment, and raw materials for production). The collective alone thus acquires the use-value of each unit of labor-power sold by setting in motion the labor of these workers with other purchased means of production."[9]

Thus, as with other competitive commodity markets, there is no reason to assume that communist enterprises could not exist with markets in which individuals sell their own labor-power. As Resnick and Wolff go on to note, the coexistence of communist enterprises and wage-labor markets may well require and/or necessitate particular laws (e.g., ones that mandate that those who sell labor-power to such an enterprise participate in the appropriative and distributive processes) and/or may change workers' understanding of their relationships to commodity producing enterprises.[10] Just as capitalist enterprises' historical relationship with wage-labor markets has exhibited extreme periods of contradiction and symbiosis, communist enterprises' relationship with labor markets would be complex and historically contingent.

Consider how a communist enterprise that contracted with a large urban municipal government to produce a sanitation service commodity would deal with the issue of finding and hiring a highly-skilled urban planner capable of designing the most sensible routes for its sanitation trucks. Presumably, it would launch a job search—just as any capitalist enterprise would do. Upon finding this individual, it would engage in a salary negotiation. The salary agreed to would be (over)determined by a number of factors, including the going wage for similarly-skilled urban planners in the area, the planner's alternative job options, and, the enterprise's class structure. It may turn out that the enterprise would have to pay the planner a salary well above existing workers.' This suggests that there is nothing inherent in a communist enterprise's class structure that would guarantee an internal wage structure that would be characterized by equality. A communist enterprise's internal wage structure could exhibit stark inequalities.

Similar to a capitalist enterprise, a communist enterprise that coexisted with wage-labor markets would have to negotiate those markets. The success of those negotiations (just as they do for a capitalist enterprise) would play an important role in determining whether or not it successfully reproduced its class process.

Communist Enterprises and Private Ownership. One important coexistence issue remains. Namely, could communist enterprises coexist with private ownership? Because this issue is dealt with in considerable detail in Chapter Seven, here I offer only some brief remarks.[11] Just as an enterprise's internal managerial processes, organizational structure, and relationship with competitive product and labor markets are separable from its class structure, so too is its relationship with ownership forms. Thus, for example, a communist enterprise could elect to issue ownership (equity) shares, just as many capitalist enterprises do. The existence of shareholders and their relationship to a communist enterprise's class structure would necessarily be complex and produce a host of important contradictions, just as they do in capitalist enterprises. As Cullenberg remarks, "Private ownership confers certain specific rights and privileges on owners, but there is no necessary right to appropriation, control, or residual claimancy, only the right of the owners of capital to whatever factor payments the capital input will bear."[12] As explained previously, share-ownership in an enterprise may entitle owners to dividends (a subsumed class distribution). In the event a communist enterprise issued equity, it may be required to pay dividends. The only difference would be that in a communist enterprise productive workers would participate in the decision-making (subsumed class) process whereby the decision to pay dividends is made.

The foregoing discussion suggests that communist enterprises could accommodate and coexist with the institutions, practices, processes, and structures that are assumed to underlie the presumed efficiency of private-sector enterprises (and, thus, by extension, constitute the *raison d'etres* for privatization processes at the municipal level). Given this, the question concerning the particular class form a municipal privatization process should take becomes politically relevant. Clearly, municipal privatizations can be structured to generate and/or encourage communist enterprise formation. The fact they have not done so is not evidence to the contrary. Instead, it underscores policy-makers' failure to recognize and/or consider the class dimension of municipal privatization processes. This prompts an important question. Namely, besides the fact that communist enterprises appear to "pass" the requisite coexistence/accommodation tests, do they possess merits that might induce municipal policy-makers to become more concerned with the class form of the privatization processes they undertake? Put otherwise, why should municipal policy-makers be concerned with the class form a privatization takes? More specifically, why might privatizations involving communist enterprises prove attractive? Before addressing these questions, one final issue must be addressed. In particular, the *sufficient* conditions for a *progressive* municipal privatization must be specified.

6.3 PROGRESSIVE MUNICIPAL PRIVATIZATIONS: DEMOCRATIC ENTERPRISE FORMATION

Municipal privatizations are deemed non-progressive from a class perspective if they generate or support undemocratic (hence, exploitative) class processes (within an enterprise). Thus, a necessary condition for a progressive municipal privatization is that it generate or support a non-exploitative class process (within an enterprise). A municipal privatization process that generated a new or relied upon an existing independent or communist enterprise would satisfy this condition. Such a privatization would not qualify as a progressive one, however. Why?

A progressive privatization would require two conditions.[13] First, it would involve an enterprise in which productive laborers *as well as* all other employees (e.g., support staff and managers) participated in appropriating and subsequently distributing the enterprise's surplus.[14] This condition rules out the possibility of an enterprise which meets the necessary condition of having a non-exploitative class process, but simultaneously excludes unproductive workers (support staff and managers) from participating in the appropriative and distributive processes. While the enterprises that would lie at the center of a progressive privatization possess a number of merits from a policy perspective (see discussion below), the democratic qualities inherent in their class processes (structures) are what make them attractive from a class perspective. As explained in Chapter Three, it is this democracy (which allows productive workers to participate in decisions regarding how the fruits of the labor (surplus value) will be used, e.g., for accumulation purposes, distributed as bonuses, directed toward social programs, etc.) that serves as the basis for deeming such enterprises' class structures non-exploitative. If one rejects the type of collective (and, democratic) appropriation (and distribution) that such enterprises afford, " . . . one also rejects the right of individuals to participate on an equal footing in making decisions concerning issues that are of central importance to their lives and that affect the better part of their waking hours."[15]

This interest in promoting democratic class processes inside enterprises underlies the necessity of requiring an enterprise's support staff and managers (in addition to its productive workers) to participate in the appropriative and distributive processes as a condition for a progressive municipal privatization. More specifically, it is difficult to square the idea that support staff and managers should be precluded from participating in these processes merely because they perform "unproductive" labor (i.e., they do not directly produce surplus value) with an interest in democracy.[16] Unproductive workers' labor, despite its specification as unproductive from a class perspective, clearly plays an important role in ensuring the production and realization of an enterprise's surplus value.

The first condition for a progressive privatization thus specifies who within the enterprise must participate in the appropriative and distributive processes. This condition alone is not sufficient for a progressive privatization, however. Specifically, something must be said about the *basis* on which those who participate in these processes do so.

A progressive privatization must not only allow both the enterprise's productive workers as well as its other employees to participate in the appropriative and distributive processes, but *it must do so on the basis of one-person, one-vote*. This condition rules out other possibilities for the basis for participation, e.g., equity-ownership in the case of an employee-owned enterprise.[17] The exact manner used to meet this second condition is left unspecified.[18] Hence, the one-employee one-vote condition might be met via a consensus decision-making process, a representative democratic one, or via some other method.

To sum up, a municipal privatization process that involved or generated (which seems the more likely scenario) an enterprise that:

1. allowed *all* of the enterprise's employees (i.e., the productive laborers as well as its support staff and managers) to participate in the appropriative and distributive processes, and,

2. which did so on the basis of one employee-one vote, would qualify as a progressive privatization from a class perspective.[19]

Enterprises whose class processes meet the above two conditions are hereafter referred to as democratic enterprises.

The above discussion prompts an important issue that must be addressed before the policy merits of progressive municipal privatizations are set out. In particular, because they satisfy a necessary condition of a progressive municipal privatization process (namely, that the enterprises such processes generate or support host non-exploitative class processes), communist enterprises were used as a model to demonstrate the viability of such enterprises. More specifically, communist enterprises were shown to pass various coexistence and accommodation tests that make them politically and economically viable. This in turn suggested that municipal privatization processes that generated or supported communist enterprises (but one type of non-capitalist enterprise) are viable. The critical question is whether or not the democratic enterprises which serve as the foundation of progressive municipal privatizations are similar enough to communist enterprises to assume their (and, thus, progressive municipal privatizations') viability.

The answer to this question is yes. As explained, the claim that a democratic enterprise's class structure is non-exploitative rests on the fact that its productive employees participate in the appropriative and distributive processes (and, further, would do so on the basis of one employee-one vote). Though not necessary, the same premise can be used to make the claim that communist enterprises' class structures are non-exploitative. If the theoretical basis for deeming communist enterprises' class processes non-exploitative requires their productive workers to *exclusively* appropriate and distribute their own surplus (unlike the situation in democratic enterprises in which productive workers would not exclusively appropriate and distribute their own surplus) then a theoretical difference between them and democratic enterprises would arise. This difference, in no way, however, would jeopardize the demonstration of communist enterprises' viability in the context of municipal privatization. It follows that the democratic enterprises which serve as the foundation of progressive municipal privatizations, similar to communist enterprises, pass the viability test. This, in turn, implies that progressive municipal privatizations are viable.

6.4 THE POLICY MERITS OF PROGRESSIVE MUNICIPAL PRIVATIZATIONS

The attempt to place progressive municipal privatizations on the policy agenda must not only address the viability question surrounding the democratic enterprises they involve, but must also provide a rationale for why the class form question (they raise) is important. Put otherwise, what are the potential payoffs that might flow from a concern with the class form of a municipal privatization process? More specifically, why might policymakers find *progressive* municipal privatizations attractive?

Democratic Enterprises and Monitoring. The issue of monitoring is among the most important surrounding privatization, as the costs associated with monitoring privatization processes must be weighed against whatever benefits they provide. Once a public good or service has been privatized, the enterprise that comes to produce the good or service may have incentives to cut corners. Corruption by private producers of public goods and services, as noted at the outset of Chapter One, has long plagued privatization efforts at the municipal level, and been a chief reason many municipalities have reverted back to public production. As far back as 1892, the head of the Chicago Board of Health declared, "There are few if any redeeming qualities attached [to the contract system]. No matter what guards are placed around it, the system remains vicious."[20]

A vast sub-literature that discusses how privatizations can be structured to minimize the risks associated with corruption has evolved within the municipal privatization literature.[21] This literature identifies several factors that impinge upon an enterprise's ability to engage in corruption. In the current context, it seems obvious that one of those factors is an enterprise's class structure. Clearly, an enterprise's class structure will impinge upon its employees' ability to engage in corrupt behavior.

It seems reasonable to assume that as the number of individuals engaged in an enterprise's key operational and strategic decision-making processes increases, the more difficult it is to engage in corrupt behavior.[22] Democratic enterprises' class structures allow *all* of its employees (managers as well as productive workers) to participate in the subsumed class process, in which, all decisions regarding how the enterprise's surplus is to be distributed are made. In this sense, the class structure of a democratic enterprise ensures that productive workers and managers actively monitor one another as a direct consequence of their participation in the distributive process. In the language of the literature devoted to monitoring problems, democratic enterprises' class structures would ensure that the monitoring costs associated with municipal privatizations were in part internalized. If follows that progressive municipal privatizations, by virtue of their generation of democratic enterprises, could help reduce the monitoring costs associated with municipal privatizations.

Reshaping the Interest Group Environment. It is obvious that any attempt to structure a progressive municipal privatization process would encounter a significant hurdle: there are unlikely to be many, if any, democratic enterprises. Thus, a municipality interested in pursuing a progressive privatization would have to structure it to ensure such enterprises were generated *via the privatization process.* This point is important because it suggests that a progressive municipal privatization could reshape the existing interest-group environment in a way that made the privatization less politically divisive.

If a progressive privatization provided for the generation of a new democratic enterprise, it is reasonable to assume that some existing municipal employees (who have the requisite skills and knowledge of the production process used to produce the good or service in question) could be encouraged (perhaps via the provision of various incentives) to form such an enterprise. Such incentives (e.g., tax breaks, subsidies, employee training, grants, loans, etc.) would be no different from those often used by municipalities in other contexts, e.g., local economic development efforts. To the extent progressive privatizations provided conditions that encouraged existing municipal employees to form democratic enterprises that produced public goods and services, they would likely be viewed in a very different light by public employees as well as, possibly, the unions that represent them.

The above possibility raises several questions. For instance, how would a collective of municipal employees interested in participating in a progressive privatization that encouraged democratic enterprise formation finance itself? There are a variety of possibilities. First, such a collective could secure private financing, e.g., a common small business loan. In the event the collective received such a loan, it would make interest payments on the loan just as any small business enterprise does. Alternatively, the municipality could provide financing to the collective. By underwriting the collective's new democratic enterprise the municipality would collect interest payments. In the future, a portion of the enterprise's surplus would be used to repay the loan. Another option is that the municipality could rent the collective the equipment and materials, including the office space, it needed to produce the newly privatized public good or service.

In contemplating how a democratic enterprise created via a progressive privatization might come to fruition—in particular, how it might be financed—it seems obvious that municipal labor unions could play a lead role. Public employee labor unions often boast significant pension funds—ones that, in many cases, carry significant institutional weight in the financial marketplace.[23] Public employee unions could not only play an important role in financing fledgling democratic enterprises (perhaps either directly or as loan guarantors), but they could also provide such enterprises various support services, e.g., payroll and insurance, etc. The result would be union-supported and perhaps financed democratic enterprises (ones possibly comprised of former municipal employees) that were the offspring of municipal privatization processes.

While it clearly lies well outside the context of U.S.-based municipal privatization, it is notable that since 1992 (i.e., since the convention of the First National Meeting on Trade Union Enterprises and Institutions) trade unions in China have been aggressively engaged in establishing economic enterprises.[24] All China Federation of Trade Unions (ACFTU) statistics indicate that, by the end of 1998, Chinese trade unions at all levels had launched 120,000 enterprises and institutions, of which 65,000 were economic entities that had income of 47.6 billion yuan and turned over (to the state) 5.66 billion yuan in profits and taxes. The same year, the number of enterprises and institutions run by trade unions increased by forty percent over the prior year. Of course, the question of whether or not these union-run enterprises qualify as democratic enterprises is an empirical question. If these union-backed Chinese enterprises exhibit communal (and/or democratic) class structures then the much ballyhooed rise of China might owe much to communal (and/or democratic) class processes (enterprises).[25] Indeed, there would be deep irony could it be shown that China's march toward capitalism had simultaneously spurred non-capitalist enterprise formation.

Progressive municipal privatizations would undoubtedly alter the interest group environment that generally surrounds municipal privatizations. Indeed, it seems possible that they could reduce the resistance policy-makers interested in privatization often face. The idea that privatization processes can be structured in ways designed to reshape interest group environments (and, thereby, make them more politically saleable) was espoused in 1988 by Reagan's Presidential Commission on Privatization. The Commission wrote:

> "For example, a proposal to divest a government business might suggest transferring it to the employees. . . . A proposal to divest government power-generating facilities might suggest giving the facilities (or selling them cheaply) to the current power customers. . . . A proposal to divest government conservation lands might suggest giving it to a current conservation organization. . . . In summary, if privatization consists simply of eliminating government programs and cutting off benefits, change may come at a slow pace. If privatization consists, however, of forming and recognizing new private rights for the beneficiaries of existing programs, the pace could accelerate."[26]

Needless to say, despite the Reagan administration's recognition that privatizations can be structured to increase the likelihood of their political realization, there is a major difference between conceptualizing them as foremost a means of reducing the size and/or scope of government, and conceptualizing them as avenues for non-capitalist (democratic) enterprise formation.[27]

Democratic Enterprises and Managed Competition. Managed competition is a form of privatization in which municipal government departments or agencies compete with private sector producers. Because the government unit and one or more private producers produce the same public good or service, managed competition simulates a competitive market environment. In many cases, the municipal departments engaged in managed competition are afforded wider-than-usual budgetary freedoms and forced to adopt standard private-sector accounting measures which allow their performance vis-à-vis their private sector competitors to be assessed. Among the most attractive features of managed competition is that it often considerably reduces political resistance to privatization, as municipal employees are given a chance to compete instead of being summarily laid off, as is often the case with the contracting-out form of privatization. Managed competition has been widely used for many years in several municipalities, especially in Phoenix and Indianapolis.

The interest in managed competition in the present context stems from that fact that its creation of small independent enterprises (comprised of municipal departments and their employees) is not substantively different than the democratic enterprises a progressive privatization would likely involve. Despite the novel class structures of democratic enterprises, their conceptual similarity to the enterprises generated via managed competition should make them more attractive to policy-makers.

Democratic Enterprises and the Preference for Local Procurement. Progressive privatizations possess another benefit. Specifically, there is a heightened sense among municipal governments that procurement must double as an economic development tool.[28] Thus, increasingly, municipalities take pains to ensure that their procurement policies support (stimulate) local economic enterprises (activity). To the extent progressive municipal privatizations provide vehicles for creating local enterprises, they would presumably prove especially attractive to municipal policy-makers. In effect, progressive privatizations would not only allow policy-makers interested in privatization to realize their primary goal (turning the production of a public good or service over to a private entity), but could, if properly structured, provide the added benefit of incubating local enterprises. Instead of benefiting large, national, or multinational enterprises with few local ties (which many municipal privatizations regularly do (which often engenders intense political backlash)), a progressive privatization would double as a generator of home-grown enterprises—albeit, ones involving novel and non-exploitative class structures.

While the above sections highlighted some of the political and economic merits of progressive municipal privatizations, it should be clear that the enterprises such privatizations would yield would *ipso facto* promote democratic principles. All levels of government ostensibly have an interest in seeing democracy promoted. And, while the democracy inherent in democratic enterprises would be substantively different than the type of political democracy so cherished in the U.S. it would nevertheless represent a rationale (for privatization) with an ethical basis that made it politically viable.

Progressive municipal privatizations clearly have several political and economic merits that should make them attractive to policy-makers. Moreover, these merits in conjunction with the fact that democratic enterprises can coexist with and/or accommodate the institutions, processes, and structures assumed to underlie the presumed efficiency of private-sector enterprises suggests that progressive privatizations are economically and politically viable.

6.5 RETHINKING MUNICIPAL PRIVATIZATION ON THE LEFT

The foregoing analysis offers the Left a new approach to municipal privatization. By recognizing the class dimensions of municipal privatization processes, this approach reconceptualizes such processes as vehicles for pursuing democratic enterprise formation. In doing so, it identifies an avenue by which the Left could pursue a more progressive class-oriented politics and local development paradigm—especially in the large urban centers in which municipal privatizations have most forcefully appeared. As David Harvey suggests in the quote that heads this chapter, class analysis is capable of revealing "a whole bundle of levers for social change . . . " Were progressive municipal privatizations realized, they would undoubtedly yield important social and class-transformative changes. These changes would reflect the democracy inherent in democratic enterprises' class structures. The reasons that warrant this new approach are clear. It is difficult to imagine that the economic, political, and ideological forces that have driven the municipal privatization movement in the United States will suddenly vanish. This suggests that the Left's current privatization strategy—which involves pouring ever more resources into fighting more and more municipal privatizations with scattered successes—is unsustainable.

It should be equally clear that this new approach does not represent an endorsement of municipal privatization processes. From a class perspective, the policy choice between pro- and anti-privatization positions is a false one. This is because it fails to recognize the class dimension—and, thereby, the class-transformative possibilities—of municipal privatizations. Indeed, it is precisely because they have tended to turn the production of public goods and services over to capitalist enterprises that the municipal privatizations carried out in the United States during the past three decades are considered unprogressive from a class perspective.

Finally, it should be clear that this approach need not be confined to the municipal privatization context. As the ensuing chapter demonstrates, it is equally applicable to all sorts of privatization processes. In particular, the class form question is especially pertinent in the context of the privatization of state-owned enterprises. Thus, the insights that flow from a class approach to municipal privatization have equally important policy implications for the global privatization discourse.

Chapter Seven
Rethinking the Privatization of State-Owned Enterprises

This chapter considers privatization in a global context and thereby extends the argument developed in Chapter Six. Specifically, I consider the privatization of state-owned enterprises and show that the class form question is just as relevant as in the municipal privatization context. I argue that privatizations of state-owned enterprises afford opportunities for pursuing progressive development policies—if certain class conditions are realized. Unfortunately, these conditions have not been articulated or recognized, nor met heretofore. Similar to municipal privatizations in the United States, privatizations of state-owned enterprises during the past twenty-five years have not been progressive forces. What these class conditions are, why their realization would contribute to a more progressive development paradigm, and how privatizations of state-owned enterprises create opportunities for pursuing their realization are the questions this final chapter addresses.

7.1 THE GLOBAL PRIVATIZATION MOVEMENT

The Magnitude of Global Privatization. In dollar terms, the magnitude of privatizations carried out by governments around the world during the past quarter-century is remarkable. The total revenue raised by governments via privatizations since 1988 climbed above $1 trillion USD during the second half of 1999, according to Gibbon.[1] As Megginson and Boutchkova point out, what began as a highly controversial concept first injected into national policy discourse by Margaret Thatcher in the early 1980s, has today, "developed into a robust, even orthodox economic policy tool that at least 100 national governments have adopted to one degree or another."[2] Of course, as noted in Chapter One, the privatization concept is considerably older than twenty-five years. Its coalescence into a global, national policy tool, however, occurred during the last quarter century.[3]

The Geography of Global Privatization. While privatizations in OECD countries have accounted for the majority of global privatizations, those outside the OECD grew significantly over the course of the 1990s—especially during the latter half of the decade. In fact, in 1997, the year in which global privatization-derived revenues peaked (at $160 billion USD), those outside the OECD accounted for roughly one-third of the total.[4] While privatizations in the developing world have occurred in every region of the world, those in South America have been particularly significant. The privatizations that occurred in the latter part of the 1990s in the South American region yielded significant revenues for the region's governments.[5]

The Sectoral Dimension of Global Privatization. Margaret Thatcher's privatization of British Telecom—the first large divestiture of a public utility in the United Kingdom—is generally cited as having jump-started the global wave of privatization in 1979. Since then, privatizations around the world have been implemented across a broad range of sectors and industries, including, among others: manufacturing, finance, banking, natural resources, and transportation. During the 1990s, privatizations related to key infrastructural segments of the economy, e.g., telecommunications, energy, water, and sanitation became increasingly significant.

7.2 THE MOTIVES FOR PRIVATIZATIONS

There exists a vast sub-literature within the global privatization literature that focuses on the various rationales used to motivate privatization programs. I do not review that literature here. Thus, the following comments highlight only the most prominent of these rationales. The privatizations that have been undertaken around the world over the past quarter-century have been carried out in very diverse economic, political, cultural, and legal environments. These differences have played important roles in influencing the ways in which privatizations have been implemented, interpreted, and rationalized.

Revenue Raising and Subsidy Shedding. One of the reasons privatizations have become (and remain) attractive to many governments is because they effectively represent free lunches. The divestiture of state-owned enterprises can provide heavily debt-burdened or otherwise fiscally constrained governments significant tax-neutral windfall revenues. Moreover, such privatizations should (it is generally assumed) generate future tax revenues. At the same time, such privatizations generally allow governments to significantly reduce or entirely eliminate the subsidies that regularly flow to state-owned enterprises.

Efficiency and Private Sector Development. As in the municipal context, the pursuit of efficiency remains a key motivating factor in many privatizations involving the divestiture of state-owned enterprises. Above all else, it is assumed that the transfer of bloated, inefficient, bureaucratic, state-owned enterprises to the private sector will result in significant efficiency gains. The competitive pressures of the marketplace, it is presumed, constitute the ultimate source of such gains. Indeed, the nurturance and development of a competitive (and, therefore, efficient) private sector, one that can compete in today's increasingly complex global marketplace, is (it is increasingly assumed) the desired and ultimately only endgame of development.[6] Even in cases where privatization results in a competitive environment that is less than what might be desired (or, required in order to motivate the usual efficiency story), it is assumed that the management practices and/or organizational structures that prevail in the private sector (in contrast to the budget-maximizing bureaucratic managerial practices thought to plague the public sector) will translate into marked efficiency improvements.

Capital Market Development. Another benefit presumed to flow from privatizations regards their role in nurturing capital market development. Efforts to empirically document the connection between capital market development and economic growth have led some to hypothesize a positive relationship between privatization and economic growth.[7] On this logic, privatizations are beneficial because they aid capital market development, which, in turn, is seen as being a key to economic growth. The promotion of wider domestic public share ownership has often been an ancillary goal of governments that have sought to use privatization as a means of aiding capital market development. (The issue of public share ownership is retuned to below.)

Structural Reform. Finally, as is well known, privatization programs have constituted a central part of the structural adjustment antidote administered to developing countries by the World Bank and (often demanded by) the IMF. Indeed, revenue raising and/or subsidy shedding, efficiency improvements (via privatization-induced competition and private sector development), and capital market development constitute important planks of the World Bank's structural adjustment framework. This framework often also includes restructuring developing countries' legal, political, and often cultural structures and processes, depending on local circumstances. As the World Bank writes:

> "In general, [privatization] programs seek to increase efficiency, expose
> state enterprises to market discipline and best practices, promote wider

share ownership and entrepreneurship, reduce government interference in the economy, strengthen competition and weaken monopolies, develop domestic capital markets, cut budget deficits, and reduce public and external debt."[8]

It is worth underscoring how the World Bank sees the efficiency concept as fitting into the structural adjustment framework and discourse:

> "The burdens of loss-making and inefficient enterprises impose on society are simply too large to bear. Continued government support for state enterprises and their employees comes at the expense of society as a whole, diverting scarce resources to subsidize loss-making operations—and benefit a small number of citizens—rather than to social sectors that benefit the economy and the poor."[9]

Above all else, however, privatization is understood to play a critical role in nurturing the developing world's private sector—a key, from the World Bank's perspective, to reducing poverty:

> "Private sector development and investment—that is, tapping private sector initiative and investment for socially useful purposes—are critical for poverty reduction. In parallel with public sector efforts, private investment, especially in competitive markets, has tremendous potential to contribute to growth. Private markets serve as the engine of productivity growth, creating productive jobs and higher incomes. And with government playing a complementary role of regulation, funding, and provision of services, private initiative and investment can help provide the basic services and conditions that empower the poor—by improving health, education, and infrastructure."[10]

Other Goals of Privatization involving the Sale of State-Owned Enterprises: Public and Employee Ownership. While the goals enumerated above have tended to be the most important in moving governments to undertake privatization programs, many governments have simultaneously pursued additional ones. Among the most important of these has been broadening public and employee ownership of the enterprises selected for privatization.

Public Ownership. Ensuring that the wealth transferred from the state to the private sector via privatization is widely distributed across the *domestic* public has been an important goal of several governments' privatization programs. Such concerns have often led governments, in conjunction with their financial advisors, to craft elaborate sales programs and incentive mechanisms in order to ensure that this goal is met. For example, when shares of British Telecom were sold the government offered shares at a fixed price to domestic retail investors, but auctioned the remaining shares to foreign and domestic institutional investors.[11] The desire to target small domestic retail investors led Argentina, France, and the U.K., among others, to offer bonuses to encourage small domestic investors to hold their shares for longer periods.[12] Domestic retail investors have also been given pricing discounts and/or offered free shares as rewards for holding purchased shares for longer periods of time.[13] Other mechanisms have been devised that allow the proportion of shares allocated to domestic retail investors to increase at the expense of institutional investors in cases where demand for shares is high.[14]

Employee Ownership. As David Binns notes, "Countries as diverse as Great Britain, France, Chile, Argentina, Hungary, Poland, Slovenia, Russia, China, Sri Lanka, Pakistan, Nigeria, and Egypt have made employee ownership a key element of their privatization programs."[15] Governments have articulated a variety of reasons for using privatization as a means of enhancing employee ownership of formerly state-owned enterprises.[16] In addition to helping ensure that the wealth transferred from the state to the private sector is widely distributed (which in many cases, especially in many transitioning Eastern European countries, dovetailed with the communitarian and egalitarian traditions and values reinforced by several decades of communism), governments have also sought to promote employee ownership in the hope that enterprise performance will be increased if employees have a direct stake in an enterprise.[17] It is often assumed that granting employees direct ownership stakes will improve labor-management relations. Finally, and certainly not least, the promotion of employee ownership may also help mitigate employee (and general public) opposition to privatizations.

As in the case of domestic public ownership, privatizing governments have often been forced to devise programs and methods in order to help ensure that their employee ownership goals are met. To take but one example, the privatization of Morocco's Banque Marocaine du Commerce Exterieur (BMCE) in the mid-1990s, which involved a mixed sale (see discussion in the next section), set aside three percent of the bank's capital for its employees. Employees were offered shares at a fifteen percent discount and offered loans to help purchase their shares.[18]

7.3 METHODS OF DIVESTITURE

There have been three principal methods of divestiture used by governments seeking to sell state-owned enterprises.[19] By far the most common method within the OECD has been public share offerings. Public share offerings on stock markets have been most often used for divestitures of large, profitable, and relatively well-known state-owned enterprises. The divestiture of British Telecom, British Gas, as well as Argentina's Yacimientos Petroliferos Fiscales (YFP) involved public share offerings. In addition to the size and quality of the enterprise privatized, the viability of the public share offering method also generally depends upon the status of a country's capital market. In particular, a country's capital market must be mature and developed enough for the public share offering to be successfully executed.

In many developing nations, this latter requirement has not been met. Thus, many privatizations outside the OECD have used so-called trade sales. There are two types of trade sales: auctions (open bidding) and negotiated sales. The former, which has been more common, involves the solicitation of multiple bids for a state-owned enterprise. Concerns about "asset-stripping" have resulted in the adoption of often elaborate bidding procedures that ensure that a privatizing government's various goals are more likely to be realized, e.g., ones related to the enterprise's continued "on-goingness," that buyers have sufficient resources and technical knowledge to run the enterprise, etc. Negotiated sales (a variant of the auction method) are used when there is only one bidder, or when one bidder has a particular advantage over other bidders. Once the government has decided upon a buyer, it negotiates an agreement acceptable to both parties.

Finally, mixed sales combine trade sales with share offerings. While a variety of forms can be used in mixed sales, in many cases, the method is used when a portion of an enterprise is sold to a strategic investor. The remaining portion is subsequently distributed via a public offering. Among other things, this method enables a government to allow various public parties (e.g., retail and institutional investors, and often enterprise employees and pensioners) to participate in the privatization.

7.4 WHAT PRIVATIZATIONS OF STATE-OWNED ENTERPRISES HAVE DONE AND NOT DONE: A CLASS ANALYTIC INTERPRETATION

Different historical experiences and traditions, along with profound differences in political, cultural, legal, and economic environments have, not surprisingly, worked to shape important differences in countries' respective state-owned enterprises around the world. As a result, there have existed stark differences among the ways different countries' state-owned enterprises operate. Some have been tightly controlled and operated by state administrators and bureaucrats, while others have enjoyed considerably more independence. Some have exhibited highly corporatized organizational and managerial structures, while others have exhibited less hierarchical structures. Some have allowed employees to actively participate in managerial processes, while others have not. Some have been highly attuned to the competitive marketplace, others less so. Some have exploited and adopted cutting-edge production techniques and processes, while others have failed or been unable to exploit such advances. Some have allowed ownership stakes (usually minority ones) to be held by outsiders, others have been owned outright by the government.

Despite these differences, the vast majority of state-owned enterprises that have been privatized over the course of the past quarter-century or so have shared one feature. Namely, they hosted *capitalist* class processes prior to their privatization.[20] The class processes within these state-owned enterprises were capitalist ones because: 1) the productive workers that produced the surpluses generated within them did not participate in appropriating and distributing them and, 2) these surpluses took the form of surplus value—that is, they were extracted from workers who, in exchange for their labor power, received a wage from their governments who, in this particular capacity, functioned just as any other industrial capitalist. In most cases, the surpluses generated in these state-owned enterprises were appropriated and distributed by state administrators and bureaucrats. In other cases, boards of private individuals (often appointed by or closely connected to state officials) performed these tasks.

The above argument implies that it is entirely possible for capitalist class processes (structures) to exist within state-owned enterprises. This argument highlights the difference between an enterprise's class structure and its ownership form and illustrates that there is no necessary connection between the two. *Thus, it is entirely possible for a state to own the majority of a nation's productive enterprises (assets) and for capitalist class structures to continue to predominate within those enterprises.* From a class perspective, this situation is deemed a "state form" of capitalism, as opposed to a "private form" of capitalism.[21] Indeed, this situation was exactly that which—as Resnick and Wolff provocatively argue—prevailed in the former Soviet Union in the post-1917 period: "the post-1917 transformations in the USSR changed but did not eliminate capitalism. A system of state (rather than private) ownership and operation of industrial enterprises and state planning (rather than markets) *amounted to a shift from a private to a state form of capitalism.*"[22] In the context of the privatization of state-owned enterprises, the argument here can be interpreted as reversing the words private and state in the italicized portion of the just-quoted passage, viz., the privatization movement that has so forcefully emerged over the course of the past quarter-century has generally involved transforming state-owned capitalist enterprises into privately-owned capitalist enterprises.

To be clear, from a class perspective, any privatization involving the transfer of state-owned enterprises to the private sector is understood to involve a host of changes in a number of economic, political, cultural, and natural processes. Moreover, such changes undoubtedly cascade across the social environment (within which the privatization takes place) in complex and contradictory ways. At the same time, the privatization programs that have been carried out around the world over the course of the past quarter century have, in general, *not involved any change in the class structures of the state-owned enterprises that have been privatized.* Whereas prior to privatization, state administrators or bureaucrats (or, boards of individuals appointed and/or closely connected to them) appropriated and then distributed the surpluses produced by the productive wage laborers employed (by the government) in state-owned enterprises, following privatization, this appropriation and distribution has been carried out by a different group of private individuals—generally, the board of directors of the private capitalist enterprises that have often become responsible for the operation of newly-privatized enterprises. In this sense, most privatizations of state-owned enterprises have amounted to a shell game: one group of individuals who do not directly participate in the production of the surplus generated within the enterprise, but who do appropriate and distribute it, is after all is said and done, exchanged for a similarly situated, but different group of individuals. Because they did not involve class structural changes—i.e., state-owned enterprises' class structures remained capitalist (hence, exploitative) ones post-privatization—these privatizations were non-progressive ones.

The above argument does not deny that these types of privatizations yielded important economic, political, cultural, and even natural changes. Both the "successes" as well as the "failures" of the privatization of state-owned enterprises have been exhaustively documented.[23] In some cases, privatizations have ostensibly contributed to the realization of many of the goals of the governments that have undertaken them. For example, many have, via various methods (including both massive capital injections as well as dramatic workforce reductions), contributed to the increase in the technical sophistication and efficiency of formerly state-owned enterprises' productive labor processes.[24] Many have helped improve the quality of the various use-values (commodities) these enterprises produce. Some have encouraged and promoted foreign investment and capital market development. Others have increased share ownership among the public. All of these changes have undoubtedly worked to produce an infinite number of still other important changes.

The managerial and organizational restructurings that have often accompanied the privatization of state-owned enterprises, a process referred to as corporatization, do not imply anything about the type of class processes that occurred within these enterprises *prior to* their privatization.[25] Thus, the fact that the managerial processes and organizational structures within state-owned enterprises are often dissimilar to those exhibited within them following privatization in no way alters the foregoing argument. The managerial processes and organizational structures of state-owned enterprises prior to their divestitures did not preclude them from hosting capitalist class structures.

To sum up, the typical privatization process in which a state-owned enterprise has been transferred to the private sector amounts to a simple substitution from a class perspective. One group of individuals who appropriates and distributes the surplus value generated within the enterprise is, after the privatization, substituted for a different group of individuals. Of course, in some cases this second (or, new) group of individuals has proven better at reproducing these enterprises' capitalist class processes. In other cases, the opposite has been the case, as recent instances of reverse privatization in some countries testify.[26]

7.5 THEORIZING PROGRESSIVE PRIVATIZATIONS INVOLVING STATE-OWNED ENTERPRISES

The above class analytic interpretation of the global privatization movement—specifically, as it has related to the sale of state-owned enterprises—leads back to the question posed at the chapter's outset. Namely, are progressive privatizations of state-owned enterprises possible? If so, what conditions would they require? The argument developed in Chapter Six concerning progressive municipal privatization provides a model. Specifically, one *necessary* condition of such a privatization is that it would transform the class structure of a state-owned enterprise in the course of its privatization. This transformation would involve changing a state-owned enterprise's capitalist (and exploitative) class structure into non-exploitative class structure (e.g., a communist or independent one) in the context of its privatization. As in the municipal privatization context, the critical question regards the viability of such a class-transformative privatization. The viability issue is in principle unknowable, however. Thus, a better line of inquiry is one that seeks to answer questions about the relationships between such transformed state-owned enterprises and the institutions, practices, and organizational structures that generally motivate privatizations. Put otherwise, could a formerly state-owned enterprise whose capitalist class structure was transformed into a non-exploitative one via a privatization process coexist with and/ or accommodate competitive markets, private property, private sector (corporate) managerial processes and organizational forms? And, if so, why else might governments find such class-transformative privatizations attractive?

The remainder of this chapter explores these coexistence, accommodation, and attraction issues. As in the municipal context, the coexistence and accommodation issues are answered in the affirmative: formerly state-owned enterprises whose capitalist class structures were transformed into non-exploitative ones via privatization could coexist with competitive markets and private property, and could accommodate a wide variety of managerial processes and organizational structures, including those regularly exhibited by large capitalist enterprises. Class-transformative privatizations, I further argue, appear to complement many of the ancillary goals (in particular, those that reflect broader concerns with social equity and fairness) world governments have deemed important in the privatization context. Additionally, many of the attractions progressive municipal privatizations afford (e.g., those related to monitoring, local procurement, and reshaping the interest group environment) have clear analogues in the context of the privatization of state-owned enterprises.

Finally, I emphasize that privatizing governments have considerable flexibility to shape and design privatization initiatives in ways that increase the likelihood of the realization of their diverse policy goals. This suggests that the goal of enterprise class-structural transformation could be accommodated. Thus, privatizations involving the divestiture of state-owned enterprises afford viable opportunities for pursuing enterprise class structural transformations. The democratic enterprises such class-transformative privatizations would yield could play an important role in an alternative and more progressive development paradigm.

Transforming State-Owned Enterprises' Class Structures in the Context of Privatization. What would a privatization of a state-owned capitalist enterprise that involved the transformation of its class structure entail? As indicated, such a privatization would transform the enterprise's capitalist class structure into a non-exploitative one. This would require the enterprise's productive workers (who produce the enterprise's surplus) to participate in the appropriative and *thereby* the distributive processes.[27] The capitalist class structures of state-owned enterprises preclude such participation.

Before developing an example that will concretize the idea of a class-transformative privatization, the concept of a *progressive* class-transformative privatization must be more clearly specified. This concept parallels the one set out in the municipal context. Specifically, a privatization of a state-owned enterprise that transformed its capitalist class structure into one that:

1. allowed *all* of its employees (productive workers, support staff, and managers) to participate in the appropriative and distributive processes and,

2. which did so on the basis of one employee-one vote,

would qualify as a progressive privatization.[28] As in the municipal context, I refer to enterprises in which the above two conditions are met as democratic enterprises. Thus, a progressive privatization involving the divestiture of a state-owned enterprise would yield a democratic enterprise.

The following example concretizes the foregoing discussion. Consider a hypothetical state-owned capitalist enterprise. The vast majority of the enterprise's workers are productive workers and thereby produce surplus value. Other workers perform various support services and functions, e.g., payroll, bookkeeping, etc. Finally, some employees are managers. The productive workers receive a wage in exchange for their labor power from the government, i.e., their employer. The support staff and managers receive wages in exchange for the various functions they perform. A board of directors that includes state officials and enterprise managers appropriates and distributes the enterprise's surplus value.

Assume this state-owned enterprise is earmarked for divestiture as part of a privatization plan. Now, consider some of the goals discussed above. For instance, assume that in addition to its desire to reduce (or, perhaps eliminate) its financial commitment to the enterprise and promote private sector development, the government also wished to ensure: 1) the enterprise's continued existence[29]; 2) that a majority of the enterprise's ownership remains in domestic hands; and, 3) that the enterprise's employees participate in the privatization in some unspecified capacity. Finally, assume the privatization was structured in such a way that it qualified as a progressive privatization.

Now, consider the just-enumerated goals. The third goal would be met as a direct consequence of the progressive privatization. Post-privatization, the enterprise's employees would actively participate in the appropriative and distributive processes as a consequence of the enterprise's new non-exploitative class structure. On the assumption that most employees would share an interest in the government's first goal (presumably they would have an interest in the enterprise's on-goingness), the enterprise's new class structure would provide them considerable leverage for realizing it. Importantly, this would be true regardless of the enterprise's post-privatization management and/or ownership structure. (See the discussion on ownership below.) Finally, the privatization's progressivity would substantively alter the importance imputed to the second goal. This would reflect the fact that the enterprise's post-privatization class structure would allow its employees to collectively appropriate and distribute its surplus value. The enterprise's owners would only hold a right to whatever factor (subsumed class) payment the enterprise could bear, i.e., they would not appropriate or play a role in the distribution of the enterprise's surplus. This implies that the government's concern with the enterprise's post-privatization ownership (generally, a concern that reflects a distaste for foreign ownership) would be obviated. (See the discussion on ownership below.)

This example suggests that a progressive privatization could support many of the goals privatizing governments have sought—in particular, those related to broader social concerns with equity and fairness. As discussed above, however, while many governments have sought these types of ancillary goals while pursuing privatizations, they are not the primary factors motivating their privatization efforts. As explained, these factors include: revenue raising and subsidy shedding; efficiency and private sector development; capital market development; and, structural adjustment. Are there reasons to believe that a class-transformative progressive privatization would undermine these goals? Answers to this question involve the coexistence and accommodation issues, i.e., could the democratic enterprises that a progressive privatization would yield coexist with competitive markets and private property (ownership), and could they accommodate corporate (private sector) managerial processes and organizational structures?

Could a class-transformative progressive privatization accommodate the goal of revenue raising and/or subsidy shedding? Clearly, it seems likely that the conditions required for such a privatization would undermine private sector interest. Indeed, the World Bank's "Privatization Tool Kit," a guidebook for governments considering the privatization of state-owned enterprises, instructs them to limit the number of conditions they place on divestitures.[30] The World Bank, for instance, remarks, "As a rule, conditions attached to privatizations by government detract from an enterprise's value because they increase uncertainty or restrain privatized firms' commercial freedom of action."[31] Needless to say, most prospective buyers would consider the class structural transformation a progressive privatization requires a major condition. In the event private sector demand for such a privatization (divestiture) was undermined owing to its class structural requirements, the government might nevertheless structure the privatization so that it would accommodate the goal of revenue raising and/or subsidy shedding. For instance, it could sell the enterprise to its existing employees. As in the municipal context, employees could finance such a purchase by securing loans and financing via traditional private channels, or the government could provide them a loan. Given the fact that privatizations are often pursued in order to ease fiscal pressures, such a loan arrangement may appear odd.

In discussing a similar situation in the context of privatization in Eastern European, Joseph Stiglitz writes, "Such questions show a confusion between the macroeconomic roles of government finance and the role of financial accounting. The government will lend the firms money to buy the firm and then receive the money back again."[32] In essence, by providing the enterprise's employees a loan that would allow them to purchase the enterprise, the government would ensure itself a future cut (interest payments) of the enterprise's surplus. Eventually, if the enterprise succeeded, the loan would be repaid.

Such a privatization may also require the government to maintain an existing stake in the enterprise for some time—a practice that has been common in many privatizations of state-owned enterprises. Over time, if the enterprise succeeded, the government could elect to sell some or all of its ownership stake—perhaps to the enterprise's employees or to private investors. While such a privatization would clearly not yield the government windfall revenue it would nevertheless provide it revenue (interest payments on the loan and taxes), and, of course, it could allow it to eventually reduce or completely eliminate subsidies to the enterprise.

If the government believed traditional private sector participation in the divestiture was necessary, it might entice private investors by offering various guarantees. For example, guarantees could be adjusted according to various levels of risk private investors were willing to assume by investing (owing shares) in an enterprise that involved a novel class structure.[33] This suggests that a democratic enterprise (one hosting a non-exploitative class structure) that was a product of a progressive privatization could be compatible with private ownership.[34] As noted, "Private ownership confers certain specific rights and privileges on owners, but there is no necessary right to appropriation, control, or residual claimancy [of the surplus] only the right of the owners of capital to whatever factor payments the capital input will bear."[35] Because this idea is critically important it deserves underscoring.

In particular, the difference between an enterprise's class structure (process) and its ownership structure concerns (among other things) a legal distinction between cash flow rights (rights on dividends and liquidation surpluses) and control rights (rights over the enterprise's surplus).[36] In many countries these rights are *effectively* separated. As Moerland remarks:

> "Common shares of equity are residual claims which give the hold-
> ers, in principle, cash flow rights and control rights with respect to the
> firm . . . These property rights are, again in principle, proportional
> rights, which, for example, are encapsulated in the maxim: 'one share-
> one vote.' However, in practice, control rights in particular are very
> often restricted in one way or another."[37]

In the present context, this idea is important because it implies that private ownership of an enterprise may entail only cash flow rights not necessarily control rights. In the case of a democratic enterprise (one generated via a progressive privatization), control (of the surplus) rights would necessarily be held by the enterprise's employees, whereas owners would have only cash flow rights, i.e., rights to whatever dividends (a subsumed class payment) might be paid out.

Thus, instead of placing their investments in the hands of a small group of individuals (a board of directors) who do not produce but appropriate and distribute an enterprise's surplus—as institutional and retail investors in publicly-traded capitalist enterprises do—investors in a *privatization-generated* democratic enterprise would effectively entrust their investments to all of the enterprise's employees who, by virtue of the enterprise's non-exploitative class structure, would collectively appropriate and distribute its surplus. And, just as they may by owning shares of capitalist enterprises, investors in a privatization-generated democratic enterprise could receive dividend payments and perhaps eventually (if a capital market in the democratic enterprise's shares developed) experience capital gains or losses.

As the above discussion suggests, democratic enterprises could also be compatible with capital markets. Thus, progressive privatizations would not necessarily undermine capital market development. Of course, as is generally the case with any new unknown enterprise, capital markets in the shares of democratic enterprises (assuming they were to coexist with private ownership) would take time to develop. There is no reason, however, to presume that such markets could not develop.

Because the managerial processes and organizational structures adopted by successful capitalist enterprises are generally assumed to play a central role in their efficiency, and because efficiency concerns are often central to privatizations involving divestitures of state-owned enterprises, the relationship between an enterprise's class structure and its managerial processes and organization structure is important. As with ownership, there need not be any one-to-one correspondence between an enterprise's class structure and its managerial processes or organizational structure. Thus, there is nothing that would preclude a democratic enterprise from exhibiting a very hierarchical managerial process and/or organizational structure. A democratic enterprise could accommodate a wide variety of managerial processes and organizational forms. Clearly, it might accommodate some more easily than other. As with capitalist enterprises, the managerial processes and organizational structure of a democratic enterprise would be expected to evolve and shift over time in response to various stimuli. It follows that there is no reason to assume that the democratic enterprise a progressive privatization would yield would, by virtue of its managerial processes and/or organizational structure, be less productively efficient than a capitalist enterprise. Just as there are more and less efficient capitalist enterprises, so too would there be more and less efficient democratic enterprises.

Further, the goals pursued by a democratic enterprise would be complexly overdetermined by a number of factors. Just as with a capitalist enterprise, whatever goals a democratic enterprise pursued would have to be balanced, would involve risks, and would likely constantly shift and change. Thus, a democratic enterprise's business behavior might be indistinguishable from a capitalist enterprise's. Most importantly, whatever goals a democratic enterprise pursued would reflect the democratic process inherent in its non-exploitative class structure.

Thus, democratic enterprises might exhibit extreme internal struggles and contradictions arising from the democratic process inherent in their class structures. Among other things, such enterprises would have to develop protocols, mechanisms, systems, and cultural and educational processes that worked to mitigate and ensure that such struggles and contradictions were overcome and normalized (i.e., came to be seen as being just as normal and proper as democratic *political* processes which regularly involve compromise and deal-making over such complex and important issues as writing laws and distributing tax revenues collected by the state). Such internal struggles and contradictions would be similar to those that regularly manifest themselves inside capitalist enterprises (e.g., boardroom and shareholder struggles over managerial pay-packages and bonuses, or over proposals to merge or acquire a competitor). The primary difference between these two cases is that whereas in a capitalist enterprise, such struggles and contradiction are negotiated and sorted out by members of the enterprise's board, in a democratic enterprise, the employees would participate in negotiating them. The following example helps clarify this point.

Imagine a hypothetical quarterly meeting in a democratic enterprise. At this meeting, the employees who have collectively appropriated the enterprise's surplus decide how to distribute it. The managers (and, perhaps employees) might present various proposals for how the surplus should be distributed. For instance, one proposal might suggest the surplus be divided as follows: twenty-five percent for research and development related to a new product line; fifteen percent to upgrade the enterprise's capital equipment; twenty percent to design a new marketing campaign; twenty percent to build a new school; ten percent retained, five percent distributed in dividends, and five percent distributed as bonuses. A different plan might suggest that: sixty percent be used to acquire an ownership stake in another communist enterprise (which may provide the enterprise dividends); twenty percent be distributed in bonuses; ten percent be used to explore entering a new market; and, ten percent retained. After various proposals were put forth, their details, implications, and merits would be discussed and debated. Then, after some period of time, the employees would vote (on the basis of one employee-one vote) to decide which proposal to adopt. Such a (subsumed class) distributive process regularly occurs in the board meetings of capitalist enterprises. The productive employees of capitalist enterprises are excluded from participating in this process, however.

Because markets and competition figure so prominently in the context of most privatization processes, the question regarding the relationship between democratic enterprises and markets and competition is critical. Could democratic enterprises coexist with markets and competition?[38] As explained in the municipal context, there is nothing inherent in a democratic enterprise (in particular, its class structure) that would preclude its coexistence with markets and/or competition. A democratic enterprise's relationship with markets and competition would give rise to all sorts of complexities and contradictions. These complexities and contradictions would impinge upon its class structure—simultaneously working to both support and undermine it—just as they support and undermine a capitalist enterprise's class structure.[39] These pressures and contradictions must be constantly negotiated by devising processes, systems, and mechanisms, and by undertaking actions that allow them to be overcome. In the event they are not, the existence of any enterprise—be it a capitalist or a democratic one—is imperiled. Some democratic enterprises would prove just as capable of successfully negotiating the complexities and contradictions that emanate from market-based competition as many capitalist enterprises are. Other democratic enterprises would not be successful and would thus perish (just as many capitalist enterprises do).

It should also be noted that there may be reasons to expect that democratic enterprises might help mitigate certain problems associated with markets, e.g., crises related to over-production, etc. For instance, to the extent democratic enterprises elected to distribute (use) their surpluses in ways that reflected the pursuit of goals other than profit-maximization (say, by building urban transport systems, schools, social centers, etc.) they would direct less surplus to their own accumulation functions. This could reduce the likelihood of imbalances developing in certain commodity markets. This could, ironically, prove beneficial to some capitalist enterprises.[40] At the same time, democratic enterprises may elect to behave exactly as capitalist enterprises. How they behave—for instance, how much surplus they decide to produce and how they elect to distribute the surplus they realize—would play an important role in how they coexist with markets and competition.

Finally, similar to the democratic enterprises a progressive municipal privatization process would yield, the democratic enterprises that would emerge from a progressive privatization involving a state-owned enterprise would have several additional attractions to policy-makers. First, a democratic enterprise's class structure could help mitigate the traditional monitoring problems associated with privatization. The collective of employees in a democratic enterprise would actively monitor one another as a direct consequence of their role in the appropriative and distributive class processes. The value of such internalized monitoring would ostensibly be similar to that inherent in the German "co-determination" corporate governance structure. And, it seems clear that if a class-transformative privatization process involved transferring the enterprise to its existing employees and management, the interest group environment surrounding the process would be dramatically altered. In particular, it seems likely that the enterprise's employees and managers might be more amenable to the privatization.[41]

Worker Cooperatives and Microenterprises in the Context of the Privatization of State-Owned Enterprises. While progressive privatizations involve transforming state-owned enterprises' class structures (and, thereby generate democratic enterprises), it should be pointed out that many privatizations involving divestitures of state-owned enterprises have resulted in the formation of additional enterprises. Such enterprises are of interest because they represent additional vehicles by which democratic enterprise formation (via privatization processes) could be realized.

The issue of labor redundancy in the context of the privatization of state-owned enterprises has long been a critical issue—one that often constitutes the chief political obstacle for governments seeking to privatize state-owned enterprises. In order to ensure that such redundancy does not undermine private sector demand for privatization divestitures, the World Bank has often advised governments to trim the workforces of the state-owned enterprises earmarked for privatization well ahead of the divestiture date. (It is generally assumed that prospective buyers are unwilling to absorb the political costs associated with purchasing an enterprise in which much of the workforce is thought to be redundant.) As a result of the need to often dramatically trim the workforces of state-owned enterprises prior to divestiture, governments along with the World Bank, have devised an array of strategies aimed at employees who lose their state enterprise jobs during this process. Two strategies that have been used involve the creation of worker cooperatives and microenterprises. In many cases, a newly privatized enterprise arranges to purchases various goods and services from these cooperatives and micro-enterprises. The World Bank provides several examples:

- In Argentina, the privatized oil company YPF entered into service contracts with 210 companies formed by 5,300 former employees. Similarly, the railways company rented out workshops performing rolling stock repairs to workers cooperatives that now compete with the private sector.

- In Congo, railroad workers have subcontracted with the railways company to manage activities that have been privatized, including marketing merchandise, handling baggage and packages, and maintaining tracks, equipment, and buildings.

- In Benin and Egypt new private owners of beverage companies gave retrenched workers the option of becoming distributors and provided assistance to get them started in the private sector.[42]

From a class perspective, the critical question in regard to these newly created worker cooperatives and microenterprises is, "what type of class structures do they host?" Clearly, empirical investigation would be required in order to answer this question. The creation of such worker cooperatives and microenterprises (as a byproduct of privatizations of state-owned enterprises) clearly afford additional opportunities for establishing enterprises that host non-exploitative class processes—whether they be ones that qualify as democratic enterprises or some other type.

7.6 THE POLICY IMPLICATIONS OF PROGRESSIVE PRIVATIZATIONS

The Neoliberal development paradigm presents the Left two formidable tasks. The first involves proposing and designing viable alternative development policies. The second task involves locating or identifying spaces (to use David Harvey's metaphor) into which progressive alternatives might be fruitfully injected or implanted.[43] A class approach to privatization suggests that transforming state-owned enterprises' capitalist class structures into non-exploitative ones could play an important role in an alternative development paradigm. Further, it reveals that privatizations of state-owned enterprises represent viable spaces into which such class-transformative initiatives could be injected.

The Left's understandable focus on the consequences of privatization (e.g., its effects on wage and employment levels, and efficiency) has had important theoretical and policy consequences. Namely, privatizations (especially those involving state-owned enterprises) are too often interpreted on the Left as reflections of a hegemonic capitalist or Neoliberal logic—one whose future course appears (to many on the Left) largely immune to substantive intervention.[44] For example, Harvey recently argued that such privatizations are part and parcel of what he refers to as "accumulation by dispossession" a central plank of what he considers a modern day form of imperialism.[45] Such interpretations serve to deepen and reinforce the discursive and theoretical *association* between privatization and capitalism that pervades the privatization discourse. Of course, the history of the privatization movement over the past quarter-century underpins this association and lends it considerable empirical support. The vast majority of privatizations that have occurred during the past quarter-century (be they those involving the sale of state-owned enterprises in a global context or those related to the production of public goods or services on the municipal level) have spawned and/or supported exploitative capitalist enterprises. Still, the unfortunate byproduct of this association is that it has worked to conceal the class dimension (and, thereby, the class-transformative possibilities) inherent in all privatizations. The idea that privatization processes could be designed to generate, promote, or otherwise encourage the formation of non-capitalist and/or non-exploitative enterprises (and, thereby, support more progressive development policies) has never been considered. This is especially unfortunate given the fact that it is clear that privatizations are always political processes, i.e., they are always carefully tailored, crafted, and designed to accommodate numerous policy goals—both those of the governments that undertake them as well as many other participant parties.'

The enterprise class-structural transformations involved in progressive privatizations could become an important part of Left efforts to craft and implement more progressive, equitable, and socially just local and global development policies. Above all, such transformations aim to inject democratic principles into one particular economic process (the class process) that occurs inside enterprises. In addressing the question of "why collective [democratic] appropriation?" Cullenberg remarks, "If one rejects collective appropriation, one also rejects the right of individuals to participate on an equal footing in making decisions concerning issues that are of central importance to their lives and that affect the better part of their waking hours."[46]

There are ample reasons to believe that privatization processes afford viable opportunities for pursuing such transformations. I interpret many governments' efforts to massage the privatization processes they undertake in ways meant to promote (what they consider to be) broader social goals (ones related to fairness and equity) as signals that they may be open to adding enterprise class-structural transformations to their list of privatization goals. More importantly, such transformations do not appear to seriously jeopardize any of the primary goals governments seek via privatizing their own enterprises. There is nothing inherent in democratic enterprises that preclude their coexistence with markets, competition, or private ownership. And, they seem readily capable of accommodating private- (or, corporate) sector managerial processes and organizational structures. Additionally, they appear to have several policy benefits, e.g., those related to monitoring, altering interest group environments, mitigating accumulation crises, etc.

Using privatization processes to pursue the goal of democratic enterprise formation (and, thereby, a more progressive development paradigm) has an additional important merit. Namely, it militates against the idea that viable alternatives to current Neoliberal development policies must be preceded by social upheaval and/or revolution.[47] Enterprise class-structural transformation via the privatization of state-owned enterprises could proceed gradually and peacefully. Such transformations thus fit well with the idea that, "Socialism in one city is not a viable concept. But then it is quite clear that no alternative to the contemporary form of globalization will be delivered to us from on high either. It will have to come from within multiple local spaces conjoining into a broader social movement."[48]

The privatization movement's envelopment of nearly every corner of the globe over the course of the past quarter-century—and, more importantly, the likelihood that this process will continue—suggests that there will be many local spaces into which democratic enterprises could be implanted in the future. Such enterprises would help ensure that future waves of privatization are more progressive than those that have passed.

One final question remains. Namely, how might those interested in pursuing progressive privatizations secure a place in future privatization negotiations? Clearly, some ingenuity and hard thinking will be required if this task is going to be successfully met. As noted in the municipal context, one way this task might be accomplished is to gain entry into such negotiations as a prospective buyer. To a far greater extent than in the U.S. municipal context, labor (and the institutions that represent it) often has a seat at the table in negotiations concerning the privatization of state-owned enterprises. Presumably, labor could use this seat to participate as a prospective buyer of state-owned enterprises slated for divestiture. Even without a seat at the table, the Left must work harder to educate and consult the parties that regularly attend such negotiations. It is hoped that the class-based theorization of progressive privatizations this book develops represents a contribution to such efforts.

Notes

NOTES TO CHAPTER ONE

1. Jeffrey D. Greene, *Cities and Privatization: Prospects for the New Century* (Upper Saddle River, NJ: Prentice Hall, 2002) 4.
2. Moshe Adler, *The Origin of Governmental Production: Cleaning the Streets of New York by Contract in the 19th Century* 3. Unpublished manuscript.
3. Most cities of course provide goods and services using a mixture of public and private production.
4. Jeffrey R. Henig, "Privatization in the United States: Theory and Practice," Political Science Quarterly 104 (1989–90): 649. Henig citing, Peter Young, "Privatization Around the World," Prospects for Privatization, ed. Steve H. Hanke (New York: The Academy of Political Science, 1987) 205; Patrick Dunleavy "Explaining the Privatization Boom: Public Choice versus Radical Approaches," Public Administration 64 (Spring 1986).
5. Ronald C. Moe, "Exploring the Limits of Privatization," *Public Administration Review* 47 (1987): 453.
6. Adapted from Greene Appendix B. Original sources: The International City/County Management Association, "Profile of Alternative Delivery Approaches Survey" (1988); The International City/County Management Association, "Profile of Local Government Service Delivery Choices Survey" (1997).
7. David Osborne, Ted Gaebler, *Reinventing Government: How the Entrepreneurial Spirit is Transforming the Public Sector* (New York: Plume, 1993)
8. Douglas Jehl, "As Cities Move to Privatize Water, Atlanta Steps Back," *New York Times*, 10 Feb. 2003, late ed.: A14. See also, Maude Barlow, Tony Clark, *Blue Gold: The Fight to Stop the Corporate Theft of the World's Water* (New York: W. W. Norton & Company, 2003)
9. These descriptions are set out in, Robin A. Johnson, Normal Walzer, eds., *Local Government Innovation* (Westport, CT: Quorum Books, 2000).
10. Johnson and Walzer, *Local Government Innovation* 4.

11. E.S. Savas, *Privatization: The Key to Better Government: Public Administration and Public Policy* (New York: Chatham House Publishers, 1988) 98.
12. The city's charter once mandated contracting out for all work done for the city. See Adler, *The Origin of Governmental Production.*
13. New York City, *The Mayor's Management Report 2001: Supplement,* (New York: New York City, 2001) 267–269.
14. *The Mayor's Management Report 2001: Supplement.*

NOTES TO CHAPTER TWO

1. Henig, "Privatization in the United States" 649. The discussion that follows draws heavily on this article.
2. Henig, "Privatization in the United States" 656.
3. Henig, "Privatization in the United States" 653. Milton Friedman, *Capitalism, Capitalism and Freedom* (Chicago: University of Chicago Press, 1962). Cited in Henig. Henig suggests that one could trace these underpinnings back well before Friedman—to Smith, for example. He duly notes that such exercises quickly devolve into infinite regress.
4. William Niskanen, *Bureaucracy and Representative Government* (Chicago: Aldine, 1971); Gordon Tullock, *Politics of Bureaucracy* (Washington, D.C.: Public Affairs Press, 1965); Anthony Downs, *Inside Bureaucracy* (Boston: Little Brown, 1967); James Buchanan, "Why Do Governments Grow?" *Budgets and Bureaucrats: The Sources of Government Growth*, ed. Thomas E. Borcherding, (Durham, N.C.: Duke University Press, 1977).
5. D.C. Mueller, *Public Choice II* (Cambridge: Cambridge University Press: 1989). Cited in Andre Blais, Stephane Dion, eds., *The Budget-Maximizing Bureaucrat: Appraisal and Evidence* (Pittsburgh, PA: University of Pittsburgh Press, 1991). The next two paragraphs draw on Blais' and Dion's discussion.
6. Niskanen, *Bureaucracy and Representative Government* 30. Cited in Blais and Dion, *The Budget-Maximizing Bureaucrat* 4.
7. Blais and Dion, *The Budget-Maximizing Bureaucrat* 4.
8. J. L. Migué, and G. Bélanger, "Toward a general theory of managerial discretion" *Public Choice* 17.1 (1974): 27–43. Cited in Blais and Dion, *The Budget-Maximizing Bureaucrat.*
9. George Stigler, "The Theory of Economic Regulation," *Bell Journal of Economics and Management Service* 2 (1971): 3–21. Cited in Henig, "Privatization in the United States."
10. Charles Tiebout, "A Pure Theory of Local Expenditures," *The Journal of Political Economy* 64 (1956): 416–424. Cited in Henig, "Privatization in the United States" 655.
11. Tiebout, "A Pure Theory of Local Expenditures" 416.
12. Sidney Sonenblum, John J. Kirlin, and John C. Ries, *How Cities Provide Services* (Cambridge, MA: Ballinger Publishing Company, 1977) 4.
13. Henig, "Privatization in the United States" 653.
14. Henig, "Privatization in the United States" 654.

15. U.S. Advisory Commission on Intergovernmental Relations, *City Financial Emergencies: The Intergovernmental Dimension* (Washington, D.C.: U.S. Government Printing Office, 1973). Cited in William Tabb, "The New York Fiscal Crisis," *Marxism and the Metropolis*, William Tabb, Larry Sawers, eds., (New York: Oxford University Press, 1978) 249.
16. Tabb, "The New York Fiscal Crisis" 248.
17. Philip Dearborn, "Bankruptcies, Defaults, and Other Government Financial Emergencies" (Washington: D.C.: U.S. Advisory Commission on Intergovernmental Relations, 1985). Cited in George E. Peterson, and Carol W. Lewis, eds., *Reagan and the Cities* (Washington D.C.: The Urban Institute Press, 1986) 28.
18. Henig, "Privatization in the United States" 657. Henig notes that a search of the Social Sciences Citation Index found Savas to be the most frequently cited author (by a wide margin) in articles written about privatization between 1972 and 1986.
19. Roger S. Ahlbrandt, Jr., *Municipal Fire Protection Service: Comparison of Alternative Organizational Forms* (Beverly Hills, CA: Sage Publications, 1973). Cited in Henig, "Privatization in the United States" 658.
20. Roger S. Ahlbrandt, Jr., "Efficiency in the Provision of Fire Services," *Public Choice* 16 (1973): 14.
21. E.S. Savas, "Municipal Monopolies Versus Competition in Delivering Urban Services," *Improving the Quality of Urban Management*, eds., Willis Hawley, and David Rogers (Beverly Hills, CA: Sage Publications, 1974) 477. The Savas quotes here are cited in Henig, "Privatization in the United States" 658.
22. Ahlbrandt, "Efficiency in the Provision of Fire Services" 3.
23. Franklin R. Edwards, and Barbara J. Stevens, "The Provision of Municipal Sanitation Services by Private Firms: An Empirical Analysis of the Efficiency of Alternative Market Structures and Regulatory Arrangements," *The Journal of Industrial Economics* 27 (1978): 133–147. E.S. Savas, *The Organization and Efficiency of Solid Waste Collection* (Lexington, Massachusetts: D.C. Heath, 1977). Eileen Brettler Berenyi, "Contracting Out Refuse Collection: The Nature and Impact of the Change," *The Urban Interest* 3.1 (1981): 30–42. Donald M. Fisk, Herbert Kiesling, and Thomas Muller, *Private Provision of Public Service: An Overview* (Washington, D.C.: The Urban Institute, 1978). Barbara Stevens, "Comparative Study of Municipal Service Delivery," (New York: Ecodata, Inc., 1984). For a comprehensive list of many of these studies, see Appendix A in Greene, *Cities and Privatization*. See also, John Hilke, "Cost Savings From Privatization: A Compilation of Study Findings" *How-to-Guide* #6 (Los Angeles: The Reason Public Policy Institute, 1993). See also, the annotated bibliography in, John Tepper Marlin, ed., *Contracting Municipal Services: A Guide for Purchase from the Private Sector* (New York: John Wiley and Sons, 1984).
24. See preceding endnote.
25. Henig, "Privatization in the United States" 663.
26. Henig, "Privatization in the United States" 662.

27. *President's Private Sector Survey on Cost Control, Report on Privatization* (Washington, D.C.: Government Printing Office, 1983), i. Emphasis in original. Cited in Henig, "Privatization in the United States" 662.

28. Stuart Butler, *Privatizing Federal Spending: A Strategy to Eliminate the Deficit* (New York: Universe Books, 1985). Cited in Henig, "Privatization in the United States" 662.

29. John M. Greiner, and George E. Peterson, "Do Budget Reductions Stimulate Public Sector Productivity? Evidence From Proposition 2 ½ in Massachusetts," *Reagan and the Cities*, eds., George E. Peterson, and Carol W. Lewis (Washington D.C.: The Urban Institute Press, 1986) 63.

30. Henig, "Privatization in the United States" 663.

31. See Greene, *Cities and Privatization* Appendix A, and Hilke, *How-to-Guide* #6.

32. George A. Boyne, "Bureaucratic Theory Meets Reality: Public Choice and Service Contracting in U.S. Local Government" *Public Administration Review*, 58 (1998): 474–484.

33. Boyne, "Bureaucratic Theory Meets Reality" 475. Boyne claims such claims are, "demonstrably untrue."

34. See: Lawrence K. Finley, *Public Sector Privatization: Alternative Approaches to Service Delivery*, (New York: Quorum Books, 1989); Richard C. Rich, *Analyzing Urban-Service Distributions*, (Lexington, MA: Lexington Books, 1982); Robert M. Stein, *Urban Alternatives: Public and Private Markets in the Provision of Local Services*, (Pittsburgh: University of Pittsburgh Press, 1990).; Tepper Marlin *Contracting Municipal Services;* Paul G. Farnham, "The Impact of Government Functional Responsibility on Local Expenditure" *Urban Affairs Quarterly* 22 (1986): 151–165; , "Contracting out: For What? With Whom?" Public Administration Review 46 (1986): 332–344; David R. Morgan, Michael W. Hirlinger, and Robert E. Englan, " The Decision to Contract Out City Services: A Further Explanation" The Western Political Quarterly (1988): 363–372; Donna Sheldon, *Contracting of Municipal Services: The Unanswered Questions* (New York: Council on Municipal Performance, 1982). Eileen Brettler Berenyi, "Contracting Out Refuse Collection: The Nature and Impact of the Change," *The Urban Interest* 3 (1981): 30–42.

35. Osborne and Gaebler, *Reinventing Government.*

36. Osborne and Gaebler, *Reinventing Government* xxi.

37. Osborne and Gaebler, *Reinventing Government* 79–80.

38. Osborne and Gaebler, *Reinventing Government* 344–345. Emphasis in original.

39. Adrian Nelson, Cary L. Cooper, "Uncertainty Amidst Change—The Impact of Privatization on Employee Job Satisfaction and Well-Being," *Journal of Occupational and Organizational Psychology* 68 (1995): 57–71; P.A. Dorwart, M. Schlesinger, and H. Davison, et. al., "A National Study of Psychiatric Hospital Care," *American Journal of Psychiatry* 148 (1991): 204–210; Alexander C. Wagenaar, HD Holder, "A Change From Public to Private Sale of Wine: Results from Natural Experiments in Iowa and West Virginia," *Journal of Studies on Alcohol* 52 (1991): 162–173; Cornheil S.

Lastarria, "The Impact of Privatization on Gender and Property Rights in Africa," *World Development* 25 (1997): 1317–1333; M. Segall, "From Cooperation to Competition in National Health Systems—And Back?: Impact on Professional Ethics and Quality in Health Care," *International Journal of Health Planning and Management* 15 (2000): 61–79; M. Schlesinger, R. Dornart, C. Hoover, et. al., "Competition, Ownership, and Access to Hospital Service: Evidence from Psychiatric Hospitals," *Med Care* 35 (1997): 974–992; Barbara Pfetsch, "Convergence Through Privatization? Changing Media Environments and Televised Politics in Germany," *European Journal of Communication* 11 (1996): 427–451; T.D. Chandler, "Sanitation Privatization and Sanitation Employee Wages," *Journal of Labor Research* 15 (1994): 137–153; Kevin Doogan, "The Marketization of Local Services and the Fragmentation of Labor Markets," *International Journal of Urban and Regional Research* 21 (1997): 286–302.

40. Cecilia Perry, "Safety Net for Sale," *New Labor Forum* 4 (1999): 78–87; Martin D. Hanlon, "Running on Two Tracks: The Public and Private Provision of Human Services," *New Labor Forum* 4 (1999): 100–111; Frank Emspak, Roland Zullo, and Susan J. Rose, "Privatizing Child Protective Services in Milwaukee County: An Analysis and Comparison of Public and Private Service Delivery Systems," (Milwaukee: Institute for Wisconsin's Future, 1996); Maryann Mason, Wendy Siegel, "Does Privatization Pay?: A Case Study of Privatization in Chicago," (Chicago: Chicago Institute on Urban Poverty, 1997). Elliot D. Sclar, "The Privatization of Public Service: Lessons from Case Studies," (Washington, D.C.: Economic Policy Institute, 1997). Mildred Warner, Amir Hefetz, "Privatization and the Market Role of Local Government," (Washington, D.C.: Economic Policy Institute, 2000). Privatization related policy briefs and case studies published by Economic Policy Institute can be found at <http://library.epinet.org/epi/catalog/subjects/1943.html>. For a comprehensive listing of American Federation of State, County, and Municipal Employees (AFSCME) privatization-related publications see: <http://www.afscme.org/private/aculink4.htm>. For industry-based privatization policy briefs and case studies see: <http://www.privatization.org/database/policyissues/golf_local.html>.

41. Stephen Goldsmith, *The Twenty-First Century City: Resurrecting Urban America* (Washington, D.C.: Regnery Publishing, Inc., 1997) 18.

42. John O. Norquist, *The Wealth of Cities: Revitalizing the Centers of American Life* (Reading, MA: Addison-Wesley, 1998)

43. On growth see: Patrick Plane, "Privatization and Economic Growth: An Empirical Investigation from a Sample of Developing Market Economies," *Applied Economics* 29 (2) (1997): 161–178. On geography see: Igor V. Filatotchev and Roy P. Bradshaw, "The Geographical Impact of the Russian Privatization Program," *Post-Soviet Geography* 36 (1995): 371–384. On enterprise formation, see, Daniel Berkowitz, Jonathan Holland, "Does Privatization Enhance or Deter Small Enterprise Formation?" *Economic Letters* 74 (2001): 53–60. On rural industry see: Hongbin Li and Scott Rozelle, "Saving or Stripping Rural Industry: An Analysis of Privatization

and Effects in China," Agricultural Economics 23 (2000): 241–252. On housing see: A. LaGrange, "Privatizing Public Housing in the Welfare Regime of a Tiger Economy: A Case Study of Hong Kong," Housing Theory & Society 16 (1999): 17–30.

44. Willis D. Hawley, David Rogers, eds., *Improving the Quality of Urban Management* (Beverly Hills: Sage Publications, 1974) 11.
45. Hawley and Rogers, *Improving the Quality* 13.
46. Henig, "Privatization in the United States" 658. Henig notes that while Savas was cited in Harpers, Ahlbrandt was cited in Readers Digest.
47. Daily News, 30 October 1975. Cited in Joshua B. Freeman, *Working Class New York*, (New York: The New Press, 2000) 267.
48. James O'Connor, *Fiscal Crisis of the State* (New York: St. Martin's Press, 1973)
49. O'Connor, *Fiscal Crisis of the State* 7–8.
50. O'Connor, *Fiscal Crisis of the State* 9.
51. Mark Gottdiener, ed., *Cities in Stress: A New Look at the Urban Crisis* (Beverly Hills: Sage Publications, 1986) 8.
52. Gottdiener, *Cities in Stress* 10. Gottdiener cites: Francis Fox Piven, and Richard Cloward, *Poor People's Movements* (New York: Vintage, 1979); Ira Katznelson, *City Trenches: Urban Politics and the Patterning of Class in the U.S.*, (New York: Pantheon, 1981); Alain Touraine, *The Voice and the Eye*, (New York: Cambridge University Press, 1981); Henri Lefebvre, *The Explosion*, (New York: Vintage, 1969).
53. Ann R. Markusen, "Class and Urban Social Expenditure: A Marxist Theory of Metropolitan Government," *Marxism and the Metropolis* 90–111.
54. Tabb, "The New York Fiscal Crisis" 247. See also: David C. Perry, and Alfred J. Watkins, eds., *Rise of the Sunbelt Cities*, (Beverly Hills: Sage Publications, 1977)
55. Tabb, "The New York Fiscal Crisis" 249.
56. Tabb, "The New York Fiscal Crisis" 246.
57. Greiner and Peterson, *Reagan and the Cities* 86.
58. Greiner and Peterson, *Reagan and the Cities* 63.
59. Gottdiener, *Cities in Stress* 11.
60. Paul Starr, *The Limits of Privatization* (Washington D.C.: Economic Policy Institute, 1987)
61. Ronald C. Moe, "Exploring the Limits of Privatization" 459.
62. Harold J. Sullivan, "Privatization of Public Services: A Growing Threat to Constitutional Rights," *Public Administration Review* 47 (1987): 461–467.
63. M. Shamsul Haque, " The diminishing publicness of public service under the current mode of governanc," *Public Administration Review* 61 (1) (2001): 65–81.
64. Barbara Stevens, "Delivering Municipal Services Efficiently: A Comparison of Municipal and Private Service Delivery" (Washington, D.C.: U.S. Department of Housing and Urban Development, 1984)

65. Barry Bluestone, Bennett Harrison, *The Deindustrialization of America* (New York: Basic Books, 1982)

66. Bluestone and Harrison, *The Deindustrialization of America* 6.

67. Alexander Ganz, "Where Has the Urban Crisis Gone: How Boston and Other Large Cities Have Stemmed Economic Decline" *Cities in Stress: A New Look at the Urban Crisis*, ed., Mark Gottdiener (Beverly Hills: Sage Publications, 1986)

68. David Harvey, *Spaces of Capital: Towards a Critical Geography* (New York: Routledge, 2001) 351. Harvey argues that this governance concept involves, "The power to organize space." This power, "derives from a whole complex of forces mobilized by diverse social agents" and is, "a conflictual process, the more so in the ecological spaces of high variegates social density."

69. Others have used different terminology to refer to this idea. See, Peter K. Eisinger, *The Rise of the Entrepreneurial State* (Madison: The University of Wisconsin Press, 1988); and, Haque, "The diminishing publicness of public service."

70. Harvey, *Spaces of Capital* 352.

71. Harvey, *Spaces of Capital* 353.

72. Harvey, *Spaces of Capital* 353.

73. The literature surrounding this topic is vast. I do not address it here. Rather, the broader point is to suggest that the growing importance of this topic, perhaps not surprisingly, further eroded whatever little academic interest in privatization on the local government level existed. For bibliographies of the Neoliberal literature see: George DeMartino, *Global Economy, Global Justice: Theoretical and Policy Alternatives to Neoliberalism*, (New York: Routledge, 2000); George Stiglitz, *Globalization and its Discontents*, (New York: Norton, W.W. & Co., Inc, 2002); Pierre Bourdieu, "The Essence of Neoliberalism," *Le Monde Diplomatique* (December 1998); Susan George, "A Short History of Neo-liberalism," paper presented at the Conference on Economic Sovereignty in a Globalising World, Bangkok, March 24–26, 1999.

74. There are often important epistemological implications involved with this practice. I do not address those here.

75. Under managed competition, a municipality continues to produce a public good or service, but competes with one or more contractors that also produce the same public good or service.

76. Greene, *Cities and Privatization*, Appendix A, Hilke, *How-to-Guide #6*, and, Boyne, "Bureaucratic Theory Meets Reality."

77. See Endnotes 39 and 43 above.

78. See Eric Lichten, *Class Power & Austerity: The New York City Fiscal Crisis* (South Hadley, MA: Bergin and Garvey Publishers, Inc., 1986). In addition to adding a financial/corporate class to the traditional capital-labor duality, Lichten's analysis expands the definition of class struggle to include those of blacks and other minorities.

79. Stevens, "Comparative Study of Municipal Service Delivery."

80. See: Eliot Sclar, *You Don't Always Get What You Pay For: The Economics of Privatization* (Ithaca: Cornell University Press, 2000); Kamal R. Desai, Carol VanDeusen Lukas, and Gary J. Young, "Public Hospitals: Privatization and Uncompensated Care," *Health Affairs* 19 (2) (2000):31–36; and, Lichten, *Class Power & Austerity*.

NOTES TO CHAPTER THREE

1. Stephen A. Resnick and Richard D. Wolff, *Knowledge and Class* (Chicago: The University of Chicago Press, 1987), 20. This seminal work set out the Marxian class theoretic framework that underlies this book's class approach to privatization. The discussion set out in this section and the next draws on this work.
2. Resnick and Wolff, *Knowledge and Class* 19–23.
3. Resnick and Wolff, *Knowledge and Class* 88.
4. Within Marxian class theory, municipal employees are generally considered *unproductive* because they do not produce commodities containing surplus. Instead, the goods or services they produce represent only use-values. Municipal employees' labor does provide various conditions of existence to other production processes, many of which yield commodities containing surplus. Municipal workers could perform productive labor under certain conditions. In the U.S. municipal context, however, they generally do not.
5. Harvey, *Spaces of Capital* 75.
6. The quoted passage rephrases, with the necessary modification, Richard D. Wolff, "Limiting the State versus Expanding it: A Criticism of this Debate" Contemporary Economic Theory: Radical Critiques of Neoliberalism, ed., Andriana Vlachou. (Basingstoke and London: Macmillan Press, 1999) 73.
7. Stephen Resnick and Richard Wolff, "Rethinking Complexity in Economic Theory: The Challenge of Overdetermination" *Evolutionary Concepts in Contemporary Economics*, ed., Richard W. England (Ann Arbor: University of Michigan, 1994) 46.
8. The quoted passage rephrases with the necessary modifications, George DeMartino, *Modern macroeconomic theories of cycles and crisis: A methodological critique*, diss., U of Massachusetts Amherst, 1992. Cited in Katherine Gibson, and Julie Graham, "Rethinking class industrial geography: creating a space for an alternative politics of class." *Economic Geography* 68 (1992): 109–128.
9. This understanding of exploitation—which links it to the presence or absence of a certain type of democracy in the subsumed class process—differs substantively from the one adopted by the Marxian class theory that the class approach to privatization developed here builds upon.
10. U.S. Department of Labor, National Commission on Employment Policy (NCEP), *The long-term implications of privatization*" (Washington, D.C.: U.S. Department of Labor, 1989). Cited in, Christi Clark, Robin

A. Johnson, and James L. Mercer, "Impact of Privatization and Managed Competition on Public Employees" *Local Government Innovation*, eds., Robin A. Johnson and Normal Walzer, (Westport: Quorum Books, 2000): 191–211

11. Barbara Stevens "Delivering Municipal Services Efficiently." Cited in Clark, Johnson, and Mercer, "Impact of Privatization and Managed Competition on Public Employees" 195.

12. Gary Hoover and James Peoples, "Privatization of refuse removal and labor costs" *Journal of Labor Research* 24 (2003): 293–306. Bin Wang, "The Influence of Privatization on Municipal Earnings" working paper, University of Wisconsin-Madison, Department of Economics, February 2004. It is worth noting (given the class analysis of Central Park's privatization developed in the next chapter), that Wang finds that privatization does not dramatically change the earnings of either nonunion or union municipal workers employed in the parks and recreation industry.

13. Hoover and Peoples, "Privatization of refuse removal and labor costs" 296.

14. Wang, "The Influence of Privatization on Municipal Earnings."

15. Wang, "The Influence of Privatization on Municipal Earnings."42.

16. Andrew Pendleton, "What impact has privatization had on pay and employment? A review of the UK experience" *Industrial Relations* (Canadian) 52 (1997): 554–583.

17. M. Bishop, and J Kay, "Privatization in the UK: Deregulatory Reform and Public Enterprise Performance," *Privatization: A Global Perspective*, ed., V. Ramanadham (London: Routledge, 199). Cited in Pendleton, "What impact has privatization had on pay and employment?"

18. J. Haskel, and S. Szymanski, "Privatization and the Labour Market: Facts, Theory and Evidence," *Privatization and Economic Performance*, eds., M. Bishop, J. Kay, and C. Mayer (Oxford: Oxford University Press, 1994). Cited in Pendleton, "What impact has privatization had on pay and employment?"

19. T. Collings, "Contracting Public Services: The Management of Compulsory Competitive Tendering in Two County Councils," Human Resource Management Journal 29 (1993): 1–15. Cited in Pendleton, "What impact has privatization had on pay and employment?"

20. Kieron Walsh, Howard Davis, "Competition and Service: The Impact of the Local Government Act 1988" (London: HMSO, 1993). Cited in Pendleton, "What impact has privatization had on pay and employment?"

21. Stephen Resnick, Richard Wolff, "A Marxian Reconceptualization of Income and its Distribution" *Rethinking Marxism: Struggles in Marxist Theory*, eds., Stephen Resnick, Richard Wolff (Brooklyn, NY: Autonomedia, Inc., 1985). This essay shows that a productive worker's wage is potentially comprised of several different money flows emanating from a variety of class and nonclass processes. As a result, observing a change in labor's post-privatization wage (e.g., an increase) precludes drawing inferences regarding the change's origins.

NOTES TO CHAPTER FOUR

1. These statistics and the ensuing discussion draw heavily on, Roy Rosenzweig and Elizabeth Blackmar, *The Park and the People: A History of Central Park* (Ithaca: Cornell University Press: 1992) 502–504.
2. Rosenzweig and Blackmar, *The Park and the People* 502.
3. E.S. Savas, *A Study of Central Park* (New York, NY, 1976). Cited in Rosenzweig and Blackmar, 502.
4. Rosenzweig and Blackmar, *The Park and the People* 503.
5. As Rosenzweig and Blackmar explain, this change in focus dated to La Guardia's appointment of Robert Moses as the city's parks commissioner in the 1930s. Moses' pragmatic vision of the city's parks as foremost places for activity and recreation constituted a rather dramatic reconceptualization of the entire park system—one far removed from its original aristocratic roots that conceptualized Central Park (as the crown jewel of the system) in primarily aesthetic terms. See, Rosenzweig and Blackmar, *The Park and the People* 447–463.
6. In fact, a $7 million appropriation of a planned ten-year $55 million rehabilitation program for Central Park was preliminarily approved in 1973. The political and fiscal forces that emerged at the same time short-circuited the program, however. See, Rosenzweig and Blackmar, *The Park and the People* 503.
7. Rosenzweig and Blackmar, *The Park and the People* 510.
8. Rosenzweig and Blackmar, *The Park and the People* 512.
9. For a discussion of this program, see, Eugene Kinkead, *Central Park: The Birth, Decline, and Renewal of a National Treasure*, (New York: W.W. Norton & Company, 1990)
10. Rosenzweig and Blackmar, *The Park and the People* 514.
11. "Agreement between The Central Park Conservancy and City of New York Parks & Recreation" (February 11, 1998) 2. The contract sets out in detail what the CPC's maintenance and repair efforts must include (e.g., cleaning, snow removal, landscape maintenance, repairs, and facilities) as well as the standards by which such efforts will be deemed as satisfying the terms of the contract. It is silent, however, on what the CPC's programming efforts must include, as well as the standards by which those efforts will be deemed as satisfying the terms of the contract.
12. Only those costs and expenses of performing these activities are included in the computation of the $5 million. In particular, the contract excludes costs and expenses attributable to the corporate or development (fundraising) offices and city- or Parks-originated contributions to the CPC in excess of $100,000. The CPC may include expenditures and costs funded with earnings on its endowment in the $5 million computation.
13. Richard Gilder, "Set the Parks Free" *City Journal* 7.4 (1997).
14. The fact that the park is not exchanged via a market mechanism, but via a privately negotiated contract, does not jeopardize its theoretical specification here qua commodity. Commodities may be (have been) exchanged via various mediums throughout history.

15. The ability to theoretically specify the performance (production) of surplus labor is but a necessary condition of the specification of a class process. Some type of exchange process must be posited to lie (in temporal terms) between production/appropriation (the first moment of the class process) and distribution (the second moment of the class process) of the surplus labor. An exchange process makes possible the realization of surplus labor and therefore must precede the subsequent distribution of it. Of course, it may turn out that the exchange value assigned to the surplus labor via the exchange process is zero. Also, the specification of a class process does not require the specification of the medium through which exchange occurs (e.g., via a market, custom, a negotiated contract, etc.), nor the form used to represent value (e.g., another use-value, currency, corvee). The importance of an exchange process to the specification of a class process, however, necessitates the positing of the existence of something that can be (is capable of being) exchanged. Prior to its privatization, Central Park, though a use-value, was not an object of exchange: its production did not entail a class process. Following its privatization, the park became an object of exchange. Its subsequent production as such meant that the theorization of a class process became possible.

16. The specification of a class process' form requires the specification of a set of economic processes—in particular, the commodity or non-commodity status of the good or service produced (distributed), and the form of productive labor's remuneration. In other words, while the definition of a class process does not require the specification of these additional economic processes, the specification of a capitalist, feudal, communal, independent class process does. See, Stephen Cullenberg, "Socialism's Burden: Towards a "Thin" Definition of Socialism" *Rethinking Marxism* 5 (1992): 64–83.

17. While this argument may seem apropos given Central Park's location in the city that serves as a key financial center for global capitalism, it is worth noting that it would prove ironic to the nation's earliest urban park visionaries, including Central Park's chief designer, Fredrick Olmstead, who conceived of urban parks as providing urbanites essential refuge and respite from the late-nineteenth century pressures of capitalist urbanization.

18. Karl Marx, *Grundrisse*, trans., Martin Nicolaus, (London: The Penguin Group, 1993) Part 10.

19. Whether or not the set of municipal workers who produced the park prior to privatization is similar to the one that came to produce it (for the CPC) following privatization is not an issue. The point is that these two sets (whatever their individual elements, i.e., workers) stand in economically different positions (from a class perspective), i.e., one set is exploited, the other is not.

20. This conceptualization of the Central Park commodity (in particular, its two dimensions) is consistent with the conceptualization of urban parks increasingly espoused in the literature on them. See, for instance, Galen Cranz, "Changing Roles of Urban Parks: From Pleasure Garden to Open

Space" *San Francisco Planning and Urban Research Newsletter* (San Francisco: San Francisco Planning and Urban Research Association, June 2000) 7; and, Chris Walker, "The Public Value of Urban Parks," *Beyond Recreation: A Broader View of Urban Parks* (Washington D.C.: Urban Institute, June 2004).

21. Walker, "The Public Value of Urban Parks."
22. Walker, "The Public Value of Urban Parks" 3.
23. Cranz, "Changing Roles of Urban Parks" 7.
24. By the early 1980s, New Yorkers perceived Central Park as unsafe. Indeed, among the earliest studies carried out by the CPC involved gauging the public's perceptions of the park's safety. See, Rosenzweig and Blackmar, *The Park and the People* 518–530.
25. Besides the fact that public education and urban parks yield similar use-values for local governments, it is noteworthy that both have increasingly become targets for privatization.
26. There is an important distinction between the use-values students and citizens realize via their consumption of public education and munici-pal parks and those realized by the municipalities that generally produce these goods. In particular, whatever the precise use-values that flow to students and citizens, municipalities realize a conceptually distinct set of use-values via students' and citizens' consumption of these goods.
27. Fred Curtis has argued that liberal arts colleges, many of which are tax-exempt nonprofit organizations, can be considered capitalist commodity producers. In this case, a liberal arts college education is the capitalist commodity produced. Curtis argues that these institutions' faculties are akin to a typical capitalist manufacturer's factory workers, and thus can be conceived as producing surplus value. The surplus value produced by liberal arts institution's faculties is appropriated by trustee-capitalists as opposed to a board of directors. See, Fred Curtis, "Ivy Covered Exploi-tation" *Re/Presenting Class: Essays in Postmodern Marxism*, eds., J.K. Gibson-Graham, Stephen Resnick, and Richard Wolff, (Durham: Duke University Press, 2001): 81–104.
28. Another important difference is the so-called "non-distribution" con-straint imposed on "charitable" non-profit organizations. This constraint implies that non-profit organizations may not pay dividends.
29. See, Jessica Peña and Alexander L.T. Reid, "A Call for Reform of the Operational Test for Unrelated Commercial Activity in Charities" *New York University Law Review*, 76 (2001) 1855–1898.
30. Gilbert M. Gaul, and Neill A. Borowski, "Nonprofits: American's Growth Industry," *Philadelphia Inquirer*, 19 April 1993, A1. This article was part of an Inquirer expose entitled, "Warehouses of Wealth: The Tax-Free Economy" cited in Peña and Reid. See also, Susan Rose-Ackerman, "Charitable Giving and "Excessive" Fundraising," *The Quarterly Journal of Economics* 97 (1982): 193–212; and, Burton Weisbrod, *To Profit or Not to Profit* (Cambridge, UK: Cambridge University Press, 1998).
31. The issue concerning gardeners' managerial responsibilities is set aside, as the primary concern here is with their role as surplus value producers.

32. This follows traditional Marxian notation.

33. That is, this magnitude of capital advanced for productive labor-power corresponds to (i.e., can be denominated in value terms) a specific amount of time (e.g., hours) spent performing productive labor.

34. This discussion draws on, Richard D. Wolff, Antonino Callari, and Bruce Roberts, "A Marxian Alternative to the Transformation Problem," *Review of Radical Political Economics* 16 (1984): 115–135.

35. Only that portion of the value of means of production consumed in the production process enters into value formation. Thus, if the *production price* of the means of production is what enters into the Central Park commodity's value formation, then, some portion of *that* price (e.g., twenty percent per annum of a lawn-mower, rake, computer, etc.) enters into the value calculation.

36. Wolff, Callari, and Roberts, "A Marxian Alternative" 126.

37. Equation one, which represents the (labor) value of the Central Park commodity is denominated in abstract labor time, e.g., hours. This idea is further explained in the next quoted passage from Marx, viz., what a commodity actually costs ("the actual cost of the commodity") is "measured by the expenditure of labor" which must be denominated in units of (abstract labor) time.

38. Karl Marx, *Capital,* vol. 3, trans., David Fernbach (London: Pelican Group, 1981) 118–119.

39. W is equivalent to Marx's C, and C_1 (in the subsequent text) is equivalent to his c.

40. Resnick and Wolff, *Knowledge and Class* 219.

41. A donation from a self-employed individual could represent a subsumed class distribution.

42. Thus, just as demand and supply conditions overdetermine a capitalist commodity's value, a number of factors overdetermine the Central Park commodity's value.

43. Within a class analytic framework, merchants constitute a subsumed class. In exchange for buying and distributing an appropriator's commodity, a merchant receives a portion of appropriated surplus labor (via a subsumed class distribution) from the appropriator in exchange for her performance of distributive services. Thus, a merchant acquires an appropriator's commodity at a discount from its value. The CPC acts as a merchant when it purchases commodities for resale in its gift shops. It thereby receives subsumed class distributions from these commodities' producers.

44. Hundreds of volunteers provide labor-power to the CPC each year. While these volunteers' labor-power is important to the production of the Central Park commodity, it represents *unproductive* labor—it does not produce surplus value. Despite the fact that no exchange process occurs between the CPC and these volunteers, the CPC's receipt (use) of volunteers' labor-power represents a specific quantum of labor time that represents nonclass revenue for the CPC. In effect, the value of volunteers' labor-power (V_{LP}) is purchased by the CPC at a price equal to zero.

45. For example, the Y_{SC2} and Y_{NC2} revenue flows that derive from the CPC's fundraising activities overdetermine Y_{FC}.
46. Investment-related expenses (i) are equal to the difference between A (net additions (withdrawals) made to the endowment portfolio each fiscal year) and the management fee the CPC pays to the financial institution that manages its portfolio. Thus, i = A—fee = D—fee. Fundraising-related expenses are represented by g. And, m represents money capital used to purchase the commodities the CPC sells in the park's visitor gift shops and via its on-line retail store. Also included in m are expenditures related to the recruitment of volunteers.
47. Modifications were made to this schedule in order to aid comprehension of the ensuing discussion.
48. The $1.6 million constituting "payroll taxes and employee benefits" represents a subsumed class distribution made by the CPC to the state and city, and providers of pension- and health-plan services.
49. Given that seventy-three percent of outlays on contracted services is allocated to construction/design, this is a reasonable assumption.
50. The amount listed for contributed services represents legal advice, office space, and utilities and is excluded from the calculation. The CPC advances no capital for such services but includes them in both its revenue and functional expensing.
51. This is an assumption.
52. Thus, for example, in fiscal year 2001, of the approximately $1 million used to purchase elements of constant capital, $0.31 million replaced worn capital equipment. I make the simplifying assumption that the $0.31 million represented as depreciation on the schedule of functional expenses is wholly attributable to depreciation of this capital.

NOTES TO CHAPTER FIVE

1. One notable exception is, Richard P. Nathan, Elizabeth I. Davis, Mark J. McGarth, and William C. O'Heaney, *The Non-profitization Movement as a Form of Devolution* (Albany, NY: Rockefeller Institute, 1996)
2. Jennifer R. Wolch and Robert K. Geiger, "Urban Restructuring and the Non-for-Profit Sector," *Economic Geography* 62 (1986): 3–18.
3. John Vickers and George Yarrow, "Economic Perspectives on Privatization," *The Journal of Economic Perspectives* 5 (1991): 111–132.
4. This model is adapted from one set out in Resnick and Wolff, *Knowledge and Class* 207–219.
5. The sector also obviously pays taxes to the state and U.S. government. For simplicity, I identify only New York City.
6. For simplicity, the model assumes that appropriated and realized surplus value (S) represents the entirety of the for-profit sector's class analytic revenues. Thus, subsumed class and nonclass revenues are excluded. This allows New York City's for-profit sector to be closed. The subsumed class and nonclass revenues that clearly exist among the sector's enterprises can be thought of as transfers (between the sector's enterprises) that affect

individual for-profit enterprise's class analytic revenues (and value profit rates), but do not necessarily alter the total surplus value appropriated/realized by the sector in New York City.

7. The $49,000 figure excludes the securities industry, which has an average wage of $230,000. Part of the wage differential between the two sectors reflects the fact that a higher proportion of employees in the non-profit sector work part-time. The nonprofit sector wage is from Seley and Wolpert. The New York City-wide and government average wages are calculated from the New York State Department of Labor's 2002 ES-202 (Covered Employment) series.

8. For-profit sector donations also of course represent deductions against tax liabilities.

9. In a similar vein, instead of raising the rate of exploitation in order to offset increases in D, the for-profit capitalist sector may elect to lower the organic composition of capital (κ). This could lead to slower job growth in the sector.

10. This dynamic occurred in New York City in the late 1990s. For many reasons—including what was heralded as a Giuliani-orchestrated quality-of-life improvement—the city's population and labor force increased significantly during the 1990s.

11. In the same vein, to the extent that a municipal privatization process helps increase a municipality's quality of life, it might also help attract visitors and tourists to the municipality, and thereby benefit the for-profit capitalist sector.

12. Burton A. Weisbrod, *To Profit or Not to Profit* 2.

13. Burton A. Weisbrod, *To Profit or Not to Profit* 3.

14. John E. Seley and Julian Wolpert, *New York City's Non-profit Sector* (New York: Community Studies of New York, Inc., and the Non-profit Coordinating Committee of New York, Inc., 2002).

15. Seley and Wolpert, *New York City's Non-profit Sector* 43–44. The discrepancy between the total and the average reflects the role of large health organizations with significant revenues with small shares of those revenues coming from contributions.

16. Seley and Wolpert, *New York City's Non-profit Sector* 14.

17. This is surprising given the fact that surveys of non-profits indicate they are aware of (and worried about) this type of competition. See, Association of Fundraising Professionals, *Association of Fundraising Professionals, State of Fundraising Report 2003* (Alexandria, VA: Association of Fundraising Professionals, 2003).

18. Rose-Ackerman, "Charitable Giving" 212.

19. Inkyung Cha and William Neilson, "Is Competition Among Charities Bad?" Working Paper Series No. 0116 (Private Enterprise Research Center, Texas A&M University, 2001)

20. Burton A. Weisbrod, *To Profit or Not to Profit* 15.

21. This argument need not necessarily rest on a zero-sum type assumption. Even if competition for donations among non-profits worked to increase the total supply of donations, an increase in the costs associated with

securing a single donation could have detrimental effects on a non-profit organization. In effect, the return to fundraising would be reduced.

22. In many cases, contracts for social and human service commodities are let via competitive request for proposal (RFP) processes, and thus contractors frequently renegotiate contract (commodity) prices with the city—for example, every year or two.

23. Seley and Wolpert, *New York City's Non-profit Sector* 62–63.

24. Burton A. Weisbrod, *To Profit or Not to Profit* 2.

25. Burton A. Weisbrod, *To Profit or Not to Profit* 15.

26. These expenditures were represented as g in Figure 4.6.

27. In collaboration with Fireworks by Grucci, America's oldest fireworks company, Cai Guo-Qiang developed state-of-the-art technology that employs programmable microchips inside firework shells that allow him to draw in the sky.

28. These continuing education-like courses generally have modest user-fees unlike the set of free programs that also comprise part of the programmatic dimension of the Central Park commodity. Despite these user-fees, I treat these courses as a constituent part of the programmatic dimension of the Central Park commodity, as the production process that gives rise to them is the same one that yields the dimension's free programs.

29. Many of these independent producers occupy other class positions in other social sites in which they participate.

30. Anonymous Central Park horse carriage operator, personal interview, 15 June 2003.

31. The exchange values of the commodities produced by the park's street performers, musicians, and bands are difficult to specify. This is due to the way in which these commodities are distributed. Specifically, these commodities' exchange values are determined post-consumption: some members of the public pay for their consumption of these commodities, others do not. This fact does not jeopardize the theoretical specification of these performances qua commodities, however. Instead, it highlights a contradiction all producers confront—one that arises from the contradictory unity between the use and exchange value of a produced commodity. Specifically, if and when these producers' performance commodities cannot be sold (i.e., those who consume their use-values do not place money in the hat following their consumption), or if the commodity is sold at less than its value (i.e., the average revenue dropped into the hat turns out to be less than the value produced) these producers face a crisis. In short, their ability to reproduce their fundamental class processes is imperiled. The regularity with which many of these performers appear in the park suggests this crisis either does not materialize and/or that these producers earn other kinds of revenue that allow them to subsidize their production of these commodities.

32. No time series data on Central Park's visitorship exist. While the tourism boom New York City enjoyed in the late 1990s likely increased park attendance, the several qualitative (capital) improvements the CPC made to the park, in addition to its increased outlays on the park's programmatic

dimension, undoubtedly increased the park's attractiveness and thereby foot-traffic through it.

33. The italicized words in this sentence reflect the difference between the park qua use-value (pre-privatization), and the park qua capitalist commodity (post-privatization).

34. The CPC's qualitative improvements to the Central Park commodity also worked to enhance (complement) carriage operators' commodity.

35. Walter Benjamin, *Illuminations* (London: Fontana, 1973). Cited in, Allen J. Scott, *The Cultural Economy of Cities: Essays on the Geography of Image-Producing Industries* (London: Sage, 2000) 326.

36. Despite its theoretical specification as a capitalist commodity, the park is literally a place in an urban locale.

37. Scott, *The Cultural Economy of Cities* 325.

38. Harvey, *Spaces of Capital* 404–405.

39. The auratic quality arising out of independent and communist production in the park is akin to a restaurant's ambiance.

40. Because government statistics do not take class into consideration, detailed geographic-by-industry-by-class employment data that might shed light on the question of whether or not the number of these produces operating in or near Central Park increased following the park's privatization do not exist. Census-based non-employer (self-employed) data do allow one to get some sense of the number of self-employed "independent, artists, writers, & performers" living in Manhattan. These data might be taken as a rough proxy for these types of independent and communist producers. In 1997, there were 22,998 of these self-employed independent, artists, writers, and performers in Manhattan. Their average annual receipts were $30,085. In 2001, these numbers were, 28,219, and $29,782. (Dollar-figures are in nominal terms.)

41. The city retained authority over the issuance of permits in Central Park following its privatization.

42. Central Park Conservancy, "The Right to Rally and the Great Lawn" Central Park Conservancy website, July, 18, 2004.

43. The protesters that took the city to court over its denial of a permit were quick to point out that the CPC's free AOL-Time Warner-sponsored New York Philharmonic summer concert series regularly draws upwards of 80,000 spectators to the Great Lawn.

NOTES TO CHAPTER SIX

1. The political Left in the United States is understood to comprise heterodox academics (especially heterodox economists), labor advocates (including labor unions), self-described progressives, and radicals. While their rationales (and politics) often differ, these individuals and institutions generally oppose privatization. Note that self-described progressives need not necessarily endorse the definition of "progressive" set out in the next endnote.

2. Progressive here and throughout the remaining chapters is meant to imply political positions, orientations, and policies broadly characterized as ones

that exhibit (either explicitly or implicitly) preferences for *non-capitalist* class processes (or, enterprises) and the institutions that enable and/or support them.

3. Individuals engaged in independent class processes are assumed to exploit themselves. Because exploitation here is linked to the undemocracy that characterizes certain class processes, the self-exploitation independents endure is obviously substantively different from the type of exploitation endured by individuals engaged in other exploitative class processes.

4. I make this point because Savas' study of the privatization of various social and health service related commodities in New York City in the mid- to late-1990s revealed that city solicitations that allowed a contractor to rent an existing structure or facility from the city resulted in more bids (which Savas takes as an indicator of how competitive the privatization was). This suggests that capital constraints reduce the number of bidders in some privatizations. The larger point (which will become increasingly important as the argument develops) is that municipalities can structure privatizations in ways that promote non-capitalist enterprises. See, E.S. Savas, "Competition and choice in New York City Social Services," *Public Administration Review* 62 (202): 82–92.

5. Gilder, "Set the Parks Free."

6. Cullenberg, "Socialism's Burden" 78.

7. Cullenberg, "Socialism's Burden" 78.

8. Consider a communist enterprise that elected to pursue the goal of providing all employees' children college scholarships. Presumably, this goal would promote an interest in efficiency.

9. Stephen A. Resnick and Richard D. Wolff, *Class Theory and History: Capitalism and Communism in the U.S.S.R.* (New York: Routledge, 2002) 60.

10. Resnick and Wolff, *Class Theory and History* 61.

11. The issue of the relationship between communist enterprises and private ownership is less important in the municipal context than in other contexts, e.g., privatizations involving the sale of state-owned enterprises. Many U.S. municipalities are not overly concerned with whether or not a contractor involved in a privatization is publicly owned, i.e., issues equity.

12. Cullenberg, "Socialism's Burden" citing, Robert Dahl, *A Preface to Economic Democracy* (Berkeley: University of California Press, 1985), and David Ellerman *The Democratic Worker-Owned Firm: A New Model for the East and West* (Boston: Unwin Hyman, 1990). I elaborate upon this topic in the next chapter.

13. My definition of a progressive privatization is based on Cullenberg's collective form of appropriation concept. See, Cullenberg, "Socialism's Burden."

14. It should be noted that this condition prompts an important theoretical issue. Namely, it appears to violate the previously specified necessary condition that the class processes of enterprises involved in progressive privatizations be non-exploitative ones. More specifically, does the required inclusion of the enterprise's unproductive workers (its management and support staff) in the appropriative and distributive processes imply that the enterprise's class process is exploitative? While space constraints preclude

a full discussion of this question, some brief remarks are warranted. The question of whether or not the inclusion of unproductive workers in the appropriative and distributive processes implies that the enterprise's class process is exploitative turns on how one understands exploitative appropriation and its relationship to the subsumed class process. Two conditions may serve as the basis for exploitative appropriation process: 1) the *presence* of non-producers of surplus labor (unproductive workers) in a process through which they receive the surplus produced by others or, 2) the *non-presence* of "producers" of surplus labor in a process through which its distribution occurs. While the two conditions are closely related, it can be shown that if the second condition is used as a basis for exploitative appropriation the aforementioned theoretical issue is circumvented.

15. In the quoted passage, Cullenberg is referring specifically to communal appropriation. His definition of communal appropriation, however, provides the foundation for my definition of a progressive privatization. See, Cullenberg, "Socialism's Burden."

16. At the same time, it should be acknowledged that this first condition precludes a situation in which all adult members of society (or, of a municipality) in addition to the enterprise's productive and unproductive laborers participate in the appropriative and distributive processes. As Cullenberg (1992) notes, there are grave theoretical and practical problems associated with the concept of a "society-wide" appropriative and distributive process.

17. Cullenberg, "Socialism's Burden" 74.

18. Cullenberg, "Socialism's Burden" 74.

19. As noted in Endnote Thirteen, these two conditions constitute Cullenberg's collective form of appropriation concept, and underlie his "thin" definition of socialism. For me, they constitute a "thick" definition of progressive municipal privatization. Clearly, one could devise other definitions, e.g., that only the productive laborers of the enterprise participate on some unspecified basis in the appropriative and distributive processes.

20. Martin Melosi, *Garbage in the Cities: Refuse, Reform, and the Environment, 1990–1980* (College Station: Texas A&M University Press, 1981) 29. Cited in Adler, *The Origin of Governmental Production*.

21. See, Philip D. Giantris, "Business Perspective—Environmental Infrastructure" *Public Sector Privatization*, ed., Lawrence K. Finley (New York: Quorum Books, 1989) 47–62; Mark H. Flener, "Legal Considerations in Privatization and the Role of Legal Counsel" *Public Sector Privatization*, ed., Lawrence K. Finley (New York: Quorum Books, 1989) 141–152.

22. As is well known, there is a point at which this would cease to be the case.

23. California's public employees' well-known pension fund, CALPERS, wields enormous clout on Wall Street, for instance. The following example helps clarify what could be at stake for public-employee unions. AFSCME, the largest public employees union in the U.S., with 1.3 million members, has a huge pension fund that it runs for its members. In mid-2002, the fund held between two and three percent (14.4 million shares valued at $432 million) of all shares in Waste Management, Inc. (WMI). WMI, a multi-national

capitalist producer of sanitation services, would undoubtedly appear on
the short-list of potential service providers that would be drawn up by
any government contemplating privatization of its sanitation services.
Concerned that new living wage ordinances and other local regulations
might cut into the profitability of WMI, AFSCME's pension launched a
shareholder campaign in 2002 to force WMI's management to release
a report indicating how such local ordinances and regulations would
impact WMI's bottom line and its ability to secure future contracts. So,
the question: is AFSCME interested in current and future pensioners'
WMI return, or is it interested in protecting the jobs of current AFSCME
members? A finer example of the contradictions that arise out of multiple class positions would be difficult to find.

24. See: <http://www.acftu.org.cn/volindus.htm>.
25. "No Sign of Landing" *The Economist* January 29, 2005.
26. David F. Linowes, *Privatization: Toward More Effective Government.
     Report of the President's Commission on Privatization* (Urbana: Univer-
     sity of Illinois Press, 1988). Cited in Henig, "Privatization in the United
     States" 649.
27. Moreover, a public employee-owned enterprise generated via a privatiza-
     tion process would not meet the requirements of a progressive privati-
     zation. The defining characteristic of democratic enterprises (which lie
     at the center of progressive municipal privatizations) is their democratic
     and non-exploitative class structures not their ownership form.
28. Betsy Gotbaum, Public Advocate for the City of New York, "Procure-
     ment in New York City: A Strategy for Local Economic Development"
     (New York: Office of the Public Advocate for the City of New York,
     June 2003).

NOTES TO CHAPTER SEVEN

1. Henry Gibbon, "Worldwide economic orthodoxy" *Privatisation Interna-
    tional* 123 (1998) 4–5. See also, Henry Gibbon, Editor's Letter, *Privati-
    sation Yearbook* (London: Thomson Financial, 2000) 1.
2. W.L., Megginson and Maria K. Boutchkova, "The Impact of Privatisa-
    tion on Capital Market Development and Individual Share Ownership."
    Paper presented at the Thirteenth Plenary Session of the Advisory Group
    on Privatisation, OECD, Paris, September 1999.
3. Despite the fact that some countries (e.g., Chile) began to undertake
    privatization programs (or pre-programs) during the 1970s, Thatcher's
    efforts, which began in 1979, are generally pointed to as the global
    privatization movement's birth date.
4. Ladan Mahboobi, "Recent Privatisation Trends in OECD Countries,"
    Financial Market Trends 82 (2002) 43–58.
5. Of the $154 billion USD of privatization-derived revenues earned in Latin
    American and the Caribbean between 1990 and 1998, those in Brazil

accounted for forty-three percent of the total. The sale of Brazil'sTelebras telecoms network in 1998 yielded over $19 billion USD. See, Ladan Mahboobi, "Recent Privatisation Trends in OECD Countries."

6. For a lucid discussion of this idea (and several closely related ones), see, George F. DeMartino, *Global Economy.*

7. Megginson and Boutchkova, "The Impact of Privatisation on Capital Market Development."

8. Dick Welch and Olivier Frémond, "The Case-by-Case Approach to Privatization: Techniques and Examples" World Bank Technical Paper no. 403 (Washington, D.C.: The World Bank, 1998). This report is one in a series of World Bank privatization toolkits. These reports provide governments contemplating privatization a variety of practical, strategic, technical, and legal advice.

9. Welch and Frémond, "The Case-by-Case Approach to Privatization."

10. The World Bank, *2004 World Development Indicators*, (Washington, D.C.: The World Bank Group) 257.

11. Welch and Frémond, "The Case-by-Case Approach to Privatization" 26.

12. Welch and Frémond, "The Case-by-Case Approach to Privatization" 26.

13. Welch and Frémond, "The Case-by-Case Approach to Privatization" 26. See also, David Bartlett, "Foreign Direct Investment and Privatization Policy: The Causes and Consequences of Hungary's Route to Capitalism" *Transitions to Capitalism and Democracy in Russia and Central Europe*, eds., M. Donald Hancock and John Logue (Westport: Praeger, 2000) 135–154.

14. Welch and Frémond, "The Case-by-Case Approach to Privatization" 26.

15. David Binns, "Privatization Through Employee Ownership: Learned From The International Experience" Working Paper. See: <http://cog.kent.edu/lib/Binns%20%20Privatization%20Through%20Employee%20Ownership.htm.>

16. Binns, "Privatization Through Employee Ownership."

17. While the privatizations that swept Eastern Europe during the 1990s took many forms, Russia's was especially noteworthy, as employee-ownership was central to it. Russian privatization, as Logue and Bell explain, "initially produced the most egalitarian structure of private ownership in the world. Much of the existing stock of housing was given to its occupants, yielding a high level of homeownership. Vouchers gave every man, woman, and child his or her equal share of the national productive wealth. The 1992–1994 privatization program yielded an astonishingly high rate of majority employee ownership, as work collectives voted overwhelmingly to acquire majority ownership of their own firms." Logue and Bell go on to note that instead of regarding this a positive outcome, "the neoliberal reform team—Gaidar, Chubais, and their associates—viewed the widespread distribution of property through vouchers and through majority ownership as a negative result." Later, as the authors explain, the rules of the privatization game were changed in order to encourage reconcentration of ownership—which has largely been successful. Still, "Russia still has the

most broadly shared ownership of productive assets in the world." In the current context, this experience illuminates the theoretical and political differences and consequences that arise from a focus on ownership versus class. Had the Russian collectives sought to establish democratic enterprises (as defined in this chapter) while simultaneously taking ownership of former state-owner enterprises (and demanded that legal structures were altered in such a way as to support such enterprise—perhaps by codifying the separation of an enterprise's ownership rights from its surplus (control) rights) the import attached to the ownership issue would have been different. See, John Logue and Daniel Bell, "Who Will Inherit the "Worker's Paradise"?: Worker Ownership and Enterprise Efficiency in Russian Privatization" *Transitions to Capitalism and Democracy in Russia and Central Europe*, eds., M. Donald Hancock and John Logue (Westport: Praeger, 2000) 29–66.

18. Welch and Frémond, "The Case-by-Case Approach to Privatization" 36.
19. Several methods have been used to divest state-owned enterprises, including: voucher schemes, coupon programs, and free distribution. The methods used to divest major state-owned enterprises, however, have tended be those highlighted here or close variants of them.
20. Empirical investigations of the class structures of *post-privatized* state-owned enterprises would put the argument developed from this point forward on firmer ground. Such investigations lie outside the scope of this book, however. Here, I am interested in presenting the basic argument. At the same time, the characterization of these enterprises' *pre-privatization* class structures is accurate, i.e., they tended to be capitalist ones. Moreover, there appear to be specific privatization cases (Russia and other Eastern European countries) which came close to qualifying as progressive privatizations on the terms I set out below. Still, in many of these cases, which involved significant employee-ownership (including, Poland and Russia) it is unclear what the relationship between employee ownership and employee control over surplus was. The literature's failure to see class makes this issue difficult to ascertain. See, Hancock and Logue, *Transitions to Capitalism and Democracy*; and, *Privatization in Latin America: New Roles for the Public and Private Sectors*, eds., Werner Baer and Melissa H. Birch (Westport: Praeger, 1994).
21. Resnick and Wolff, *Class Theory and History* 52–59. See also, Richard Wolff, "Limiting the State versus Expanding it: A Criticism of this Debate."
22. Resnick and Wolff, *Class Theory and History* 86. Emphasis added.
23. The class theory that underlies the class approach to privatization this book develops has been used to demonstrate that the terms success and failure are necessarily relative to a theoretical perspective. Thus, in the current context, what might be deemed privatization failures from one theoretical perspective might be deemed successes from another. To the extent that the vast majority of the past quarter-century's worth of privatizations involving divestitures of state-owned enterprises have not changed these enterprises' capitalist class structures, they might be said to have been resounding

successes in capitalist class terms. See, David Ruccio, "When Failure Becomes Success: Class and the Debate over Stabilization and Adjustment" *World Development* 19 (1991): 1315–1334.

24. Whereas some might view these developments positively, from a class perspective, they could reflect dramatic increases in the rate of exploitation of workers.

25. For political reasons, governments have often carried out such organizational and managerial restructurings (which have often included significant labor reductions) prior to privatization. This process is called corporatization, and is usually strongly encouraged by the World Bank, as it ensures that private demand for a divestiture is not undermined.

26. In 2001, the New Zealand government was forced to reacquire over eighty percent of Air New Zealand as a result of the collapse of Air New Zealand's Australian subsidiary. In the U.K., the privatized rail infrastructure company, Rail Track, was put under administration after its failure to secure additional government funding. The company had been privatized in 1996 and had experienced mounting financial difficulties in the aftermath of an accident in 2000. See, Ladan Mahboobi, "Recent Privatization Trends in OECD Countries."

27. As explained in Endnote Fourteen in Chapter Six, I believe exploitative appropriation involves an exclusionary dimension. It is this dimension that grants appropriators control rights to (over) the surplus' distribution. Hence, the word *thereby* is italicized for a specific reason.

28. Again, it should be noted that the mechanism that might be used to execute the one-employee one-vote condition, e.g., representative democracy, consensus decision-making, etc, is left unspecified.

29. The goal is that the enterprise not be shutdown (or its various pieces sold off) following its privatization. In the context of the divestiture of state-owned enterprise, this practice is referred to as asset-stripping. Privatizing Western European nations have been especially sensitive to American- and British-led asset-stripping.

30. Welch and Frémond, "The Case-by-Case Approach to Privatization" 39.

31. Welch and Frémond, "The Case-by-Case Approach to Privatization" 35.

32. Joseph E. Stiglitz, *Whither Socialism?* (Cambridge: The MIT Press, 1994) 188.

33. Beyond government-backed loan guarantees, this might be accomplished by offering different classes of shares, or convertible (and, perhaps, government-backed) bonds.

34. Resnick and Wolff, *Class Theory and History*. See also, Cullenberg, "Socialism's Burden" 78–79.

35. Cullenberg, "Socialism's Burden" citing, Robert Dahl, *A Preface to Economic Democracy* and David Ellerman, *The Democratic Worker-Owned Firm*.

36. Pieter W. Moerland, "Changing Models of Corporate Governance in OECD Countries" *Privatization, Corporate Governance and the Emergence of Markets*. eds. Eckehard F. Rosenbaoum, Frank Bonker, and Hans-Jurgen Wagener. (London: Macmillan Press Ltd., 2000) 75.

37. Moerland, "Changing Models of Corporate Governance."
38. For a detailed exposition of this idea, see Resnick and Wolff, *Class Theory and History* 59–65.
39. Resnick and Wolff, *Class Theory and History* 63.
40. The idea here regards the complex relationship between time, space, money, and the rates of turnover of different forms of capital. See, David Harvey, *Consciousness and the Urban Experience* (Baltimore: The Johns Hopkins University Press, 1985). Here, I am suggesting that to the extent democratic enterprises directed portions of their surpluses to projects with longer turnover periods—e.g., longer-lived infrastructure (urban transport systems, school construction, housing, etc.) that is often funded out of public monies because it precludes private capital from quickly realizing surplus—this could work to lower the average rate of accumulation by slowing the average rate of capital turnover. Generally speaking, capitalist enterprises are interested in increasing their rates of turnover. The economy-wide rate of turnover plays an important role in determining the sequencing, duration, and depth of accumulation crises. Thus, competition between capitalist and democratic enterprises could prove to have salutary effects for capitalist enterprises.
41. In many Eastern European cases, privatization programs relied on transferring state-owned enterprises to existing employees and managers because foreign direct investment was often limited or highly targeted. Because they would involve novel class structures, progressive privatizations would likely have to rely on transferring enterprises to their existing employees and managers.
42. These examples are set out in, Sunita Kikeri, "Privatization and Labor: What Happens to Workers When Governments Divest?" World Bank Technical Paper No. 396 (Washington, D.C.: The World Bank, 1998).
43. Harvey, *Spaces of Capital*.
44. Where an individual stands on this issue will play an important role in her assessment of the argument developed in this chapter. Those that believe Neoliberal development is largely immune to policy intervention posit (consciously or unconsciously) a structured global totality. This structure's boundaries (it is assumed) work to hem in and constrict alternatives (e.g., democratic enterprise formation in the context of privatization). Among other things, this implies that even if a democratic enterprise was successfully generated via a privatization process, this structured totality would undermine its class process and/or force it to behave like a capitalist enterprise. For class analysts, the articulation of the possibility of progressive privatizations as well as potential future realizations of such privatizations will change the structured totality. This implies that whatever boundaries this totality is presumed to have are constantly changing and evolving. These changes and evolutions reflect, in part, not only theory-making (e.g., articulations of alternatives like progressive privatizations), but also political interventions (attempts to politically realize alternatives like progressive privatizations). Thus, from a class perspective, it is nonsensical to assume this totality's boundaries somehow *a fortiori* make impossible the political

realization of a progressive privatization. It might be added, that this was *the* point of Marx's 11th Thesis on Feuerbach.

45. David Harvey, "The 'New' Imperialism: Accumulation by Dispossession" *The New Imperial Challenge: Socialist Register 2004*. Eds. Leo Panitch and Colin Leys. (London: Merlin Press, 2003) 63–88.

46. Cullenberg, "Socialism's Burden" 78.

47. J.K. Gibson-Graham and O'Neill make a similar point in a different context. See, J.K., Gibson-Graham and Phillip O'Neill, "Exploring a New Class Politics of the Enterprise" *Re/Presenting Class: Essays in Postmodern Marxism*. Eds. J.K. Gibson-Graham, Stephen Resnick, and Richard Wolff. (Durham: Duke University Press, 2001) 56–80. See also, Julie Graham, "Subjects of Justice?" *Rethinking Marxism* 16 (2004): 355–359.

In particular, note Graham's hesitancy over the violence that the "universalism" of DeMartino's (*Global Economy, Global Justice*) Social Index Tariff Structure (SITS) policy would likely involve. Progressive privatization processes would certainly not constitute a comprehensive SITS-like policy. Rather, they are more modest interventions, and would emerge in step with the pace of privatization.

48. Harvey, *Spaces of Capital* 411.

Bibliography

"No Sign of Landing." *The Economist* 29 January 2005: 21.

"Private Sector Should Saddle up With OTB" *Newsday* 6 June 2002: Queens ed., A52.

"Rudy's Airport Wish Has Price/New Costs in Push for Privatization" *Newsday* 5 January 2001: Queens ed., A02.

Adler, Moshe. *The Origin of Governmental Production: Cleaning the Streets of New York By Contract in the 19th Century*. Unpublished manuscript in author's possession.

Agreement between The Central Park Conservancy and the City of New York Parks & Recreation. 11 February 1998. Unpublished contract in author's possession.

Ahlbrandt, Roger S., Jr. "Efficiency in the Provision of Fire Services." *Public Choice* 16 (1973): 14.

Ahlbrandt, Roger S., Jr. *Municipal Fire Protection Service: Comparison of Alternative Organizational Forms*. Beverly Hills: Sage Publications, 1973

Akyuz, Yilmaz., Detlef J. Kotte, Andras Koves, and Laszlo Szamuely. eds., *Privatization in the Transition Process: Recent Experiences in Eastern Europe*. Geneva: United Nations Conference on Trade and Development, 1993.

Alcaly, Roger E., and David Mermelstein. *The Fiscal Crisis of American Cities*. New York: Vintage Books, 1977

All China Federation of Trade Unions. <http://www.acftu.org.cn/volindus.htm>.

Althusser, Louis. *Lenin and Philosophy and Other Essays*. New York: Monthly Review Press, 1971.

Althusser, Louis, and Etienne Balibar. *Reading Capital*. London: Verso, 1997.

Althusser, Louis. *For Marx*. London: Verso, 1996.

Amariglio, Jack, and David F. Ruccio. "Postmodernism, Marxism, and the Critique of Modern Economic Thought." Rethinking Marxism 7 (1994): 7–35.

Anonymous Central Park horse carriage operator. Personal interview. 15 June 2003.

Arvidson, Enid. "Beyond Economism? Or, Beyond *Economics:* Urban Political Economy and the Challenge of a Postmodern Marxism." Unpublished working paper. 2003.

Arvidson, Enid. "Remapping Los Angeles, or, Taking the Risk of Class in Postmodern Urban Theory." *Economic Geography* 75 (1999): 134–156.

Ascher, Kate. *The Politics of Privatization: Contracting Out Public Services.* London: Macmillan Education Ltd., 1987.

Association of Fundraising Professionals. *Association of Fundraising Professionals, State of Fundraising Report 2003.* Alexandria, VA: Association of Fundraising Professionals, 2003.

Baer, William, and Melissa H. Birch. *Privatization in Latin America: New Roles for the Public and Private Sectors.* Westport: Praeger, 1994.

Bai, Matt. "The New Boss." *New York Times Sunday Magazine* 30 January 2005.

Barlow, Maude, and Tony Clark. *Blue Gold: The Fight to Stop the Corporate Theft of the World's Water.* New York: W. W. Norton & Company, 2003.

Bartik, Timothy J. "Local Economic Development Policies." *Management Policies in Local Government Finance.* Eds. Richard Aronson, and Eli Schwartz. Washington, D.C.: International City/County Management Association, 2003. 355–390.

Bartlett, David. "Foreign Direct Investment and Privatization Policy: The Causes and Consequences of Hungary's Route to Capitalism." *Transitions to Capitalism and Democracy in Russia and Central Europe.* Eds. M. Donald Hancock, and John Logue. Westport: Praeger, 2000. 135–154.

Baumol, Willaim J. "Macroeconomics of Unbalanced Growth: The Anatomy of Urban Crisis." *The American Economic Review* 57 (1967): 415–426.

Benjamin, Walter. *Illuminations.* London: Fontana, 1973.

Berenyi, E., and Barbara Stevens. "Does Privatization Work: A Study of the Delivery of Eight Local Services." *State and Local Government Review* 20 (1988): 11–21.

Berenyi, Eileen Brettler. "Contracting Out Refuse Collection: The Nature and Impact of the Change." *The Urban Interest* 3 (1981): 30–42.

Berkowitz, D., and S. Holland. "Does Privatization Enhance or Deter Small Enterprise Formation?" *Economic Letters* 74 (2001): 53–60.

Berkowitz, Daniel, and Jonathan Holland. "Does Privatization Enhance or Deter Small Enterprise Formation?" *Economic Letters* 74 (2001): 53–60.

Binns, David. "Privatization Through Employee Ownership: Learned From The International Experience." Unpublished Working Paper.

Blais, Andre, and Stephane Dion, eds., *The Budget-Maximizing Bureaucrat: Appraisal and Evidence.* Pittsburgh, PA: University of Pittsburgh Press, 1991.

Block, Fred. "Deconstructing Capitalism as a System." *Rethinking Marxism* 12 (2000): 83–98.

Bluestone, Barry, and Bennett Harrison. *The Deindustrialization of America.* New York: Basic Books, 1982.

Bluestone, Barry, and Bennett Harrison. *The Deindustrialization of America.* New York: Basic Books, 1982.

Borcherding, T.E., W. Pommerehne, and F. Schneider. "Comparing the Efficiency of Private and Public Production: Evidence from Five Countries." *Journal of Economics* 2 (1982): 127–156.

Borcherding, Thomas E., ed. *Budgets and Bureaucrats: The Sources of Government Growth.* Durham: Duke University Press, 1977.

Bourdieu, Pierre. "The Essence of Neoliberalism." *Le Monde Diplomatique.* December 1998.

Boycko, Maxim, Andrei Shleifer, and Robert W. Vishny. "A Theory of Privatization." The *Economic Journal* 10 (1996): 309–319.

Boyne, George A. "Bureaucratic Theory Meets Reality: Public Choice and Service Contracting in U.S. Local Government." *Public Administration Review* 58 (1998): 474–484.

Brick, Howard. "Optimism of the Mind: Imagining Postindustrial Society in the 1960s and 1970s." *American Quarterly* 44 (1992): 348–380.

Buchanan, James. "Why Do Governments Grow?" *Budgets and Bureaucrats: The Sources of Government Growth*.Ed.Thomas E. Borcherding. Durham: Duke University Press, 1977.

Butler, Stuart. *Privatizing Federal Spending: A Strategy to Eliminate the Deficit.* New York: Universe Books, 1985.

Cain, Rita Marie. "Marketing activities in the non-profit sector—recent lesson regarding tax implications." American Business Law Journal 36 (1999): 349–371.

Callen, David. "Hard times hit charities, too." *The Christian Science Monitor* 22 April 2003.

Callen, Jeffrey L., April Klein, and Daniel Tinkelman. "Board Composition, Committees, and Organizational Efficiency: The Case of Nonprofits." *Nonprofit and Voluntary Sector Quarterly* 32 (2003): 493–520.

Castells, Manuel. *The Urban Question.* London: Edward Arnold, 1977.

Central Park Conservancy. *Central Park Conservancy 1993 Annual Report.* New York, 1993.

Central Park Conservancy. *Central Park Conservancy 1994 Annual Report.* New York, 1994.

Central Park Conservancy. *Central Park Conservancy 1995 Annual Report.* New York, 1995.

Central Park Conservancy. *Central Park Conservancy 1996 Annual Report.* New York, 1996.

Central Park Conservancy. *Central Park Conservancy 1997 Annual Report.* New York, 1997.

Central Park Conservancy. *Central Park Conservancy 1998 Annual Report.* New York, 1998.

Central Park Conservancy. *Central Park Conservancy 1999 Annual Report.* New York, 1999.

Central Park Conservancy. *Central Park Conservancy 2000 Annual Report.* New York, 2000.

Central Park Conservancy. *Central Park Conservancy 2001 Annual Report.* New York, 2001.

Central Park Conservancy. *Central Park Conservancy 2002 Annual Report.* New York, 2002.

Central Park Conservancy. *Central Park Conservancy 2003 Annual Report.* New York, 2003.

Central Park Conservancy. *Central Park Conservancy 2004 Annual Report.* New York, 2004.

Chandler, TD. "Sanitation Privatization and Sanitation Employee Wages." *Journal of Labor Research* 15 (1994): 137–153.

Chandler, Timothy D., and Peter Feuille. " Municipal Unions and PrivatizationPublic Administration Revie 51 (1991): 15–22.

Chandler, Timothy D., and Peter Feuille. "Cities, Unions and the Privatization of Sanitation Services." Journal of Labor Researc 15 (1994): 53–71.

Clark, Christi, Robin A. Johnson, and James L. Mercer. "Impact of Privatization and Managed Competition on Public Employees." *Local Government Innovation.* Eds. Robin A. Johnson and Normal Walzer. Westport: Quorum Books, 2000. 191–211.

Clarke, David B., and Michael G. Bradford. "Public and Private Consumption and the City." *Urban Studies* 35 (1998): 865–888.

Clifton, Judith, Francisco Comin, and Daniel Diaz Fuentes. *Privatization in the European Union: Public Enterprises and Integration.* Boston: Kluwer Academic Publishers, 2003.

Cordes, Joseph J., and Burton Weisbrod. "Differential Taxation of Nonprofits and the Commercialization of Nonprofit Revenues." *Journal of Policy Analysis and Management* 17 (1998): 195–214.

Cortez, Albert. "Origins of Public Education and the Voucher Debate." *Intercultural Development Research Newsletter* San Antonio: Intercultural Development Research Association, 1999.

Cranz, Galen. "Changing Roles of Urban Parks: From Pleasure Garden to Open Space." *San Francisco Planning and Urban Research Newsletter* San Francisco: San Francisco Planning and Urban Research Association, 2000.

Crecine, John P. ed. *Financing the Metropolis: Public Policy in Urban Economics.* Beverly Hills: Sage Publications, 1970.

Cross, John C. "Street Vendors, Modernity and Postmodernity: Conflict and Compromise in the Global Economy." *International Journal of Sociology and Social Policy* 21 (2000): 29–51.

Cullenberg, Stephen. "Socialism's Burden: Towards a "Thin" Definition of Socialism." *Rethinking Marxism* 5 (1992): 64–83.

Curtis, Fred. "Ivy Covered Exploitation." *Re/Presenting Class: Essays in Postmodern Marxism.* Ed. J.K. Gibson-Graham, Stephen Resnick, and Richard Wolff. Durham: Duke University Press, 2001. 81–104.

Dahl, Robert. *A Preface to Economic Democracy.* Berkeley: University of California Press, 1985.

Dearborn, Philip. "Bankruptcies, Defaults, and Other Government Financial Emergencies." Washington: D.C.: U.S. Advisory Commission on Intergovernmental Relations, 1985.

DiLorenzo, Thomas J., and James T. Bennett. "The profits of nonprofits: unfair competition in the computer software and audiovisual industries." *Journal of Small Business Management* 26 (April 1988): 17–25.

DeMartino, George F. *Global Economy, Global Justice.* New York: Routledge, 2000.

DeMartino, George. *Modern macroeconomic theories of cycles and crisis: A methodological critique.* Diss. U of Massachusetts-Amherst, 1992. Amherst: U of Massachusetts-Amherst, 1992.

Desai, Kamal R., Carol VanDeusen Lukas, and Gary J. Young. "Public Hospitals: Privatization and Uncompensated Care." *Health Affairs* 19 (2000): 31–36.

Dilger, Robert J., Randolph R. Moffett, and Linda Struyk. "Privatization of municipal services in America's largest cities." *Public Administration Review* 57 (1997): 21–26.

Doogan, Kevin. "The Marketization of Local Services and the Fragmentation of Labor Markets." *International Journal of Urban and Regional Research* 21 (1997): 286–302.

Dorwart, P.A., M. Schlesinger, and H. Davison. "A National Study of Psychiatric Hospital Care." *American Journal of Psychiatry* 148 (1991): 204–210.

Downs, Anthony. *Inside Bureaucracy.* Boston: Little Brown, 1967.

Edwards, Franklin R., Barbara J. Stevens. "The Provision of Municipal Sanitation Services by Private Firms: An Empirical Analysis of the Efficiency of Alternative Market Structures and Regulatory Arrangments." *The Journal of Industrial Economics* 27 (1978): 133–147.

Ehrenreich, Barbara. "Spinning the poor into gold: how corporations seek to profit from welfare reform." *Harper's* August 1997: 44.

Eisinger, Peter K. *The Rise of the Entrepreneurial State.* Madison: The University of Wisconsin Press, 1988.

Ellerman, David. *The Democratic Worker-Owned Firm: A New Model for the East and West.* Boston: Unwin Hyman, 1990.

Emspak, Frank, Roland Zullo, and Susan J. Rose. "Privatizing Child Protective Services in Milwaukee County: An Analysis and Comparison of Public and Private Service Delivery Systems." Milwaukee: Institute for Wisconsin's Future, 1996.

Farnham, Paul G. "The Impact of Citizen Influence on Local Government Expenditure." *Public Choice* 64 (1990): 201–212.

Farnham, Paul G. "The Impact of Government Functional Responsibility on Local Expenditure" *Urban Affairs Quarterly* 22 (1986): 151–165.

Feigenbaum, Harvey B., Jeffrey R. Henig. "The Political Underpinnings of Privatization." *World Politics* 46 (1994): 185–208.

Ferris, James, and Elizabeth Gradd"Contracting out: For What? With Whom?" Public Administration Review 46 (1986): 332–344.

Ferris, James, and Elizabeth Gradd. "Contracting out: For What? With Whom?" Public Administration Review 46 (1986): 332–344.

Fershtman, Chaim. "The Interdependence between Ownership Status and Market Structure: The Case of Privatization." *Economica* 57, New Series (1990): 319–328.

Filatotchev, Igor V., and Roy P. Bradshaw. "The Geographical Impact of the Russian Privatization Program." *Post-Soviet Geography* 36 (1995): 371–384.

Fine, Ben. "Privatisation: Theory and Lessons from the UK and South Africa." *Seoul Journal of Economics* 10 (1997): 373–414.

Finley, Lawrence K. *Public Sector Privatization: Alternative Approaches to Service Delivery.* New York: Quorum Books, 1989.

Fixler, Philip E., Jr., and Edward C. Hayes. "Contracting Out for Local Public Services." *The Hidden Wealth of Cities: Policy and Methods for American Local Government.* Ed. Edward C. Hayes. Greenwich, CT: JAI Press, 1989.

Flener, Mark H. "Legal Considerations in Privatization and the Role of Legal Counsel." *Public Sector Privatization.* Ed. Lawrence K. Finley. New York: Quorum Books, 1989. 141–152.

Freeman, Joshua B. *Working Class New York.* New York: The New Press, 2000.

Friedman, Milton. *Capitalism and Freedom, Freedom and Democracy.* Chicago: University of Chicago Press, 1962.

Frumkin, Peter, and Mark T. Kim. "Strategic Positioning and the Financing of Nonprofit Organizations: Is Efficiency Rewarded in the Contributions Marketplace?" *Public Administration Review* 61 (2001): 266–282.

Ganz, Alexander. "Where Has the Urban Crisis Gone: How Boston and Other Large Cities Have Stemmed Economic Decline." *Cities in Stress: A New Look at the Urban Crisis.* Ed. Mark Gottdiener. Beverly Hills: Sage Publications, 1986. 39–59.

Goodman, Robert. *The Last Entrepreneus.* New York: Simon and Schuster, 1979.

Granett, Robert F., Jr. "Marx's Value Theory: Modern or Postmodern?" *Rethinking Marxism* 8 (1995): 40–60.

Gaul , Gilbert M., and Neill A. Borowski. "Nonprofits: American's Growth Industry." *Philadelphia Inquirer* 19 April 1993, A1.

Giantris, Philip D. "Business Perspective—Environmental Infrastructure." *Public Sector Privatization.* Ed., Lawrence K. Finley. New York: Quorum Books, 1989. 47–62.

Gibbon, Henry. "Worldwide economic orthodoxy" *Privatisation International* 123 (1998): 4–5.

Gibbon, Henry. Editor's Letter, *Privatisation Yearbook.* London: Thomson Financial, 2000.

Gibson, Katherine, and Julie Graham. "Rethinking class industrial geography: creating a space for an alternative politics of class." *Economic Geography* 68 (1992): 109–128.

Gibson-Graham, J.K. "Althusser and capitalism: an encounter in contradiction." *Postmodern Materialism and the Future of Marxist Theory: Essays in the Althusserian Tradition.* Eds., Antonino Callari, and David Ruccio. Middletown, CT: Wesleyan University Press, 1996. 212–231.

Gibson-Graham, J.K., and Phillip O'Neill. "Exploring a New Class Politics of the Enterprise." *Re/Presenting Class: Essays in Postmodern Marxism.* Eds. J.K. Gibson-Graham, Stephen Resnick, and Richard Wolff. Durham: Duke University Press, 2001. 56–80.

Gibson-Graham, J.K., Stephen Resnick, and Richard Wolff, eds., *Re/Presenting Class: Essays in Postmodern Marxism.* Durham, NC: Duke University Press, 2001.

Gilder, Richard. "Set the Parks Free." *City Journal* 7.4 (1997).

Gilmour, Robert S., and Laura S. Jensen. "Reinventing Government Accountability: Public Functions, Privatization, and the Meaning of "State Action."" Public Administration Review 58 (1998): 247–258.

Glade, William. ed. *Privatization of Public Enterprises in Latin America.* San Francisco: ICS Press, 1991.

Goldsmith, Stephen. *The Twenty-First Century City: Resurrecting Urban America.* Washington, D.C.: Regnery Publishing, Inc., 1997

Gorton, Gary, and Frank Schmid. "Class Struggle Inside the Firm: A Study of German Codetermination." Working Paper, April 2002.

Gotbaum, Betsy. Public Advocate for the City of New York. "Procurement in New York City: A Strategy for Local Economic Development." New York: Office of the Public Advocate for the City of New York, June 2003.

Gottdiener, Mark, ed., *Cities in Stress: A New Look at the Urban Crisis*. Beverly Hills: Sage Publications, 1986.

Gough, Jamie, and Aram Eisenschitz. "The Construction of Mainstream Local Initiatives: Mobility, Socialization, and Class Relations." United Nations Conference on Trade and Development. 72 (1996): 178–195.

Graham, Julie. "Subjects of Justice?" *Rethinking Marxism* 16 (2004): 355–359.

Green, Jeffrey D. *Cities and Privatization: Prospects for the New Century*. Upper Saddle River, NJ: Prentice Hall, 2002.

Green, Jeffrey D. "How Much Privatization? A Research Note Examining the Use of Privatization by Cities in 1982 and 1992." *Policy Studies Journal* 24 (1996): 632–640.

Green, Jeffrey D. "Cities and Privatiztaion: Examining the Effects of Fiscal Stress, Location, and Wealth in Medium-Sized Cities" *Policy Studies Journal* 24 (1996): 135–144.

Greiner, John M., and George E. Peterson. "Do Budget Reductions Stimulate Public Sector Productivity? Evidence From Proposition 2 ½ in Massachusetts." *Reagan and the Cities*. Eds. George E. Peterson, and Carol W. Lewis. Washinton, D.C.: The Urban Institute Press, 1986. 63–97.

Greytak, David, Donald Phares, and Elaine Morley. *Municipal Output and Performance in New York City*. Lexington, MA: Lexington Books, 1976.

Hanlon, Martin D. "Running on Two Tracks: The Public and Private Provision of Human Services." *New Labor Forum* 4 (1999): 100–111.

Hanlon, Martin D. "Running on Two Tracks: The Public and Private Provision of Human Services." *New Labor Forum* 4 (1999): 100–111.

Haque, M. Shamsul. " The diminishing publicness of public service under the current mode of governanc." *Public Administration Review* 61 (2001): 65–81.

Harden, Blaine. "Neighbors Give Central Park a Wealthy Glow." *New York Times* 22 November 1999, A1+.

Hart, Oliver, Andrei Shleifer, and Robert Vishny. "The Proper Scope of Government: Theory and an Application to Prisons." *The Quarterly Journal of Economics* 112 (1997): 1127–1161.

Harvey, David. "The 'New' Imperialism: Accumulation by Dispossession." *The New Imperial Challenge: Socialist Register 2004*. Eds. Leo Panitch, and Colin Leys. London: Merlin Press, 2003. 63–88.

Harvey, David. *Consciousness and the Urban Experience*. Baltimore: The Johns Hopkins University Press, 1985.

Harvey, David. *Spaces of Capital: Towards a Critical Geography*. New York, Routledge, 2001.

Hawley, Willis D., David Rogers, eds., *Improving the Quality of Urban Management*. Beverly Hills: Sage Publications, 1974.

Hebdon, Robert. " Contracting Out in New York State: The Story the Lauder Report Chose Not to Tell" Labor Studies Journa (Spring 1995): 3–29.

Henig, Jeffrey R. "Privatization in the United States: Theory and Practice." *Political Science Quarterly* 104 (1989–90): 649–660.

Hevesi, Dennis. "Takeover of Agency For Buildings Is Proposed." *New York Times* 1 December 2000, late ed.: B8.

Hilke, John. "Cost Savings From Privatization: A Compilation of Study Findings." *How-to-Guide #6*. Los Angeles: The Reason Public Policy Institute, 1993. 1–17.

Holtmann, A.G. "A Theory of Non-profit Firms." *Economica* 50 (1983): 439–449.

Hoover, Gary, and James Peoples. "Privatization of refuse removal and labor costs." *Journal of Labor Research* 24 (2003): 293–306.

Inkyung, Cha, and William Neilson. "Is Competition Among Charities Bad?" Working Paper Series No. 0116. Private Enterprise Research Center, Texas A&M University, 2001.

Jacobs, Jane. *The Economy of Cities*. New York: Random House, 1969.

Jameson, Fredric. *Postmodernism, or, The Cultural Logic of Late Capitalism*. Durham: Duke University Press, 2001.

Jaret, Charles. "Recent Neo-Marxist Urban Analysis." *Annual Review of Sociology* 9 (1983): 499–525.

Jeffrey R. Henig, "Privatization in the United States: Theory and Practice." *Political Science Quarterly* 104 (1989–90): 649–670.

Jehl, Douglas. "As Cities Move to Privatize Water, Atlanta Steps Back." *New York Times* 10 Feb. 2003, late ed.: A14.

Johnson, Robin A., and Normal Walzer. eds., *Local Government Innovation*. Westport, CT: Quorum Books, 2000.

Katznelson, Ira. *City Trenches: Urban Politics and the Patterning of Class in the U.S.* New York: Pantheon, 1981.

Kemp, Roger L. *Managing America's Cities*. Jefferson, NC: McFarland & Company, Inc., Publishers, 1998.

Kikeri, Sunita. "Privatization and Labor: What Happens to Workers When Governments Divest?" *World Bank Technical Paper No. 396*. Washginton, D.C.: The World Bank, 1998.

Kincaid, John. "De Facto Devolution and Urban Defunding: The Priority of Persons Over Places." *Journal of Urban Affairs* 21 (1999): 135–168.

Kodrzycki, Yolana K. "Privatization of local public services: Lessons for New England," *New England Economic Review* (May/June 1994): 31–48.

KPMG LLP. *Central Park Conservancy, Inc., Independent Auditor's Reports 1997–2002*. New York.

Laban, Raul, and Holger C. Wolf. "Large-Scale Privatization in Transition Economies." *The American Economic Review* 83 (1993): 1199–1210.

Laffont, Jean-Jacques, and Jean Tirole. "Privatization and Incentives." *Journal of Law, Economics, & Organization* 7 Special Issue (1991): 84–105.

LaGrange, A. "Privatizing Public Housing in the Welfare Regime of a Tiger Economy: A Case Study of Hong Kong," *Housing Theory & Society* 16 (1999): 17–30.

Lambooy, Jan G., and Frank Moulaert. "The Economic Organization of Cities: An Institutional Perspective." *International Journal of Urban and Regional Research* 20 (1996): 217–237.

Lastarria, Cornheil S. "The Impact of Privatization on Gender and Property Rights in Africa." *World Development* 25 (1997): 1317–1333.

Latour, B., and S. Woolgar. *Laboratory life: The construction of scientific facts.* Princeton: Princeton University Press, 1986

Lefebvre, Henri. *The Explosion.* New York: Vintage, 1969.

Lefebvre, Henri. *Writings on Cities.* Trans. and eds., Eleonore Kogman and Elizabeth Lebas. Cambridge, MA: Blackwell Publishers, 1996.

Li, Hongbin, and Scott Rozelle. "Saving or Stripping Rural Industry: An Analysis of Privatization and Effects in China." *Agricultural Economics* 23 (2000): 241–252.

Lichten, Eric. *Class Power & Austerity: The New York City Fiscal Crisis.* South Hadley, MA: Bergin and Garvey Publishers, Inc., 1986.

Linowes, David F. *Privatization: Toward More Effective Government. Report of the President's Commission on Privatization.* Urbana: University of Illinois Press, 1988.

Logue, John, and Daniel Bell. "Who Will Inherit the "Worker's Paradise"?: Worker Ownership and Enterprise Efficiency in Russian Privatization." *Transitions to Capitalism and Democracy in Russia and Central Europe.* Eds., M. Donald Hancock and John Logue. Westport: Praeger, 2000. 29–66.

Lopez-de-Silanes, Florencio, Andrei Shleifer, and Robert W. Vishny "Privatization in the United States." *The Rand Journal of Economics* 28 (1997): 447–471.

Luxemburg, Rosa. *The Accumulation of Capital: An Anti-Critique.* Tran. Rudolf Wichmann. London: Penguin Press, 1972.

Mahboobi, Ladan. "Recent Privatisation Trends in OECD Countries." *Financial Market Trends* 82 (2002) 43–58.

Manzetti, Luigi. "The Political Economy of Privatization through Divestiture in Lesser Developed Economies." *Comparative Politics* 25 (1993): 429–454.

Marginson, Simon. "Value creation in the production of services: a note on Marx." *Cambridge Journal of Economics* 22 (1998): 573–585.

Marglin, Stephen. "What Do Bosses Do?" *Review of Radical Political Economics* Summer (1974): 60–112.

Markusen, Ann R. "Class and Urban Social Expenditure: A Marxist Theory of Metropolitan Government." *Marxism and the Metropolis.* Eds. William Tabb, and Larry Sawers. New York: Oxford University Press, 1978. 90–111.

Marlin, John Tepper, ed., *Contracting Municipal Services: A Guide for Purchase from the Private Sector.* New York: John Wiley & Sons, 1984.

Marx, Karl. *Capital: A Critique of Political Economy.* Ed. Frederick Engels. Trans. Samuel Moore and Edward Aveling. Vol. 1. New York: International Publishers, 1967.

———. *Capital: A Critique of Political Economy.* Tran. David Fernbach. Vol 2. London: The Penguin Group, 1992.

———. *Capital: A Critique of Political Economy.* Tran. David Fernbach. Vol. 3. London: Penguin Books, 1981.

———. *Grundrisse.* Tran. Martin Nicolaus. London: The Penguin Group, 1993.

———. *Wage-Labour and Capital.* New York: International Publishers, 1933.

Mason, Maryann, and Wendy Siegel. "Does Privatization Pay?: A Case Study of Privatization in Chicago." Chicago: Chicago Institute on Urban Poverty, 1997.

Masten, S.E. "The Organization of Production." *The Journal of Law and Economics* 27 (1984): 403–417.

McFaul, Michael. "State Power, Institutional Change, and the Politics of Privatization in Russsia," *World Politics* 47 (1995): 210–243.

McGuire, Robert A., Robert L. Ohsfeldt, and T. Norman Van Cott. "The determinants of the choice between public and private production of a publicly funded service." *Public Choice* 54 (1987): 211–230.

Megginson, W.L., and Maria K. Boutchkova. "The Impact of Privatisation on Capital Market Development and Individual Share Ownership." Paper presented at the Thirteenth Plenary Session of the Advisory Group on Privatisation, OECD, Paris, September 1999.

Megginson, William. "Privatization." *Foreign Policy* 118 (2000): 14–27.

Melosi, Martin. *Garbage in the Cities: Refuse, Reform, and the Environment, 1990– 1980.* College Station: Texas A&M University Press, 1981.

Merrifield, Andy. *Metromarxism.* New York and London: Routledge, 2002.

Migué, J. L., and G. Bélanger. "Toward a general theory of managerial discretion." *Public Choice* 17 (1974): 27–43.

Miller, Gary J. *Cities By Contract:* The Politics of Municipal Incorporation. Cambridge, MA: The MIT Press, 1981.

Miller, Hugh T., and James R. Simmons. "The irony of privatization." *Administration & Society* 30 (1998): 513–533.

Miller-Millesen, Judith L. "Understanding the Behavior of Nonprofit Boards of Directors: A Theory-Based Approach." *Nonprofit and Voluntary Sector Quarterly* 32 (2003): 521–547.

Milne, Robin, and Magnus McGee. "Compulsory Competitive Tendering in the NHS: A New Look at Some Old Estimates." *Fiscal Studies* 13 (1992): 96–110.

Moe, Ronald C. "Exploring the Limits of Privatization." *Public Administration Review* 47 (1987): 461–468.

Moe, Terry M. "The New Economcs of Organization. *American Journal of Political Science* 28 (1984): 739–777.

Moerland, Pieter W. "Changing Models of Corporate Governance in OECD Countries." *Privatization, Corporate Governance and the Emergence of Markets.* Ed. Eckehard F. Rosenbaoum, Frank Bonker, and Hans-Jurgen Wagener. London: Macmillan Press Ltd., 2000. 69–82.

Mommaas, Hans. "Modernity, Postmodernity and the Crisis of Social Modernization: A Case Study in Urban Fragmentation." *International Journal of Urban and Regional Research* 20 (1996): 196–216.

Morgan, David R., Robert E. England. "Two Faces of Privatization." *Public Administration Review* 48 (1988): 979–987.

Morgan, David R., and John P. Pelissero. "Urban Policy: Does Political Structure Matter?" *American Political Science Review* 74 (1980): 999–1006.

Morgan, David R., Michael W. Hirlinger, and Robert E. Englan. The Decision to Contract Out City Services: A Further Explanatio The Western Political Quarterly (1988): 363–372.

Nathan, Richard P., Elizabeth I. Davis, Mark J. McGarth, and William C. O'Heaney. *The Non-profitization Movement as a Form of Devolution.* Albany, NY: Rockefeller Institute, 1996.

National Council For Public-Private Partnerships. *For the Good of the People.* Washington D.C.: National Council For Public-Private Partnerships, 2002.

Nelson, Adrian, and Cary L. Cooper. "Uncertainty Amidst Change—The Impact of Privatization on Employee Job Satisfaction and Well-Being." *Journal of Occupational and Organizational Psychology* 68 (1995): 57–71.

New York City Independent Budget Office. "End of the Green for Parks After a Four-Year Rise May Tumble" *Inside the Budget* 98 (May 2002).

New York City. *The Mayor's Management Report 2001: Supplement.* New York: New York City, 2001.

Niskanen, William. *Bureaucracy and Representative Government.* Chicago: Aldine, 1971.

Norquist, John O. *The Wealth of Cities: Revitalizing the Centers of American Life.* Reading, MA: Addison-Wesley, 1998.

O'Connor, James. *Fiscal Crisis of the State.* New York: St. Martin's Press, 1973.

Organisation For Economic Co-Operation and Development. *Mass Privatization: An Initial Assessment.* Paris: Organisation For Economic Co-Operation and Development, 1995.

Osborne, David, and Ted Gaebler. *Reinventing Government: How the Entrepreneurial Spirit is Transforming the Public Sector.* New York: Plume, 1993.

Ostrom, Vincent, Charles M. Tiebout, and Robert Warren. "The Organization of Government in Metropolitan Areas: A Theoretical Inquiry." *The American Political Science Review* 55 (1961): 831–842.

Painter, Joe. "The Geography of Trade Union Responses to Local Government Privatizatoin." *Transactions of the Institute of British Geographers* 16 New Series (1991): 214–226.

Peña, Jessica, and Alexander L.T. Reid. "A Call for Reform of the Operational Test for Unrelated Commercial Activity in Charities." *New York University Law Review.* 76 (2001): 1855–1897.

Pendleton, Andrew. "What impact has privatization had on pay and employment? A review of the UK experience." *Industrial Relations* (Canadian) 52 (1997): 554–583.

Perry, Cecilia. "Safety Net for Sale." *New Labor Forum* 4 (1999): 78–87.

Perry, David C., and Alfred J. Watkins, eds., *The Rise of the Sunbelt cities.* Beverly Hills: Sage Publications, 1977.

Peterson, George E., and Carol W. Lewis, eds., *Reagan and the Cities.* Washington D.C.: The Urban Institute Press, 1986.

Pfetsch, Barbara. "Convergence Through Privatization? Changing Media Environments and Televised Politics in Germany." *European Journal of Communication* 11 (1996): 427–451.

Phillipps, Lisa. "Taxing the Market Citizen: Fiscal Policy and Inequality in an Age of Privatization." *Law & Contemporary Problems* 63 (2000): 111–131.

Piven, Francis Fox, and Richard Cloward. *Poor People's Movements.* New York: Vintage, 1979.

Plane, Patrick "Privatization and Economic Growth: An Empirical Investigation from a Sample of Developing Market Economies." *Applied Economics* 29 (1997): 161–178.

PR Newswire Association, Inc. "Waste Management Shareholder Letter Urges Support For Resolution Accounting for Effects of Anti-Privatization Policies by Local Governments on Trash Hauling Business." Washington, D.C., 30 April 2002.

President's Private Sector Survey on Cost Control, Report on Privatization Washington, D.C.: Government Printing Office, 1983.

Quigley, John M. "Urban Diversity and Economic Growth." *Journal of Economic Perspectives* 12 (1998): 127–138.

Reiner, Thomas A., and Julian Wolpert. "The Non-Profit Sector in the Metropolitan Economy." *Economic Geography* 57 (1981): 23–33.

Resnick, Stephen A., and Richard D. Wolff. "A Reformulation of Marxian Theory and Historical Analysis." *The Journal of Economic History* 42 (1982): 53–59.

———. "Marxist Epistemology: The Critique of Economic Determinism." *Social Text* 6 (1982): 31–72.

———. "A Marxian Reconceptualization of Income and its Distribution." *Rethinking Marxism: Struggles in Marxist Theory*. Ed., Stephen Resnick, Richard Wolff. Brooklyn, NY: Autonomedia, Inc., 1985. 319–344.

———. *Knowledge and Class: A Marxian Critique of Political Economy*. Chicago: The University of Chicago Press, 1987.

———. "Rethinking Complexity in Economic Theory: The Challenge of Overdetermination." *Evolutionary Concepts in Contemporary Economics*. Ed. Richard W. England. Ann Arbor: University of Michigan, 1994. 39–59.

———. "*Empire* and Class Analysis." *Rethinking Marxism* 13 (2001): 61–69.

———. *Class Theory and History: Capitalism and Communism in the U.S.S.R.* New York: Routledge, 2002.

Rich, Richard C. *Analyzing Urban-Service Distributions*. Lexington, MA: LexingtonBooks, 1982.

Roelofs, Joan. "The third sector as a protective layer for capitalism." *Monthly Review* (September 1995): 16–26.

Rose-Ackerman, Susan. "Charitable Giving and "Excessive" Fundraising." *The Quarterly Journal of Economics* 97 (1982): 193–212.

———. ed. *The Economics of Nonprofit Institutions: Studies in Structure and Policy*. New York: Oxford University Press, 1986.

Rosenzweig, Roy, and Elizabeth Blackmar. *The Park and the People: A History of Central Park*. Ithaca: Cornell University Press, 1992.

Savas, E.S., *A Study of Central Park*. (New York, NY, 1976).

———. "Privatization in Post-Socialist Countries." *Public Administration Review* 52 (1992): 573–581.

———. "Municipal Monopolies Versus Competition in Delivering Urban Services." *Improving the Quality of Urban Management*. Eds. Willis Hawley, David Rogers. Beverly Hills, CA: Sage Publications, 1974. 473–500.

———. *Privatization: The Key to Better Government: Public Administration and Public Policy*. New York: Chatham House Publishers, 1988.

————. "Competition and choice in New York City Social Services." *Public Administration Review* 62 (202): 82–92.

Schamis, Hector E. "Conservative Political Economy and Privatization: Comparative Reflections on Chile and Great Britan." Paper prepared for, "The Right in Latin American Democracies," Research Conference. 20–21 April 1990. Columbia University.

Schlesinger, M., R. Dornart, C. Hoover, et. al., "Competition, Ownership, and Access to Hospital Service: Evidence from Psychiatric Hospitals." *Med Care* 35 (1997): 974–992.

Schmidt, Klaus M. "The Costs and Benefits of Privatization: An Incomplete Contracts Approach." *Journal of Law, Economics, & Organization* 12 (1996): 1–24.

Sclar, Elliot D. *You Don't Always Get What You Pay For: The Economics of Privatization* Ithaca, NY: Cornell University Press, 2000.

————. "The Privatization of Public Service: Lessons from Case Studies." Washington, D.C.: Economic Policy Institute, 1997.

Scott, Allen J. *The Cultural Economy of Cities: Essays on the Geography of Image-Producing Industries*. London: Sage, 2000.

Screpanti, Ernesto. "The Postmodern Crisis in Economics and the Revolution against Modernism." *Rethinking Marxism* 12 (2000): 87–111.

Segall, Malcolm., "From Cooperation to Competition in National Health Systems—And Back?: Impact on Professional Ethics and Quality in Health Care." *International Journal of Health Planning and Management* 15 (2000): 61–79.

Seley, John E., and Julian Wolpert. *New York City's Non-profit Sector*. New York: Community Studies of New York, Inc., and the Non-profit Coordinating Committee of New York, Inc., 2002.

Sheldon, Donn. "Contracting of Municipal Services: The Unanswered Questions." New York: Council on Municipal Performance, 1982.

Simon,Herbert, and Clarence E. Ridley. *Measuring Municipal Activities*. Chicago: International City Managers' Association, 1948.

Soja, Edward W. *Postmetropolis*. Malden, MA: Blackwell Publishers, 2000.

Sonenblum, Sidney, John J. Kirlin, and John C. Ries. *How Cities Provide Services*. Cambridge, MA: Ballinger Publishing Company, 1977.

Soukup, David J. "A Markov Analysis of Fund-Raising Alternatives." *Journal of Marketing Research* 20 (1983): 314–319.

Starr, Paul. "The Limits of Privatization." Washington D.C.: Economic Policy Institute, 1987.

Stein, Robert M. "The Budgetary Effects of Municipal Serive Contracting: A Principal-Agent Explanation." *American Journal of Political Science* 34 (1990): 471–502.

————. *Urban Alternatives: Public and Private Markets in the Provision of Local Services*. Pittsburgh: University of Pittsburgh Press, 1990.

Stevens, Barbara. "Delivering Municipal Services Efficiently: A Comparison of Municipal and Private Service Delivery." Washington, D.C.: U.S. Department of Housing and Urban Development, 1984.

Stigler, George. "The Theory of Economic Regulation." *Bell Journal of Economics and Management Service* 2 (1971): 3–21.

Stiglitz, George. *Globalization and its Discontents.* New York: Norton, W.W. & Co., Inc, 2002.

Stormes, James Ryan. *A Class Analysis of the U.S. Poor.* Diss. U of Massachusetts-Amherst, 1988. Amherst: U of Massachusetts-Amherst, 1988.

Sullivan, Harold J. "Privatization of Public Services: A Growing Threat to Constitutional Rights." *Public Administration Review.* 47 (1987): 461–467.

Sweezy, Paul M. *The Theory of Capitalist Development.* New York: Monthly Review Press, 1942.

Tabb, William K. *The Long Default.* New York: Monthly Review Press, 1982.

Tabb, William K., and Larry Sawers, eds., *Marxism and the Metropolis.* New York: Oxford University Press, 1978.

Tabb, William. "The New York City Fiscal Crisis." *Marxism and the Metropolis.* Ed. William Tabb, and Larry Sawers. New York: Oxford University Press, 1978. 241–266.

Tiebout, Charles. "A Pure Theory of Local Expenditures." *The Journal of Political Economy* 64 (1956): 416–424.

Touraine, Alain. *The Voice and the Eye.* New York: Cambridge University Press, 1981.

Tullock, Gordon. *Politics of Bureaucracy.* Washington, D.C.: Public Affairs Press, 1965.

Twombly, Eric C. "Human Service Nonprofits in Metropolitan Areas during Devolution and Welfare Reform." *Charting Civil Society.* 10. Washington, D.C.: The Urban Institute, 2001.

U.S. Advisory Commission on Intergovernmental Relations. *City Financial Emergencies: The Intergovernmental Dimension.* Washington, D.C.: U.S. Government Printing Office, 1973.

U.S. Department of Labor, National Commission on Employment Policy (NCEP). *The long-term implications of privatization.* Washington, D.C.: U.S. Department of Labor, 1989.

Venuti, Elizabeth K. "The Going-Concern Assumption Revisited: Assessing a Company's Future Viability." *The CPA Journal* LXXIV (5), May 2004.

Vickers, John, and George Yarrow. "Economic Perspectives on Privatization." *The Journal of Economic Perspectives* 5 (1991): 111–132.

Vlachou, Andriana. "The Socialist Transformation of China: Debates over Class and Social Development." *Rethinking Marxism* 4 (1993): 8–39.

Wagenaar, Alexander C., and HD Holder. "A Change From Public to Private Sale of Wine: Results from Natural Experiments in Iowa and West Virginia." *Journal of Studies on Alcohol* 52 (1991): 162–173.

Walker, Chris. "The Public Value of Urban Parks." *Beyond Recreation: A Broader View of Urban Parks* Washington D.C.: Urban Institute, 2004.

Wallin, Bruce A. "The Need for a Privatization Process: Lesson from Development and Implementation." *Public Administration Review* 57 (1997): 11–20.

Wang, Bin. "The Influence of Privatization on Municipal Earnings." Working paper, University of Wisconsin-Madison, Department of Economics, February 2004.

Warner, Mildred, and Amir Hefetz. "Privatization and the Market Role of Local Government." Washington, D.C.: Economic Policy Institute, 2000.

Weiner, Ross D. "The Effects of Broadcasting on Professinal Baseball: A Marxian Analysis." *Rethinking Marxism* 14 (2002): 8–28.

Weisbrod, Burton A. "The nonprofit mission and its financing: Growing links between nonprofits and the rest of the economy." *To Profit or Not to Profit.* Ed. Burton A. Weisbrod. Cambridge: Cambridge University Press, 1998.

Weisbrod, Burton A. ed., *To Profit or Not to Profit?* Cambridge: Cambridge University Press, 1998.

Welch, Dick, and Olivier Frémond. "The Case-by-Case Approach to Privatization: Techniques and Examples." *World Bank Technical Paper* no. 403. Washington, D.C.: The World Bank, 1998.

Wessel, Robert H. "Privatization in the United States." *Business Economics* 30 (1995): 45–51.

Wiles, P.J.D. *The Political Economy of Communism.* Cambridge: Harvard University Press, 1964.

Williamson, Oliver E. "The New Institutional Economics: Taking Stock, Looking Ahead." *Journal of Economic Literature* 38 (2000): 595–613.

Willis, Jane. "A Stake in Place? The Geography of Employee Ownership and Its Implications for a Stakeholding Society." *Transactions of the Institute of British Geographers* 23 New Series (1998): 79–94.

Wolch, Jennifer R., and Robert K. Geiger. "Urban Restructuring and the Non-for-Profit Sector." *Economic Geography* 62 (1986): 3–18.

Wolff, Richard D., Antonino Callari, and Bruce Roberts. "A Marxian Alternative to the Transformation Problem." *Review of Radical Political Economics* 16 (1984): 115–135.

Wolff, Richard D., and Stephen A. Resnick. *Economics: Marxian versus Neoclassical.* Baltimore: The Johns Hopkins University Press, 1987.

Wolff, Richard. "Markets Do Not a Class Structure Make." *Marxism in the Postmodern Age.* Ed. A. Callari, S. Cullenberg, and C. Biewener. New York: Guilford Press, 1995.

———. "Limiting the State versus Expanding it: A Criticism of this Debate." *Contemporary Economic Theory: Radical Critiques of Neoliberalism.* Ed. Andriana Vlachou. Basingstoke and London: Macmillan Press, 1999. 72–85.

———. "Marxism and Democracy." *Rethinking Marxism* 12 (2000): 112–122.

———. "Capitalist Hegemony and Contesting Concepts of Class." Paper presented to the Socialist Scholars Conference. Cooper Union, New York. 14 April 2001.

———. "Efficiency?: Whose Efficiency?" *Post-Autistic Economics Review* 16, 16 September 2002, article 3

———. "The Critique of Economic Policy." *Post-Autistic Economics Review* 22, 24 November 2003, article 4.

World Bank. *2004 World Development Indicators.* Washington, D.C.: The World Bank Group, 2004.

Index